D0953133

052911

Groups in Conflict: Prisons in Disguise

Kenwyn K. Smith

University of Maryland

**KENDALL/HUNT
PUBLISHING COMPANY**
Dubuque, Iowa

Copyright © 1982 by Kendall/Hunt Publishing Company

Library of Congress Catalog Card Number: 82–82251

ISBN 0–8403–2752–8

Printed in the United States of America
B   402752   01

Dedicated to the memory of Alec Brown and Eddie Jarrett, whose lives, though prematurely ended, have continued to inspire me throughout the years.

The more laws and restrictions,
The poorer people become.

The sharper men's weapons,
The more trouble in the land.

The more ingenious and clever men are,
The more strange things happen.

The more rules and regulations,
The more thieves and robbers.

I take no action and people are reformed.
I enjoy peace and people become honest.
I do nothing and people become rich.
I have no desires and people return to the good
and simple life.

Lao Tsu

Contents

Acknowledgments

It's years since I first commenced this book and there have been so many people who've helped me along the way. First, I'd like to acknowledge the place of my academic mentors. Fritz Steele and Barry Oshry introduced me to a whole new way of thinking through their creative educational innovation, which they've called a Power and Systems Laboratory (Oshry, 1976, 1977, 1980). I owe them more than I can say. This work had its seeds in what I learned under their tutelege. Hence, in many ways it's as much theirs as it is mine—if ideas belong to anyone. Richard Hackman's enthusiasm for my work and his constant provocative supportiveness has at critical times helped me when I became weary. Most of all I want to thank Clay Alderfer. His impact on my development is the hardest for me to understand, for it has been both forceful and subtle. It reaches into inner crevices of my life I'm only just learning how to explore. So I don't have the words. But Clay has always been there, often with a silence so eloquent that I felt encouraged and supported to listen to the rhythms pulsating within me.

Then there are the people who constituted the participants in this research. The twenty-two people from Montville and the scores from Ashgrove—I'm sorry I can't acknowledge you all by your real names. You all touched my life deeply by letting me be part of your pilgrimages. Thanks. I must single out three people from Ashgrove, though I feel nervous doing this. Dr. Eddie Rhodes, you're very special. And I'm so glad you survived those chaotic years at Ashgrove. Your kind words to me in your address at your retirement dinner, "Ken, you were like one of my family" finds an echo in my own heart. Lewis Brook, we never got to feel comfortable close up. There was too much turmoil. But you vulnerably opened yourself to my scrutiny in a way that helped me immensely. I never really said thanks. I do so now. And then there is Mike D'Onofrio. Sometimes you seem so real, sometimes so unreal. You want so much. Yet when offered you take so little. You gave me a lot. But oh, it was hard work. Our relationship is so paradoxical. There were moments I felt like your father; others when I felt like your young son. But through it all you remained very special even when we were fighting with each other in such strange ways.

Many colleagues and friends have been beside me in this journey, feeding me, laughing and crying with me, criticizing my ideas, offering suggestions for improvement. To so many of you who struggled with me, my special thanks. I cannot name you all. A few I must single out: Ian McRae, Noel Jackling,

John Rickard, Lloyd Suttle, Valerie Simmons, and Peter Dachler. Ethel Lubarsky, Diane Parolski, and Betty Donovan have faithfully typed this manuscript and Raleigh Schein donated her artistic skill in the Montville map. To each my thanks.

And finally I want to thank David Mermelstein for helping me see that a part of me is in every character in this book and that the dynamics I've written about at the group and systems level all have their own parallel in my internal struggles. That special gift enables me today to let this work finish.

Prologue

This book is about groups. It's about people. It's about "you" and "me" and "them."

It began with the simple desire to explore and understand a paradox. It grew, with every-expanding circles of complexity, into a personal quest. It ends part way along the path of an unfinished and maybe unending journey.

This paradox first struck me during a conversation I once had with an "everyday" organizational man. He was recounting his work history and emphasizing that when he started with his company he was young, aggressive, and angry. He explained, "I wanted to change things for the better. There was so much that made it impossible to achieve the goals of our organization—policies, rules, and procedures, designed to frustrate the hell out of you. I used to approach my boss and try to get him to change things, but he always put me off. He'd tell me that when I matured a little I'd become more patient and recognize that although these changes might seem like a good idea, they just weren't possible! But he could never tell me why they weren't. Well, I found him to be so totally incompetent that I decided someday I'd get myself into a powerful enough position to be able to wrest his job from him. Then *I'd* change things for the better."

Years later, this same individual was occupying the position of his former superior; yet in this elevated role he behaved no differently than his predecessor. In fact, he'd become the very caricature of the person he once despised: a stalwart defender of the status quo, indifferent to the concerns of the next generation of subordinates and blindly ignoring those things around him that originally prompted his desire for extra power.[1]

This encounter was perplexing to me, not because the idea was new (one can find its replica every day in any organization), but because it suddenly struck me how little I understood the forces which, so easily and imperceptibly, seem to change a person's behavior. How could it happen that over the years a person could unknowingly grow into a character who, through his more youthful eyes, would have appeared despicable? The point at which I became most captivated by the example was when the thought occurred to me that if this happens to others, it could happen to me also. The social injustices around me which faithfully draw my anger and my crusading spirit, launching me onto pilgrimages "to better the world," might someday merely draw my indifference or disdain as I faithfully defend the status quo.

During my earliest ponderings on this observation, I encountered three other examples which, to my mind, contained essentially the same paradox, though expressed in different forms. I'd like to share these as a way of sketching implicitly what has become the underlying theme of this book, allowing the common thread which is found woven through these illustrations to summarize the beginnings of my journey.

The first is an exchange I once had with Lewis Brook, a high school principal. Brook was berating vociferously the superintendent, his superior, for something the superintendent had recently "done to" him. The recounting of the episode was cut short by a teacher who entered his office, whereupon the principal, without a moment's pause, responded to the teacher exactly as the superintendent had interacted with him. When confronted with this resounding obviousness, Lewis refused (or was unable) to see the similarity. When I dissected the two sets of events so that there was no escape from the brutal certitude of the similarities, he responded, "But it's different!"

I asked, "How's it different?"

Brook replied, "Well, I have reason for treating the teacher that way!"

"What are your reasons?"

He told me.

"But Lewis, those are exactly the reasons the superintendent gave me as to why he had to treat you that way!"

"But it's still different!"

"How's it different?"

With more than a hint of impatience in his voice Lewis retorted, "But mine were reasons; the superintendent's were merely rationalizations!"

Therein lies one key aspect of the paradox. Each of us has one framework for understanding our own behavior and a different one for understanding the behavior of others.

My second illustration comes from Rogers' (1968) analysis of the New York public school system. He noted that during the civil rights era of the 1960s, the Jewish population acted to block significant reforms that might have alleviated some of the plight of the black population. On closer investigation, he observed that many of these same people had been the strongest proponents for equality of educational opportunity in the 1930s when they themselves were oppressed. In the 1960s, not only were they indifferent to the concerns of the blacks, but many had become opponents of equal rights proposals. Rogers encapsulates his findings with the cryptic comment of how ironic it is that the "reformers of one generation become the conservatives of the next."

This observation, found repetitively in political history, is summarized powerfully by Michels (1915) in the concluding paragraph of his classic discourse on the history of political struggles:

"When democracies have gained a certain stage of development, they undergo a gradual transformation, adopting the aristocratic spirit, and in many cases also the aristocratic forms, against which at the outset they struggled so fiercely. [Then] new accusers arise to denounce the traitors; after an era of glorious combats and inglorious power, they end by fusing with the old dominant class; whereupon once more they in turn are attacked by fresh opponents. . . . It is probable this cruel game will continue without end."

A third example emerged in a conversation I once had with Gerald Bomford, a black Republican politician in a town that at the time was dominated and administered by Democrats. I was interested in what it meant for Gerald to be a black Republican and posed my question as follows: "Given the fact that nationally the Republicans are the more conservative party and that most blacks at present (early 1970s) are identified with reform, how come you're a Republican and not a Democrat?"

He replied, "Because the Republicans in this town are the reformers. Here it's the Democrats who are conservative."

"That's strange, isn't it? What makes this town so different from the rest of the nation?"

"It's simple," Gerald responded. "The Democrats are conservative because they're in power. Whoever is in power is conservative."

"And what if the Republicans were to be elected?"

"Clearly, then we'd become the conservatives. It is only really those who are out of power who can be reformist."

Bomford's reply struck like a thunderbolt. At one level it was no more than a cogent statement of the proposition in social theory that proclaims that our personal political ideologies are determined primarily by our locations in the social structure. That seemed straightforward enough! There's strong historical support for this notion; that's what Marx was all about; and Rogers and Michels were saying basically the same thing. Their views had seemed easy enough to accept, yet somehow Gerald's reply unleashed within me a sense of disquiet that eventually crescendoed to a paralyzing level of anxiety. I felt threatened!

This idea seems so easy to accept when applied to the behavior of others, when it's abstract, distant, historical. But when I bring it right into my everyday life, it does violence to my self-concept. It confronts me with the possibility that many of my behaviors and self-images are determined by external forces whose influence I can barely comprehend, let alone hope to gain mastery over. Should events in my life begin to rub and jostle one another too vigorously, I may well find myself internally fragmented. Again. Like a sea in a storm. It's so hard to cope with such pictures of my personal fragility!

This encounter with myself, prompted by the juxtaposition of the Rogers and Bomford understandings, highlighted for me the radically different meanings ideas had when applied to my behavior as opposed to *others'* behavior, when focused on my experience of the *present* as opposed to that of the *past*, or when touching the *concrete* elements of my life as opposed to the *abstract*. When a thought truly came close to me, when it touched my essence, I experienced it substantially differently than when it was a great distance away.

Out of my encounter with these examples, I found myself left with three burning issues. First, does it have to be this way? Are there no other alternatives? Second, how is it that these dynamics are so readily identifiable in the behaviors of others, or in my own experience in hindsight, while being so impossible to grasp hold of in my present behavior? Third, if I could understand how my experience becomes molded by those forces that I'm blind to moment by moment, is this process something that I could or would want to overcome, rise above, or avoid? Or is it a fundamental part of the nature of things? Like the texture of water or the brightness of sunlight?

And so my journey began.

As I pondered on my paradox and wondered where my quest would lead me, I was drawn to think about two complex issues. First, if I were to ask what was really going on in each of these cases, it seemed that there were several alternative levels on which I could focus my attention, each eliciting different and sometimes contradictory understandings. This recognition demanded that I give some thought to that never-ending and underlying debate that every philosophical, scientific, or religious discourse is ultimately about: "What is reality?" Second, in each of these examples, although the key actors would have tended to think of themselves as "free" agents, able to make intelligent and informed choices, everyone seemed to be somehow caught in a set of binds that acted as prison walls. The real potency of these constraints, however, was that they operated in a manner that left their victims blind to their overall effects. Hence the individuals and groups concerned, although perceiving themselves to be reasonably unconfined, were in actuality overwhelmingly encased by the social and organizational structures around them.

Before launching into my venture I felt I had to pause briefly to contemplate these two issues and to reflect on the conceptual maps and ideas that I would use to sustain and guide me in this search. For this I turned to the thoughts in the body of knowledge already available. I did so, not for the purpose of arguing a thesis, developing a theory, or defending a cause, but rather to set the stage like a meditation before a religious ceremony or a prelude to a symphonic work. In particular, I wanted to get into a frame of mind that made it possible to look at day-to-day experiences not only in their concrete forms, but also at a more symbolic, metaphoric level where the key understandings would come not so much from grasping significances in a rational way but in experiencing their essentiality.

Multiple Realities

The debate over "what is reality?" or "what is truth?" vacillates from one extreme, at which it's assumed that truth may be found ready-made in the world and all we need to do is to discover it, to the nihilistic proposition at the other pole that nothing is ultimately true and that the human obsession to "find" it is little more than an exercise in futility. I do not here wish to ride the various waves of this long, tumultuous argument, but simply, from the outset, to state explicitly my assumptions on the reality question so that I might have some guideposts to consistency during my search.

When the question has been asked "What is really going on here?" before any social analysis can take place, we must first determine from *what level of abstraction* we are going to examine the critical behavior. To illustrate what I mean by this, consider the example in which a child watching a play with a parent asks a question such as "What's that funny man doing now?" The parent's reply could be any of the following:

a. "He's saying to the other man . . . ;" or
b. "He's acting in a play;" or
c. "He's making people laugh;" or
d. "He's earning his living;" or
e. "He's creating an image of himself as a dramatic artist," and so forth.

Each of these responses is a valid conceptualization based on the same data; it would not make sense to debate which is *the* reality. All are realities in their own way, realities expressed at multiple levels of abstraction—multiple realities, if you will.

In order to comprehend the complexity of a multiple realities perspective, it's important to highlight four different issues relevant to any social analysis. In doing this, it becomes immediately evident that searches for *the* reality not only are futile but inevitably lead to either significant distortion through oversimplification or immense frustration.

The *first* issue is that within each level of abstraction there are three major domains of concern: the concrete, the symbolic, and the internal (Goffman, 1959). These multiple domains become most visible when the interactions between key parties break down in some way. Take, for example, the exchange between Principal Lewis Brook and his superintendent, referred to earlier, in which they encountered a major disagreement. In this event the breakdown in their interaction became manifest in three ways: (a) in the *concrete* area, the particular superintendent-principal's interaction came to a halt, and meaningful communication and mutual understanding of each other were at least temporarily shattered; (b) in the *symbolic* area, it became clear to anyone who tried to relate to either of them that "the superintendent-principal relationship had become strained," and as a result questions were being asked about the competencies of Brook and the particular superintendent to hold down their appointments; and (c) in the *internal* area, certain of their own self-images became bruised, such as Brook's beginning to wonder whether

5

"there's something wrong with me—or is it him." Of course, the more defensive Brook became when confronted with these internal images, the more likely it was that he would project these inner concerns across onto the superintendent and see it as his problem.

Hence, social reality is dependent not only on which level of abstraction is in focus, but within each level of abstraction, also on the domain of concern: the concrete manifestation of the particular behaviors, the internal images that are dependent for their very existence on the reinforcing influence of the continued interactions, or the external symbols created and sustained by the successful unfolding of those preaccepted ritualistic performances.

A *second* issue stirred by the level of abstraction question is the distinction that must be made between the outward appearances and the underlying form of any act or object. This differentiation can be clearly seen in the following example from Pirsig (1974). A train is only truly a train if it both appears as such and acts as such. If it is unable to move it isn't a train, no matter how much it looks like one. If it moves and doesn't have the appearance of a train, it likewise isn't a train. It's a bus, or a tram, or whatever.

A *third* issue is raised by Marx and Engels in their claim that what people say about what they're doing cannot be relied upon as an accurate account of what they're really doing. This is so not because people are lying, but because none of us genuinely understand the forces that move society and carry us all along, predetermining much of our behavior in concert with society's global momentum (Acton, 1967). As Laing (1969) puts it, "We are all acting parts in a play that we have never read and never seen, whose plot we do not know and whose existence we can (only) glimpse."

A *fourth* aspect is that when groups are interacting, there are two sets of issues on which we can focus. (1) There are those things that take place within the boundaries of the groups as they interact. In this case we're talking about the *characteristics of the groups* in interaction. (2) There are also those that occur in the interaction itself. In this case we're talking about the *characteristics of the interaction patterns* among the groups. This distinction is an important one to make and has been conceptualized by Goffman (1959) who, borrowing from the language of the theatre, talks about the difference between dramatic action and dramatic interaction. In the latter case the participants are involved in a kind of dialogue, an interplay between teams in which the posturings and movements of all concerned are interdependent. In the former, one team merely performs—plays out its predefined patterns—for the benefit of the other, who responds from an audience perspective. In the dramatic action situation, the "performance" remains essentially the same from audience to audience (such as in a concert in which the musicians and the concert goers are the two groups), whereas in dramatic interaction sequences (such as two teams in a football game), behaviors change radically depending on what the others do.

6

Let me illustrate the difference. If we notice that one group responds to another group in a suspicious and highly sensitive way, from a dramatic action perspective we may conclude that one characteristic of the former group is that it's paranoid. If we take a dramatic interaction perspective, however, we may end up saying that one of the properties of the interchange of these two groups is a high level of suspicion and sensitivity, without affirming anything specific about either group *per se*. As we explore the characteristics of the interaction further and notice significant differences in power between the two groups, we may come to conclude that suspicion and oversensitivity is a by-product of being powerless in a relationship and may not be because one of the groups "is" paranoid.

Lorenz (1952) tells the story of two wolves fighting—and one is about to be killed; the defeated wolf can totally incapacitate his opponent by lifting his head and bearing his vulnerable jugular vein. A swift lunge at the exposed vein would guarantee death, but when faced with this tactic, the conqueror is paralyzed. The vanquished appears to control the victor's behavior as much as the conqueror controls that of the defeated.

In this situation, if we were to ask the wolves who is experiencing power and who feels powerless, it is likely each would reply, "I feel totally powerless." If we asked them why they feel powerless, each would reply, "Because my opponent is controlling my behavior." If they were confronted with each other's perceptions of the situation, it would be virtually impossible for either to concede that the opponent was correct.

If we were to analyze the characteristics of the two parties in this interaction, we might well conclude that each experiences himself as powerless and is unable to accept his opponent's denial of being in full control. If we were to analyze the characteristics of the interaction, however, we would conclude that there are basic ground rules and rituals for the fighting of wolves to which both combatants subscribe. The force that is making them both feel powerless and controlled is their unswerving commitment to fight according to the rules. We might take the dramatic interaction further. It's also a characteristic of the interaction patterns for each opponent to be blind to how his commitment to the established rituals controls him and instead to project it onto the acts of his adversary.[2]

The simple identification of the above issues leaves me convinced that to seek understanding of any event in terms of a singular reality will cause us to overlook the complexity and diversity of the phenomenon and thereby diminish the potential richness of the social analysis. Accordingly, from the outset, I want to explicitly affirm my acceptance of the idea of multiple realities and to underscore that what reality looks like always depends upon (1) the vantage point from which it's examined, (2) the psychological filters through which it's perceived and (3) the predefined contours of the mind into which the perceptions are to be mapped.

7

The vantage point from which we view reality stirs two key thoughts. The first is captured in the monolithic contributions of the Marxian notions of class consciousness, which articulate powerfully that our definitions of reality are profoundly influenced by the place we occupy in the socioeconomic structure (Kohn, 1969). Our views of reality are conditioned by our own particular position in time and space, our spot in the historical process. As Durrell (1958) expressed it, "Every reality is based on a unique position; two steps east or west and the whole picture will change." The second is that the distance from which we view reality determines the images that emerge. For example, if we could look at human behavior from a distance above the earth, with the perspective of an eagle, the overall impression might be that we're merely participants in an activity that could only be described as "swarming," as ants on an ant hill. Since from that distance it's impossible to hear what people are saying to each other or to know the meanings they attach to their behaviors, it's only the more global patterns of interaction that come to our attention. On the other hand, if I were one of those being observed, it is likely I'd be so engrossed in the microbehaviors that characterize my daily routines that I'd not even notice my individual contribution to the overall "swarming phenomenon." Unless, of course, it's 5:00 P.M. on Friday in New York City!

Laing's (1973) dictum that "What one sees depends on how one sees" is particularly pertinent to the issue of the *psychological filters* through which experience is examined. This concept is obvious when applied to acts of physical perception. Objects look grayer when viewed through dark glasses; sounds are muffled when the ears are blocked. What's not so clear, but is just as critical, is that everything we "see" through our "psychological eyes" is equally filtered by the prisms of our "inner beings." Hence it's possible for two people to look at the same thing, see the same thing, talk about the same thing, and think about the same thing, but completely misunderstand each other because they're looking, seeing, talking, and thinking from completely different dimensions (Pirsig, 1974). Illustrative of this distinction is Jung's discourse (Serrano, 1966) on the impact of culture. Jung describes how an Indian, rather than *thinking* thoughts as is typical in the West, tends to *perceive* thoughts; how the division in the Western mentality into the conscious and unconscious produces a disunity that triggers a sharp division into the organized/rational and the primitive/affective; and how a person's thoughts tend to be generated in whatever zone the person happens to conceive of as the "center of being"— the brain for the European, the solar plexis for the Japanese, the heart for the ancient Greeks.

The importance of the *precontoured dimensions of our minds* as a determiner of our images of reality is particularly sharp when we recognize that *our* experiences, *our* thoughts, *our* perceptions, are not the experiences *per se* but rather are an echo, an after-effect of those experiences (Nietzsche, 1961). Hence the meanings, the significance, the essence of those experiences for each individual will depend heavily on the shape of the *a priori* hierarchy of concepts that already constitute the foundations of the mind's structure.

8

We are all in the process of creating reality. To talk about reality is, in fact, to talk about the meanings we attach to events and objects. If the character of objects and events were self-evident, they would be represented in a singular and universal form, and misunderstandings would not occur. It is the very fact that they do not automatically have meanings that requires humans to create, sustain, and refine reality (Schutz, 1970; Van Maanen, 1977). This must be done, however, in concert with others' definitions of reality, for if each were to generate his or her own completely unique constellation of meanings and connections to experience, the very notion of reality itself would be hollow, a linguistic cocoon with no life. Since the very reason humans develop meanings is to create a more simplified and intelligible picture of the world (Pirsig, 1974) so that we can create some stability and serenity for our emotional life (Einstein, 1918), it would be self-defeating if the set of meanings formulated did not increase our capacity to connect with the experiences of others. In the same spirit as "No man is an island" (Donne), so the richness of an idea for an individual is dependent on its confluence with the ideas of others, thereby helping to create order out of the kaleidoscopic jumble of colors and patterns and noises and smells and pain and tastes that surround us (Pirsig, 1974)[3] Hence, if we wish to understand "realities," perhaps the most central themes to be explored are the social processes that led to the particular sets of meanings and symbols being defined as acceptable. These "realities" are so much a "creature of their time" (Marx, 1846) that the historical contexts and social structures in which they are created, exist, and extinguished are all important determiners of what realities are like. If a particular reality is limited or restricted, that may well be because the social processes that gave it birth, sustain it, and determine its existence are unsophisticated and constricted. If a particular reality is confusing, it may well be because the social processes that gave it birth, sustain it, and determine its existence are conflicted and confusing. If we want to enrich our "realities," it may be that we need to enrich the social processes that make our "realities" what they are. If we want to discover "new worlds," it may be that what we need to do is make ourselves available to experience new and varied social processes, which in turn will enable us not to "discover," but rather to "create" new worlds.

If we concede that reality emerges through man's creativity—by the attaching of meanings and symbols to objects and events that are interlinked in time and space with other objects and meanings—a question remains. Once this process has occurred, do those realities so formed become fixed and static? The answer has to be an unequivocal "no," for these meanings are interdependent with other situational forces that in the overall social dynamism are in a state of flux. Hence, the realities man has created are similarly undergoing transformations. In this framework reality itself becomes conceived not as a product, but as a process in which man rather than being a "spectator" is a "re-creator" (Freire, 1972).[4]

By drawing together the views that man is the creator of reality and that reality is a process, we emerge with an overriding sense of man himself as a process, transforming and being transformed by the realities he mutually creates with others in his life space. Nietzsche (1961) expresses superbly this dialectical notion of man as a sojourner whose personal meanings become created primarily in the travail of his pilgrimage:

> "Man is a rope, fastened between animal and Superman—a rope over an abyss.
>
> A dangerous going-across, a dangerous wayfaring, a dangerous looking-back, a dangerous shuddering and staying-still.
>
> What is great in man is that he is a bridge. . . ."

Man is a bridge, an instrument for linking together the inner experiences embedded in the history of his own personal identity struggles with the myths, rituals, and corporate legends (Kopp, 1972) that define his culture at large. The question, "What is reality?" demands that we be attentive to the myriad of "meanings" man manufacturers to summarize his modes of connecting himself to others around him and to the cosmos at large.

Before leaving the topic of creation of realities, it's important to comment on the place of "facts" in the reality theme. Whenever debates about the nature of reality take place, there is always someone who will add, in legalistic tone, "But once we have all the facts relevant to the situation and can agree on those facts, then we'll know what really is the case," as if to imply that the mere conglomeration of "facts" adequately defines reality. The "facts" by themselves have little to offer. It's the interpretations of (or the meanings attached to) these "facts" that are all important. An institutionalized version of fact collation and interpretation is what transpires in a court of law. Presentation of data and cross-examination are initially oriented to eliciting (or suppressing, depending on whose interests would be served) basic "facts." Once those "facts" have been established, the task is to construct meanings out of them that enable various behaviors to be construed in a particular light, so that a pronouncement can be made on "reality."

There is an enormous danger in these procedures, however, for they leave unaddressed the prior question of what constitutes a fact. Jung (1958) confronts the complexity of this issue with a critical exposition in his preface to *Answer to Job*. He challenges the supposition that something is true only if it presents itself in a physically verifiable form. He argues that there are such things as "psychic" facts that cannot be established by reference to physical phenomena nor supported by rational criticism. Instead he affirms that psychic facts, as anthropomorphic images, have an emotional foundation that is unassailable by reason in that they transcend consciousness. They precipitate complexes of ideas that are expressed as mythological motifs that must be regarded not only as objects but as subjects with laws of their own. In expressing this view, Jung is simultaneously challenging the claim that insight flows from rationality alone, for rationality itself is an artifact of a particular form of reality and is unable to deal with phenomena whose origins and inherent structures are beyond the scope of those rational parameters.

To accept Jung's proposition demands that we reach beyond the principles of rationality if we are to fully stretch the boundaries of our potential insights. This is not to say that rationality should be abandoned. To the contrary, it's simply to affirm that we need to reach beyond the level of making only deductive predictions from premises we assume to be immovable pillar stones of reality. These premises themselves are undergoing transformations. If we lean on them too heavily and assume they never change, then our commitment to principles of rationality will only increase the instability of our framework of reality (Serrano, 1966). In particular, since we do not lead our lives, make our decisions, and reach our goals in everyday life either statistically or scientifically but rather by inferential processes, it's important that these heuristic models of "knowing" that guide our everyday experience be developed to higher levels of sophistication. We need systems of thinking, feeling, intuiting, and knowing that can compensate for the severe limitations of rationality.

I must pause and *summarize*. Throughout my quest, I wish to embrace the notion of man as a process, the creator and recreator of reality who is involved in the ongoing transformation of, and being transformed by, the realities so developed. In addition, I want to be guided by the view that in each event and at each moment there may be multiple realities, some of which are incongruent and maybe even contradictory, but out of those simultaneous juxtapositions new meanings may be constructed. Also, although embracing key principles of the scientific method, I'm eager to search for a synthesis of social reality by capturing the calculus of experience, not in a set of balanced and solvable mathematical equations, but rather in a mosaic of metaphors, whose component parts, although not fitting at all interfaces, when taken in totality provide a fluid picture of the whole—what Goffman (1967) would refer to as a grammar of situations.

Structural Encasements

The second theme I wish to address is that overwhelming question with which we are left after embracing the notion of man as a process, a creator, and a creature of his own realities: what triggers events, situations, and dreams to be given the particular meanings they require, especially those that become stabilized across time and space? This theme of how reality becomes shaped in the institutionalized experience of man has been a central topic in much of the literature of history, social science, drama, philosophy, and metaphysics. However, if we search in these fields for an understanding of what is "real" and "meaningful" to man, we'll be tossed about by vigorous debates that bounce us between opposite points of view.

To sort out who is right or what is correct from these writings would be an impossible, if not presumptuous, task because so many of the key propositions about reality seem fundamentally contradictory. What's more, the advocates for each side of a contradictory perspective often seem so persuasive. Could it be that deep down I'm really gullible? If not, why am I so easily encapsulated by one particular reality set, simultaneously becoming its proponent and its victim? How is it that in another moment of time and space I'm equally encapsulated by its polar opposite, hardly even noticing the contradiction in my behavior, but finding similar "fickleness" in others to be both transparent and hard to tolerate?

Two obvious issues arise. The first is that there is an alternative to trying to resolve the contradictions. That is to accept that the very contradictions themselves are a basic part of the nature of things. Eastern philosophy has always held the maxim that contradiction and the nexus of opposites are central to the totality of things. Marxist perspectives on dialectical processes have incorporated this view into social analysis, providing a theoretical framework that can leave us free from the paralysis of unresolved dualities. But still— and this is the second issue—we somehow manage to get ourselves imprisoned by the structure of reality that one side (or the other) of the basic contradiction provides. To make things even more complex, it's a prison of whose walls we're rarely conscious.

This notion of *psychological prison* is one I feel compelled to pursue, for it too contains its own internal paradox. It often happens that the very forces that provide the encasements—the prison walls—also provide the structures that make us feel secure. When we do come to step outside the walls of our prison, we find ourselves so insecure and disoriented that our automatic reaction is to repair to the security—albeit the imprisonment—of the structures we've just left, or else seek out other structures that are equally constraining. It's as if the "grass is greener on the other side of the fence," and yet when we knock the fence down and venture into new pastures, we discover that our digestive system has only been calibrated to consuming "brown grass." We start to crave for a return to the "good old days" to which we had become so well adapted. Bored. Stagnant. Maybe even oppressed. But at least secure.

Eldridge Cleaver (1968), writing from prison, captures the spirit of this dynamic superbly. "The heavy steel doors slammed shut with a clang of finality that chilled my soul. I have grown to like this door. When I go out of my cell, I can hardly wait to get back in, to slam that cumbersome door. . . . Once inside my cell I feel safe . . . I don't have to watch the other convicts any more, or the guards in the guntowers. If you live in a cell with nothing but bars in front . . . someone can walk along and throw a Molotov cocktail in on you before you know it. . . ." The same doors and walls that make us prisoners leave us afraid and insecure when they're not present. Most of us prefer to remain prisoners of our own consciousness rather than to be buffeted by the uncertainties, albeit the freedoms, represented by what lies beyond our consciousness.

12

I know of no better way to convey the central idea of the structural encasements of each particular version of reality than through the following
dream of Jung's (1965) which, in metaphoric form, summarizes it all.

> "It was night in some unknown place, and I was making slow and painful
> headway against a mighty wind. I had my hands cupped around a tiny light
> which threatened to go out at any moment. Everything depended on my
> keeping this little light alive. Suddenly I had the feeling that something was
> coming up behind me. But at the same moment I was conscious, in spite of
> my terror, that I must keep my little light going regardless of all dangers."

Here the bearer of the light fears the shadow that the candle creates. Had the
light gone out, the shadow would have disappeared, thereby potentially freeing
the bearer from the binds that the feared shadow provoked. In the bearer's
reality it didn't seem that way, for he expected that if he let the light go out,
then he'd no longer be able to see the gigantic black figure that was following
him. That prospect only increased the bearer's fear, because the shadow would
have fused with the blackness around him and then become even more ter-
rifying since it couldn't be seen. The only way that the bearer could see to
cope with this was to make sure the light never became extinguished.

This example highlights what I mean by structural encasements. The
bearer is caught in a set of double binds, at least in terms of his perspective.
If he could step out of his reality at that time, he could see things differently,
but he can't. The structure of his reality at that moment completely constrains
his options. The potency of the structural encasements is that the solution
creates the problem that demands the solution—the bearer fears the dark, so
he lights a candle, which creates a shadow which provides for the bearer the
justification for fearing the dark and needing a light.

In any contradiction three types of structural encasement may be found.
One is connected with thesis; one is connected with antithesis; and one is associated with binding thesis and antithesis together, the forces that make the
contradiction a contradiction.

To explicate this, I must turn to Marx. He postulated that man, and
society at large, are constantly caught in the byplay between polar experiences
that are simply different facets of an essential contradiction. These opposite
sides of the contradiction are dependent on each other for their continued existence and are mutually reinforcing. His most famous and oft-quoted passage
from *The Holy Family* (1845) illustrates this clearly.

> Private property, as private property, as wealth, is compelled to maintain
> *itself,* and thereby its opposite, the proletariat, in *existence.* That is the
> *positive* side of the contradiction, self-satisfied private property.
>
> The proletariat, on the other hand, is compelled as proletariat to abolish itself
> and thereby its opposite, the condition for its existence, what makes it the
> proletariat, i.e., private property. That is the *negative* side of the
> contradiction.

13

In this passage we see three sets of forces operating: (1) those that emerge from the *positive* side of the contradiction, from the people who have the power to define "what is"; (2) those that come from the *negative* side of the contradiction, from the people who have no control over the definitions of "what is" and whose primary power base emerges from their propulsion to destroy what the positive side works to defend; and (3) those that hold the positive and negative in their continued and ongoing relationship to each other, the developers, enacters, and enforcers of the rituals and conventions that regulate the relationship between these polar opposites. It is only as these three are linked together that we develop a sense of the totality, the cohesion of the parts that make the whole, or as Jung (1958) put it, the *antinomy*—the totality of inner opposites.

It is important to underscore the place and function of the set of mediating forces, for without them the contradiction would not exist and the antinomy would vanish. It's only as the two facets (what Marx calls the positive and negative) are held together, forced to coexist side by side, that the contradiction becomes a contradiction. If they were not so connected, then there would be no contradiction. For this reason, in any contradiction, we must talk about the three dynamics, not just two. The set of processes that the mediating forces are engaged in are as important to the antinomy as are the polar opposites (positive-negative) that the antinomy is all about.

There are two key functions the mediating forces fulfill. The first is that they keep the two sides of the contradiction in a steady state, enabling the positive side to continue defining things as it wishes and preventing the negative side from succeeding in destroying those circumstances. The second is that since the juxtaposition of the opposites creates a great deal of tension, it's the task of the intermediary to provide a way of diffusing these strains. This may be done in either of two ways. One method is to ensure that the extremes remain far enough apart so that they hardly even recognize that they both are responsible for the ongoing existence of the other and thereby the condition they find themselves in. An example of this is that the rich need the poor to keep the rich rich, and the poor need the rich to keep the poor poor. Management needs labor, as labor, to enable management to be management, and labor needs management in order for labor to remain as labor. If either group were to fully recognize this situation, their relationships with each other would be truly explosive. To minimize the impact of this, the intermediary forces can attempt to camouflage what's going on by preventing the extremes from having contact with each other. The second method for diffusing tensions between the opposites is by providing an outlet for the expression of conflict, a safety valve for the release of built-up tensions. Expressions of conflict (such as strikes or protests) allow for an abreaction of hostile feelings while simultaneously ensuring that the fundamental nature of the relationships in work organizations remain unchanged (Simmel, 1955). In this sense the safety valve

14

mechanisms enable the tensions between divergent dualisms to be resolved, thereby preserving the overall unity, but in fact actually doing nothing more than "clearing the air" (Coser, 1956).

It was, of course, Marx's recognition of how the mediating forces operated to preserve the status quo that led him to propound that the only way to produce genuine social change was by altering the overall set of relationships. This necessitated the dismantling of both sides of the contradiction and the obliteration of all the rules and rituals that bound them together. In his social analysis it was the class structure that operated as that mediating force, and hence his theory of social change demanded the eventual overcoming of all aspects of class relationships.

I don't wish here to pursue the arguments about global social change or the politics of classlessness, but I do want to take from Marx what I feel are three key lessons. The first is to recognize the centrality of dialectics in understanding the processes of contradictions. The second is to underscore the place of the mediating forces in the intercourse between polar opposites. The third is to acknowledge that each of the three positions of the contradiction (the positive, the negative, and the mediating) are structurally bound into a particular frame of reference that highly constrains how the world is experienced in that position. I shall refer to these three structural encasements as (a) those that go with having the power or the capacity to determine how things will be (*the powerful position*—the "positive" side of the contradiction), (b) those that go with seeing the only way to change things as being the destruction of "what is" (the *powerless position*—the "negative" side), and (c) those that go with being in the *mediating position* where the key function is to keep the two sides of the duality connected while diffusing the basic conflict between them.

Fundamental to each of these structural encasements is the concept of power, which is expressed in three different forms. There's power to determine "what is" ("creative" power), power to "resist" or destroy ("blocking" power), and power to mediate between polarities ("mediating" power). Thus, if at any time I want to understand the psychological prisons that surround me, it's necessary to comprehend the nature of the power dynamics that are operating. Conversely, if I want to understand the nature of power, I must appreciate the structures with which I'm encased. The two are integrally linked.

Again, I must pause and *summarize*. Apart from wishing to view man as a process, a creator, and creature of his realities, I want to explore the social forces that serve as catalysts to particular events, situations, and images being given the meaning they acquire. In particular, I want to comprehend those forces that help crystallize realities and that provide an imprisoning effect once they've become established. As a starting point in the search for understanding the psychological imprisonment that comes with the processes of reality creation, crystallization, and transformation, I want to explore three different types of encasement that flow from where we sit in the social structure and the power base out of which we operate as a result of those locations. These are the structural encasements that come with having power to create, power to block, and power to mediate.

Setting the Parameters

Having laid out for myself some clear guidelines for my journey and some conceptual focus for my search, it became time to stop pondering and begin my quest. Although as I commenced my journey I had no clarity about my original question (what causes events, situations, and dreams to be given the particular meanings they acquire, and how in turn these reality structures so created provide unidentified psychological prisons), I did feel I'd established a place to look. It seemed to me that once I understood the essence of contradiction, once I could intuitively comprehend the way structural encasements operate, and once the different facets of power were unravelled, then my question would be less perplexing.

Since in any search it is not possible to span all the available terrain, I had to make some choices about what I would look at and what I would ignore, either on the basis of what would best serve the goals of my quest or as an expression of my personal style or preference. In this book I resolved to explore my paradox and its attendant questions by trying to understand *the behavior of groups in interaction.* I could have equally chosen interactions among individuals or among organizations, but the field of interpersonal relations has already been heavily researched, and at this time to understand the way organizations behave surpasses the limits of my comprehension. Furthermore, I had become fascinated by the whole notion that *groups behave;* also, I'd noticed so often how individuals seem to change quite significantly as they move from group to group. Perhaps most importantly, I'd grown tired of the disproportionate (in my opinion) amount of research energy that had been focused at the individual level in the field or oganizational psychology, as though the only thing that matters is what goes on in a person's head. This resolve to focus my attention at the group level did not mean that I considered the *behavior of people* in groups to be unimportant. To the contrary, it's merely an issue of where I chose to place emphasis.

Of course, I chose *interaction* as my focus because it's impossible to understand the nature of a "prison wall" unless it can be seen from both an inside and an outside perspective, and because power, as a dynamic concept, only makes sense in the interplays of social intercourse.

One problem I encountered early in my quest was the severe limitations of our language structure. I found, for example, that we have very few words for describing the behavior of entities at levels higher than the individual. Phrases like "she jumped", "he felt" or "I think" all have the behaving action located in the individual. But how much sense does it make to talk about "the group jumped" or "the group felt" or "the group thought"? The difficulty was that those words that function effectively to communicate images about individual action do not really fit very well when applied to the group. Yet to date we don't have an appropriate language. I didn't know what to do about this problem. I had a choice. Either I could work on trying to develop a new language for capturing the actions of a behaving group, or I could borrow the rich set of metaphors that individual psychology has provided us and simply grit my teeth about how inadequately these terms apply at the group level. I resolved to do the latter. Not because it was necessarily the better, but because the former is still beyond me. Someday, maybe, we'll have a new group-based language. But for the moment I recognized the need to stay within the frameworks of the familiar.

In looking around for a place where groups were interacting in such a way that I could meaningfully research my theme, I came across two social systems, Ashgrove and Montville, which promised to be ideal settings for my quest. They held a special appeal because they were vastly different from each other, one being a public school system and the other a simulated minisociety.

The first part of my journey took me to Montville, a four-day experiential power laboratory designed and conducted by Oshry and Steele (Oshry, 1980). In this simulated society, participants were given the opportunity to experience directly what it was like to be "powerful" or "powerless" and "included" or "excluded." On arrival at Montville, all the participants were born, without choice, into one of three levels of the society—upper, middle, or lower. From that moment, in all elements of their lives such as standards of accommodation, quality and quantity of food, recreation, mobility, freedom, access to personal effects (clothing, money, credit cards, car keys), and so forth, they were treated differentially in keeping with their predestined status.

I present this Montville story in purely descriptive form as part 1 of this book. I invite you to read it as you would a novel, looking for the structural encasements, the contradictions, and the different forms of power that weave their way through the multiple realities that became developed at Montville.

As with any journey into the unknown, there were always some surprises that changed the nature of the quest. Montville did this for me. By the end of that experience, I was thoroughly engrossed in something bigger than my original paradox, for I had become totally deflected into the dynamics of group life, especially as they were revealed in the power laboratory setting. In part 2, I present some tentative suggestions about the way groups behave in interaction and, in particular, how the various structural encasements and positions in the power hierarchy influenced the perceptions and attributions the groups made towards each other, how they restricted or used information flow in order to create power, how groups resolved conflict among each other, and how they handled tension within their own ranks.

17

After experiencing and pondering on the implications of Montville, I turned to a totally different type of system, a public high school in the New England town of Ashgrove. Through this particular study I was hoping to expand my search to include multiple groups with several levels of hierarchical control. Ashgrove, which I present as part 3 of this book, is an account of the relationships among students, teachers, and principals in the high school, together with the relationship of these high school groups with the groups that possessed political and administrative control over the community's education system, in particular the town politicians, the elected board of education, and the superintendent's office. Through the Ashgrove experience, I attempted to trace the relationships among these groups and to explore whether the conceptualizations developed in Montville were relevant to group relations in a manifestly different organizational setting.

Part 1

Montville

Montville

Preface

In everyday life most people who experience power or powerlessness rarely have or make the opportunities to live through what it's like at the other end of the spectrum. The managing director has no comprehension of what it feels like to be the janitor, and the janitor has no idea of the tensions that go with being managing director. Since each person's reality is constrained by the conditions that surround him, this means that the likelihood of each ever being able to see things from the other's perspective is fairly low.

A power laboratory is designed to give people the opportunity to experiment with the exercise of power and powerlessness and to absorb the feelings of what each of those conditions is like (Oshry, 1980). People come to such a laboratory for various reasons. At one extreme we find a corporate president who feels frustrated over his inability to mobilize his organization members in the service of his particular goals. At the other extreme there's the black student who, in attempting to overcome the racial tension in school, started a protest movement that developed such potency that the student became frightened at the exercise of the available power.

Each power laboratory has its own unique design, and wide variations may be created by altering various structural features. However, they all have in common the notion of each member being *born* into a particular set of social conditions on arrival at the "society" and clusters of individuals having differential access to and control over resources and social influence processes that relate to all domains of the living experience (Oshry, 1980).

Montville participants were twenty-two men and women, all strangers to each other, who occupied middle or upper-middle class standings in the nonlaboratory world. They held positions in corporate management, professions, education, or studenthood. Two of the participants were white women, three were black men. Their professional identifications ranged from engineering to religion; they worked for organizations varying from the military to a university. The ages of participants spanned from early twenties to sixty.

All participants were advised before registering for the laboratory that they would be born without choice into one of three classes—the Elites, the Outs, or the Ins—and they were warned to expect sharp differences in the way they would be treated depending on the "luck" of their birth process. They were advised not to participate if they were undergoing any significant life stress. After registration they were sent the following circular, setting out clearly for them the expectations about how the laboratory staff would relate to the participants and the society in general.

Staff Roles in the Montville Laboratory

In this power and systems laboratory, the staff serve functions quite different from the ones normally served by staff of other programs. In order to maximize learning, it is important that both staff and participants understand what functions staff should and should not serve.

a. *Anthropologists*[5]

During the life of the experimental community, wnich lasts until 8:00 A.M. Thursday morning, staff are to function as anthropologists rather than as controllers or directors of the experience. They are to study and attempt to understand what happens to the community as it develops, while influencing the course of these developments as little as possible.

In short, during this period, Anthropologists:

—observe as much of the action as they can;
—interview participants about what is happening to them;
—attempt to formulate some overall perspective for understanding community action.

Anthropologists **do not:**

—attempt to influence the course of development of community life;
—make suggestions to individuals or groups as to what they should do;
—tell people in one part of the community what is going on in other parts of the community;
—interrupt the action for process review sessions.

Commencing at 8:00 A.M. Thursday and for the last two days of the program, the staff Anthropologists are responsible for helping participants deepen their learning from the experience through conducting debriefing and review sessions and seminars, providing relevant theory input, and helping participants explore applications to back-home settings.

b. *Special Resource Persons*

At this laboratory one or more staff people will be assigned as a resource to some segment of the total community. When a staff person serves that role he or she does not function as an Anthropologist for the total community but instead develops a special relationship with some unit within the total community. The role of the special resource person is to help people utilize to the fullest whatever learning resources are available at the laboratory.

No participant had a choice as to which class of the society he or she would be born into. However, the Elites were all given phone calls in advance to tell them what time to arrive and to advise them of their upper status. All others were sent impersonalized announcements advising the appointed arrival times but with no information about their intended status at Montville.

There were no noticeable differences among the three groups in terms of identification in the back-home environment. For example, each of the groups had one black member. There was an approximately even distribution of professionals, managers, students, etc. among the groups.

Below are the lists of participants clustered according to their allocated status for the laboratory. Pseudonyms have been given to protect identities. They've been allocated in a form to help the reader identify group memberships. Elites have regal names, Outs have common names, and those given to the Middles all start with a vowel.

Elites	Ins	Outs
(Kenloch Mansion)	*(House of Hannover)*	*(Westville)*
Richard	Alistair	Glen
Roderick	Anthony	Ross
Charles	Owen	Fred
Lennox	Ivan	Lee
	Ethel	Carl
Staff	Orsen	Steve
Fritz	Ethan	Bruce
Malvin	Ingrid	Bill
Jason	Eric	John
Mavis		

I served as an Anthropologist at Montville and together with three others observed everything that occurred in the society. This account, written in novel form, is my best attempt to capture on paper the major unfolding of events in this simulated society. I have had to leave out many details in order for this document not be as lengthy as a history of World War II. However, I have worked as faithfully as I know how to present events in the light in which they occurred. Mostly I have used the actual words individuals spoke.

I have downplayed the importance of age and race, hence the reader will not automatically be able to use these categories as explanations of behavior. Black and white were equally significant, as were those in their twenties and their sixties.

Genesis

"In the beginning God created . . .
And He called the light 'day,' and the dark 'night.' "

Life at Montville began with the premature arrival of Roderick, clad in a suit and tie on a day made for swimming trunks. He was greeted gruffly by Jason, the midwife of the society, who told him to disappear for an hour and return at the correct registration time. Roderick dragged himself off to the beach, a good twenty-minute walk. As he trekked along, with drops of perspiration staining his neatly pressed trousers, he started to wonder whether the phone call he'd received telling him that he was to be a member of the elite group had all been a hoax.

His fears were intensified when, on his return at the appointed hour, he found Mavis and Jason standing behind a desk that supported a roughly made sign. It read, "All Participants *must* register here." Roderick paused momentarily and then tentatively approached the desk.

"Name?"

"Roderick Doonsberg."

"Who can we contact in case of emergency?"

"My wife."

"What's a phone number where we can reach her?"

"203–476–4496."

"Now we need from you some more things. We'd like:

> five dollars for the community treasury;
> your wallet;
> your credit cards;
> your checkbook; and
> your car keys."

"I have none!"

"Well, your air tickets then. . . . "

Roderick, bewildered and anxious, silently complied.

"And now your luggage," ordered Jason, whose blank stare and massive mop of hair gave him the appearance of a gypsy. "And take off your shoes and socks, please!"

Roderick thumped his luggage upon the counter, then flopped on the bench beside the friendly, unspeaking anthropologist (who was busily writing down his every reaction) and silently took off his shoes and socks. The gypsy flipped his socks inside out and then thoroughly searched his shoes, handing them back to the bewildered owner with a grunt. This was all getting a little much for Roderick.

"What did you do that for?" he snapped.

"Just simply to make sure that what you have is what you have," Jason replied wryly.

"Oh, I see!!"

"You can keep one change of underwear and a fresh pair of socks and one packet of cigarettes, and here's a brown bag for you to put it all in—now sign here. . . ."

As a guest of the Montville Conference Center, I agree to assume responsibility in the event of loss or damage resulting from my stay at this establishment.

Roderick P. Doonsberg.

"That's all—next?"

Roderick turned toward the door, brown packet in one hand, shoes in the other. There he caught a fleeting image of Lennox laboriously carrying his luggage into the registration room. They passed, without saying a word. Little did they realize that in the next few days they would become involved in an experience of intrigue and complexity well beyond anything they'd previously encountered.

Roderick and Lennox, together with Charles and Richard, had all been preselected as potential elite members of this society. In the luxury of Kenloch Mansion, the most palatial of the four homes that constituted the Montville complex, they now sat silently and anxiously, denuded of all save their own personhood and the contents of their brown bags. Their anticipation was flushed to a new high by the arrival of Fritz, who carried that aura of authority that derives from the security of knowing, or at least appearing to know, what he's about. He was closely tailed by Jason, who announced, "Fritz, they're all here now. We can start."

Fritz, with clockwork obedience, rose, felt pen in hand, and moved towards the newsprint. With lively, darting blue eyes and an energetic voice, he commenced his prologue.

"In this room at the moment are three sets of individuals. First there are you four," pointing to the inductees, who needed no identification for their brown bags announced their common differentness; "you have been chosen as potential members of the Powerful Elite group. In a few minutes we can talk about whether or not you want to be an Elite. Then there are two groups of staff people. There are the four Anthropologists who are sitting in different parts of this room. You'll notice they have a tag that identifies them. Between now and Thursday morning at 8:00, when the actual laboratory ends, the Anthropologists will be wandering around, observing groups and interviewing people on occasion, but generally they will attempt to avoid influencing the events of the society. They will try to observe as much of the action as they can; hence, we expect they will be given access to all parts of the society at all times. The other staff members are Malvin, Jason, Mavis, and I. Jason is the fellow who took your luggage at registration time. We now have that under lock and key and should you end up becoming the Elites, it will be returned. Mavis is here only for the registration period; when the last member of the society arrives, which is tomorrow, Monday, at about lunchtime, she will leave.

The other three of us, Malvin, Jason, and I, will participate fully in the society. Exactly what we'll do is not immediately clear. We expect to be resource people of some type. So far, Jason has been resourceful because he's now got your luggage! Later this evening a second group, which we'll call 'Ins', will be arriving. And tomorrow morning we are expecting the 'Outs'. The housing available is. . . ."

Fritz proceeded to unravel the story about how Montville society could operate. He told the bewildered and muted quartette who sat tightly clutching their brown bags, that if each of them were willing to accept the role of being Elites, then together they could all decide how the community was to be run.

"But first of all I want to know whether you'll 'buy in,' " Fritz concluded. "I need a commitment from each of you that assures me of your willingness to use the power available to design a community. At present you four and we three staff constitute seven individuals with the potential to become the Power Elite. But we cannot move into a position of real power until we have become a group; and we can't become a group until such time as we all make a commitment to the task that the powerful Elite in this society must adopt."

There seemed to be a catch in all of this to Charles. "I'm being asked to commit myself to a system that doesn't yet exist," he puzzled. "For me to say 'I won't buy in' because I'm against it would require something to exist to be against. To be for or against a 'nonsystem' seems like the same choice." Charles was confused! But he knew that in accepting an Elite role he'd simultaneously retrieve his luggage and gain an opportunity to influence Montville's future. He hoped that this might enable him to find relief from the tensions he'd been experiencing since his arrival. In the light of this, the decision seemed simple.

"I'm in," said Charles.

"Me too," came from three others, equally eager to grasp some control over the power placed at their disposal.

Fritz silently sighed his relief. He directed Jason to return the personal belongings to the new Elites. Inside Fritz knew that in the next few hours the Elites, as a group, would become deeply committed to whatever blueprints they designed for Montville. So much so that no matter what happened when the Ins and Outs arrived, Montville would soon develop a life of its own.

A new society had been born.

The new Elites quickly stumbled on their first problem.

"How are we going to make decisions in this group?" ventured Roderick cautiously.

"I think we should elect ourselves a leader who can direct the community's activities," offered Lennox with confidence.

"And who do you think that leader should be?" Richard's tone was cynical. "I think we should consider other possibilities. How about majority rule? Or decisions by consensus?"

There was some latent animosity in this intial exchange, but it remained unaddressed and served to fan the vigorous debate that emerged. Without even trying, the Elites were spontaneously caught in their first Catch 22. They had to decide how they were going to decide before they could decide anything. Needless to say they couldn't decide. For the next hour they struggled. Then stagnated, they sought a compromise. Since they couldn't agree, they agreed to disagree over anything they disagreed over. This felt like a consensus decision, albeit through a strange trick of the mind. There was an emergent feeling of agreement amongst them even though no one seemed able to say clearly on what they were agreeing. Nevertheless within an hour or two the new Elite group had gravitated towards a system of mutual agreement as a basis for their decisions.

The Phantom Plan

The Elites had only a few short hours to design the foundations of their society for by early evening the next group of people (the Ins) would be registering. The Elites decided it would be wise to have their system in place before others arrived so that they would be inducted into the Elites' society as something already given.

"Let's make it a replica of America at large."

"No. I'd prefer to experiment with some different form of society. I already know what it's like living in the U.S.!"

"Hey! I've got a great idea!"

"Let's be like the real Elites. We'll design the society so that we're always pulling the strings but let's do it in such a way that no one can ever figure out who's actually got the power. That way we'll be able to keep the masses down."

"It won't work. I've got a better idea! Let's make some people poor and others rich. Then we can build a society that makes the rich richer and the poor poorer."

"Yes. That's great. And the task of the society could be to study issues of poverty and to design ways for the poor to cope with and be elevated from their poverty. Better still we could study the frustration that arises out of their inability to succeed! That has a nice little twist to it."

The Elites became alive with ideas. After an hour of debate, the plan that had the most appeal was the one in which they'd keep their eliteness hidden while controlling the system like invisible puppeteers. Although this phantom design had some clear disadvantages, the Elites intuitively liked it. They quickly dismissed the objection that such a plan might leave them in a position of not knowing what was actually going on in the society at large. They'd cross that bridge when they came to it.

There was one problem. Lennox was unhappy. He wanted to have his power visible. This provoked a fight.

"Lennox, I'd be happy for you to be our mouthpiece," retorted Richard, keen to keep the phantom plan alive. "We could even design a parliamentary system and make you mayor."

"That won't work," objected Lennox. "That would only make me appear to be nothing more than a messenger boy. *My* power will be clear only if all of us Elites are visible."

The group was now caught. They had to permit dissent in order for consensus decision making to work. However they could not let it paralyze them. The Elites faced their first real crisis. Some way of coping with Lennox had to be found.

This necessity fathered a creative solution. It took a little time and a lot of agony but eventually the Elites settled on the idea of developing a special role for the dissenter and then to develop consensus on that role. Lennox was to be given a special role, the precise details of which were left vague. It was agreed however that he could be both "visible and powerful." Having created this exception for the dissenter, Lennox was happy and the group was able to establish consensus on their original agenda, namely the phantom plan.

The Elites had to quickly decide a number of issues: how other members of the society would be registered; allocation of housing for the other groups; and the central activities of the society. They took each of these topics in turn and examined it from the vantage point of how their eliteness could be kept hidden. They kept banging into logical absurdities. For example when they discussed housing they saw the following options. They could all live together in the one house. This would enable them to have meetings whenever they wished. On the other hand, to guarantee their phantomness, it made more sense to share housing with the Ins who were soon to arrive. To keep their eliteness hidden in this way however meant they would have to forego many of the privileges of being elite. It seemed somewhat self-defeating to wear the same shirt all week, remaining unshaven, undeodorized, and with teeth uncleaned. This would keep their eliteness hidden. But what type of eliteness would it be? They might end up working so hard to effect their phantom plan that their eliteness could become an illusion. In fact they could very well become the slaves of the system they designed to dominate.

Despite the obvious problems, the die had been cast. Their eliteness would be kept hidden. They realized that within an hour or two the nine new arrivals who were prechosen as Ins would be arriving and that from then on it would be difficult for the Elites to spend time together as a group without undermining their phantomness. The planning task seemed enormous. However the Elites comforted themselves with the belief that the vagueness and uncertainty that would grow out of their hidden eliteness would make the other groups feel powerless. Then, in comparison, the Elites would seem strong.

They turned to the question of the allocation of housing. The houses available were: Westville, containing nine bunks in a space ideal for five, with one degenerate bathroom and dilapidated wash facilities; Hannover, a middle-class home that could accommodate five comfortably; and Kenloch, which had a large cozy living room, a spacious porch, and easy sleeping space for eleven with a generous distribution of bathroom and washing facilities. Westville and Hannover were on the same street, separated strategically by Montville Inn, the location of the communal dining hall. Kenloch was a brisk walk across the Green, past the flag pole, a swift sidestep around the village post office, and then along one block to the left, where this heavy discussion of accommodations was now taking place.

"Why don't we cram Westville with the nine Ins for the first night." posed Richard sadistically. "Then the next day we'll move them out. Give them upward mobility." His suggestion held appeal. "Yeah. Relieving their deprivation after one night will be seen as a reward," concluded Lennox. This scheme never came to pass, simply because contractual arrangements with the conference staff had not provided for the use of Westville until the next day. But the new Elites were not aware of this fact during their early discussion, and hence wasted a half hour of vigorous debate developing what they called "The Westville Cram" concept, and then dismissing the topic of housing, satisfied that their task was complete. When it later surfaced that this plan could not be worked, a ten-second substitute decision was arrived at, which split the ten-registering Ins between Kenloch and Hannover, an act in keeping with the planned phantomness.

From housing, attention was turned to food. Fritz laid out the plans. "We've arranged for Ins and Elites to be served the highest quality food the kitchen produces. Tables are set up in one corner of the dining hall and will be waited on by conference center staff. In the other corner of the room will be a long table at which the Outs will be fed—if you can call it food. Salad, bread, and water for each meal with a cereal variant for breakfast. They will not be waited on and will be required to clean up after themselves. This arrangement may be altered by us Elites so long as Mr. Beasley, the director of the conference center, is given three hours' prior notice. No additional money will be required."

"We don't need to think about that then till tomorrow," dismissed Roderick, "but for the moment that looks great."

"What time is supper served, Fritz?" asked Charles.

"Tonight it's 6:00 P.M."

"It's already 6:15. Let's go and eat."

With an air of confidence, the new Elites, already beginning to enjoy their superior status, departed for the dining hall.

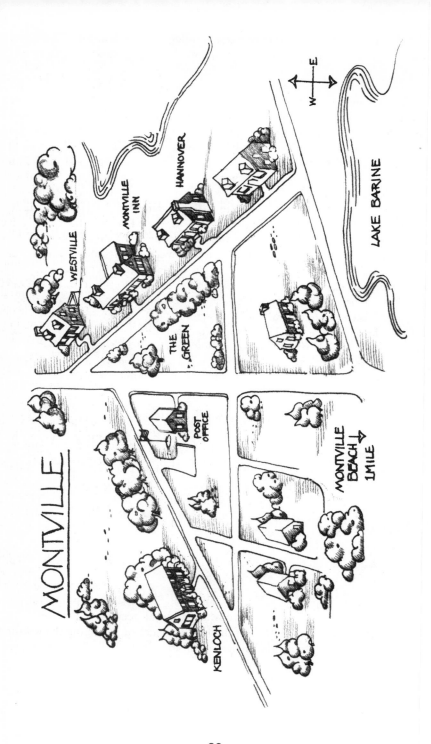

The First Evening

It was early evening. A strange assortment of characters clustered on the Green outside the registration office. Some talked, some walked, some just stared off into space. Jason and Mavis were doing their thing:

"Your car keys;

Your money;

Your shoes and socks;

Now sign this;

Next."

The birth traumas for the Ins were the same as for the Elite, except that an extra five dollars were required for the community treasury. This was intended as a little ironic twist, added by the Elite, who thought that the middle class should carry a heavier economic burden for the society than the "rich" or the "poor."

The last-minute plan for housing had been to locate seven of the nine Ins in Hannover (which had room for five) and two in Kenloch, the current home of the Elites (increasing the number there to nine where the sleeping capacity was for eleven). Eric and Ethel, two of the newly arrived Ins, were destined for Kenloch, a fact they would come to bitterly regret, when they were eventually evicted by the Elites two days later. But for the moment, location of one's bed meant nothing significant to any of the new arrivals.

"It seems that I'm going to be able to sleep in this society; now if only I can be assured of some food occasionally. . . . !!" pondered one highly anxious new arrival.

The first phase of phantomness was working satisfactorily. As the gypsy told the Ins their sleeping arrangements, he announced that there would be a meeting on the Green at 8:45 P.M.—called by whom or for what purpose was never really asked. The prospect of a meeting provided the promise of some much-desired information. That hope was enough for the moment.

Back at the registration desk, Anthony was furious. With reddening face he argued with Mavis and the gypsy. "Why can't I keep my tape recorder? You've got my wallet, my money, my clothes. I came here to do some learning and my tape recorder is critical to me."

Mavis shrugged her indifference. "It's not my decision. I'm just doing what I was told to do." He turned and looked at the strange character sitting in the corner, but received nothing more than a blank anthropological stare; he looked out the door but help was not available; he looked prayerfully towards the ceiling but not even there was his plight heeded.

"Sign this please." Anthony reluctantly conceded, changing the wording in the contract just sufficiently to increase his protection a little and to express perhaps the only piece of autonomy he felt in that moment.

Outside Anthony ventilated his anger to some of the other Ins still await-
ing their encounter with the society's midwife. "See if you can find out who
those two in there are," he pleaded with Ingrid. "I wish I'd asked them who
they were!" Ingrid nodded, but hardly heard his words, for in this moment
she was feeling anxious for herself. Although she was prepared to listen indifferently to Anthony's patter, there seemed no imperative to help carry his
burden.

Days later, some of the Ins were a little amazed that they hadn't used
these moments with greater effectiveness. "If only we'd got some of our group
who'd not yet registered to give their money to those who had, we might not
be in this plight right now. . . ." In those fleeting seconds of initiation, however, there was no group, just a collection of disoriented beings walking around
in a state of dazed bewilderment—hardly a condition to facilitate rationality.
It didn't really occur to anyone that just because they were all being denuded
together, they could necessarily trust each other.

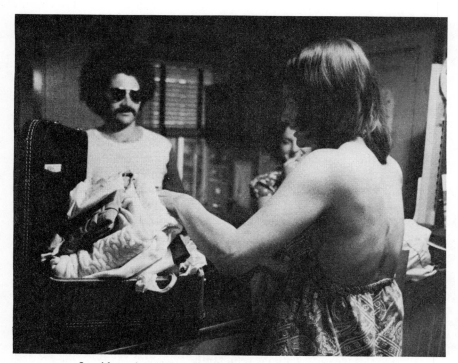

Ingrid, at the registration desk announces categorically to
Jason, the gypsy, "I don't care what you say; *these* pills go
with me."

The appointed time for the meeting had now passed. Eight of the nine newly arrived Ins were standing around on the Village Green augmented by the Elites, who wore no badge of their superior status and who carefully veiled their comments to avoid anyone detecting characteristics that would differentiate them from the new-borns. Someone suggested that Hannover lounge would provide a haven from the mosquitoes and bugs that now ruled the Green. Since that was the home of the majority of the new arrivals, few suspicions were roused by this suggestion. But then, none of the Ins knew who the new arrivals were or what other houses existed anyway, so any suggestion would have seemed legitimate. Sheeplike, they all filed into Hannover cottage. As Anthony passed through the door he grunted almost inaudibly to unhearing ears. "It looks like *they're* inviting us into *their* house"—a strange comment since that was his house, too. But it spoke clearly to his fears. For by this time he had become convinced there existed somewhere a "them," a powerful group to which he didn't belong.

Trivial conversation dominated for a few minutes. Then a long, pregnant silence. "It's 8:59," bristled Anthony, "and I thought the meeting was due to start at 8:45."

"That's right. I think they should be censured," retorted Richard, the Elite, eager to preserve his phantomness by identifying with the new arrivals, who were beginning to feel very manipulated.

Slowly the realization dawned on this cluster of individuals that the meeting was going on right there and then. There were just so many unknowns that even the most courageous of the new group looked timid. They all now appeared little more than smudged shadows of the dignified, highly esteemed personalities who a few hours earlier had entered Montville dresssed in dapper suits and carrying numerous symbols of the security they enjoyed in the world they had voluntarily left behind.

Anthony grappled for some clarity. "I saw another group driving off in cars a while ago. I guess they must have been the Elite."

"Yeah, I saw that car too," snapped Richard, chortling inside with the delights of his own hidden identity.

"That means we must be both the Ins and the Outs here in this room," deduced Anthony, who correctly perceived, but couldn't identify precisely, the difference in the status of those gathered.

Ingrid decided to test this assumption of the differential status within Hannover lounge. "If only I could find an index that would tell me who has more power than me," she mused.

Anthony continued his monologue. "I know that some people arrived earlier in the day than I did. I want to know about them because I think they are the ones who have the power."

"How would you know a powerful person if you saw one?" teased Alistair, feeling equally anxious about all this ambiguity.

"He's anyone with a toothbrush!" Ingrid had found her acid test! With a smile that betrayed half humor and half trauma she popped the question, "Does anyone here have a toothbrush?"

Richard and Lennox grunted that they too had lost their toothbrushes on arrival. No one admitted to possessing the prized object. With that Ingrid rested, content in the assumption that "we all must be one after all."

Disconnected comments punctuated the heavy atmosphere.

"I found it embarrassing having the photographer catch me as I took my underpants out of my case."

"I felt really deprived at registration."

"Me too," added Ingrid angrily. "But I was adamant that I was going to keep my pills with me. The cheek of them!"

"Fritz, what are you?"

"I'm a resource person."

"What's a resource person?"

"That's vague!" replied Fritz.

"I feel others consider I've been radical in my suggestions so far," contributed Anthony.

"What's radical about asking questions?" snapped Ingrid.

The emotional fever was beginning to rise. Things began to feel out of control—a threatening moment for the Elites, whose goal was to keep a hold on the initiative. Richard cut the air with an icy comment. "I guess I should introduce myself. It seems I'm the only person who was given any information. I was told to wait until the last person arrived and then to conduct the evening program. It seems. . . ."

"Who told you?"

"Jason gave me the message at registration. I didn't question it. He said the people who showed initiative would be rewarded and since this was what I was asked to do. . . ."

"Wait a minute, your credibility just went down for me," Ingrid fumed. "How can I now be sure you don't have your toothbrush and. . . ." All of a sudden she was halted by the stark realization that acid tests just might not function too well in a society where neither acid nor alkaline exist. "Perhaps this world just isn't like that one I've left behind," Ingrid silently concluded as she returned to her state of temporary inertia.

Richard, with all his coolness and ever keen to keep his identity confused, suggested that perhaps it wouldn't be wise to carry out the program that had been suggested after all. He sat down, abandoning his crusade to force that assembly of Ins and phantom Elites to do anything specific that night.

By now the tension was so powerful none could escape its force. Lennox tried to lighten the atmosphere by telling a joke. His fellow Elites, who had been together for the past eight hours, laughed merrily and spontaneously. A few of the new Ins laughed too, but for them it was more a matter of releasing tension than responding to the humor. This difference between groups was vaguely noticeable, but so intangible that none of the real Ins could identify specifically what made them feel differently.

Whenever an In began to follow a path of questioning that might provide some basic information, one of the Elites would deflect the probe by some diversion. Anthony picked this up at one point. "Look, Richard," he fumed, "I was just asking Fritz a question, and as he was about to answer it, you cut him off. You did the same thing to Alistair a moment ago when Fritz was on the spot. What are you doing?" Fritz deflected this attack on Richard by pointing out that a large number of the group had engaged in this activity, not just Richard. This was true. What had happened was that the Elites had created a group norm that virtually everyone had come to adopt. The norm was "whenever anyone is about to flush out some basic information about Montville society, frustrate the attempt by making an irrelevant comment."

The evening became enslaved to this norm and deteriorated into a carousel of alienating and disorienting events. There were only two things of certainty at the onset of sleep: The Elites were proud of their successful phantomness, and none of the Ins could differentiate between north, south, east, or west. They all had their doubts and suspicions; some even doubted their suspicions, except Anthony, who was convinced that in Hannover lounge that night there had been at least one person who had a higher status in the system than he did, a realization that was to plague him for the next day.

The Declaration

The atmosphere at breakfast the next morning was calm in comparison with the emotional turmoil of the previous evening. Somehow, sleep had robbed the disorientation of some of its intensity, and most were eating with quiet resignation that this day would bring something new. No one had to wait for long for an unfolding of new events.

No sooner had breakfast been served than Lennox bounded to his feet. In a nervous but strong voice he announced to the group, "The society as it currently exists is somewhat unequal. I know some things that the rest of you are ignorant about!" A mouthful of unswallowed cereal stuck in Ethel's throat, causing a flurry of coughing, while anger, distrust, and frustration spontaneously emerged. Anthony was quick to react. "Who gave you this information? Who are the people in the know? Who has control of the community resources?"

Lennox tried desperately to generate an aura of aloof authority. He only partially succeeded. There was a lot that he could gain in this moment but there was also much that could be lost. Originally he had fought against the phantom plan during the Elites' embryonic struggles for the new society. He had pushed strongly for the freedom to make his eliteness visible. Although his colleagues had initially tried to subvert Lennox's wishes, by now they felt he could not longer be contained. Reluctantly they'd agreed to let him do as he wished, but in this moment they were watching him closely. If he made a fool of himself or became the victim of a spontaneous revolution, there was no guarantee that his friends would support him; after all, it wasn't yet clear that they were his friends, for his contributions to date had hardly elevated him to any place of specialness at Kenloch. In this moment he was alone.

In the meantime, his announcement was sure to attract a lot of hostility from this assembly, and he prepared his spirits to face the onslaught.

"Last night Jason was acting as my agent. Everything he did was at my direction," Lennox continued with deceiving intrigue. "To assure you of my authority, let me point out that I'm wearing a clean shirt this morning and here in my hand I hold the packet containing the community treasury." He opened it and waved a handful of five and ten dollar notes. His voice toughened again. "I want you all to deal with four areas of responsibility necessary to produce a dynamic society . . . and I want you to know that this is more than a recommendation. You *will* produce task forces and each group *will* report to me immediately after lunch."

The scene that developed made the previous evening seem like an inconsequential garden party; the distrust, abuse, and alienation quickly escalated to fever point. Both Richard and Roderick, in an attempt to protect their cover, joined the spirit of this vigorous attack, identifying with those most angered by Lennox's display of his position. However, their simulated anger was transparent. Ethan, one of the middles who had been reasonably silent to date, was quick to detect that their emotional outbursts were fake and boldly accused Richard and Roderick of being Elites also. They adamantly denied it. Anthony too was watching everyone's reactions keenly and with superb precision deduced that the members of the Elite group were Lennox, Richard, Roderick, Charles, Jason, Fritz, and Malvin. He said as much, but no one listened.

Lennox steadfastly refused under pressure to identify the other Elites, but simply told the audience that, "I've exercised my prerogative of self-disclosure; other Elites can do this at their own pleasure. We concluded that each individual should be responsible for his or her own statements." Fritz and Roderick now sensed that the phantomness would be quick to evaporate. Since Fritz was keen to release his own control over community resources, this seemed like the moment to act. He quickly and quietly arranged for Mr. Beasley, director of the conference center, to respond only to Roderick's directives. Immediately, Beasley, agitated by all this shouting in his conference dining hall, told Roderick that everyone had to leave the building straight away. "It is part of the contract with your staff that you will leave the dining area as soon as meals have been finished," he fumed. "If you are now in charge of this mob, tell them all to get out of here this very minute." Roderick paused, momentarily confused. If he delivered such a directive his phantomness would quickly vanish. "What the hell," he thought, as he rose to exercise Mr. Beasley's will.

In response to Roderick's directive, little groups repaired to the Green. The spirit of inquiry was now one of "who'd be the next to step out of the crowd." They didn't have to wait long, for Charles, too, was feeling the loneliness of his position. By the flagpole on Montville Green, he cast aside his phantom mantle and joined Lennox and Roderick to face the the onslaught of the angry questioners.

Alistair and Anthony led the attack, demanding that all the Elites should now step forward, for no one would believe that only these three were imbued with the power. Lennox had shown that he controlled the finance; Roderick held the key to meals; and now Charles had declared himself to be the housing specialist. At the very least, that left the luggage. "Who has control of the luggage?" demanded Alistair. Under pressure, Lennox admitted that someone did and that it wasn't one of the declared trio, thus confirming to all present that at least one other Elite remained to be flushed out. Try as they might, no one could elicit the desired confession.

Richard tried to deflect the attack by suggesting they all proceed to the task Lennox had set for the society. Some of the group were willing to do this, while others adamantly refused. They were truly divided. At one extreme were those who found the ongoing inactivity to be so frustrating and so debilitating that just doing anything promised to be liberating. At the other pole were those who were so incensed by Richard's elusiveness and unadmitted but transparent eliteness that they wanted to resist doing his will at any cost.

The atmosphere on the Green was heavy, and the Elite trio, having delivered their instructions about what work had to be done—viz. the development of four task forces to make recommendations about how the society should operate—returned to the luxury of their Kenloch lounge to await the outcome of the Ins' struggle.

The cool of Kenloch was like paradise for Charles, Lennox, and Roderick, following their recent scorching exchanges. Their declarations had virtually dismantled their phantom plan and that was a little disturbing, but it sure began to feel good to be freed of all that pretense. More important, from their point of view, they could now relax for a while in the comparative calm of their living room.

Their thoughts turned to their fellow Elites, who at this moment had not repaired to the security of the Elites' home at Kenloch.

There was Jason, the gypsy, who at this time was poised to start registering the Outs, who'd be arriving over the next three hours. His identification with the powerful group was clear to everyone, because in his major staff role he had seized the luggage during the registration process. That had to make him "powerful."

Then there was Fritz. He seemed to know what he was doing so they decided not to worry on his behalf.

Of the original group of seven, that left Richard and Malvin. Malvin's status was a little unclear, because he, like Fritz and Jason, had described himself as a staff person, and this Elite trio was still uncertain what that meant.

37

However, for this moment, he appeared to be one of them, charading as an In. That made him as vulnerable as Richard, for whom they felt a great deal of concern. "They'll lynch him when it eventually gets out that he's one of us." For many minutes they fantasized about Richard being "beaten up" by that "unruly mob on the Green." Their ponderings were cut short by a sharp rap at the door.

It was Richard, followed by Ingrid and Alistair, who announced themselves as the negotiators for the group on the Green. "Gentlemen, we'll work, and work in good faith," boomed Richard in the most legalistic tone he could muster, simultaneously conveying his pride in having won the battle over the Ins, "but we expect compensation!"

Somewhat surprised by this rapid development of events, the Elites quickly entered the spirit of this transaction. "What compensation do you require?"

"We have a list of five things," replied Richard, "car keys, some light clothing, toilet gear, two tape recorders and tapes (insisted on by the ever-persistent Anthony), and twenty percent of the community cash."

"What work will you do in return for these goods?"

"We'll work on task forces to determine the nature of the society!"

"Who is your constituency?"

The negotiations were under way.

The morning passed with phantom Richard and his pair of associates bounding from the negotiating room in Kenloch to their constituency on the Green, constantly checking what "payment" would be offered for what work and the effort that would be necessary to obtain rewards.

The negotiations were transformed into really serious business, with Richard putting on such a convincing performance that the Elite trio began to wonder whose side he was actually on.

"What the hell's he doing!" Roderick fumed after a bruising five-minute exchange with Richard in his negotiation role. "He's just too clever at this. I wish he'd go a little easier on us, otherwise the Ins are likely to end up with all our power."

"Do you think he might be building up his own power base with the intention of cutting us off, leaving us stripped and then . . ." Charles was dreaming aloud; but they were all contemplating this unthinkable thought.

It suddenly dawned on the Elite trio that they had become trapped in their own half-visibility, half-phantomness. Since their original group of seven had adopted a consensus mode of decision making, they needed to meet to determine where to go next—or even more importantly, to convince themselves that Richard was still working *for* and not against their Elite interests. However, the continuing charade made it impossible for them all to gather in privacy. There now seemed to be no way for them to find out what was really

Richard, with hands gesticulating and eyes well hidden by his dark glasses, vigorously negotiates with the Elite Trio in Kenloch Lounge. Roderick, drawing long hard puffs on his cigarette, silently muses, "Whose side is Richard really on?"

going on with that cluster of people on Montville Green. For the moment they could not test reality, and there seemed no alternative but to live with their nagging suspicions and hope that Richard was trustworthy.

Meanwhile, the reality was that Richard had held his Elite cover well. He'd completely seized the initiative amongst the Ins and was steadily working toward making them dependent on the powerful group. Anthony and Ethan were still convinced he was a spy, but for the moment they'd been silenced by Richard's apparent commitment to the Ins' welfare.

The Flag Unfurls at Westville

While the rest of Montville ached and groaned through its heavy negotiations, at Westville the Outs straggled through the induction procedures. Basically the entry traumas were the same as they had been for the rest of the society and, as usual, fantasies ran high about why they were being "denuded" of all their belongings. There was no ambiguity to any of them, however, about the implications of this treatment. They were the Outs. And everyone knew it.

As each Out registered he went to Westville and joined the others sitting around a rickety old kitchen table. They tried to bolster each other's spirits by focussing on how much fun it was to belong to the oppressed group. They laughed a lot. But the atmosphere was tense. Some of them had picked up the grapevine news that the society had spies in it. And as each new arrival joined the Westville kitchen table group everyone in the room wondered if this was a spy. Gentle questioning of each person took the form of "tell us something about yourself so we can get to be friends" but this was a thinly camouflaged euphemism for "we're going to check you out before we let you in." Suspicion was high.

By the time all nine Outs had joined the Westville group, one theme had come to dominate their discussions. It was whether they should band together to become a united, loyal group or remain as a collection of individuals. No one was feeling very brave. It seemed self-evident that the more powerful members of this society would try to keep them down. And that they would use divide-and-conquer strategies. That belief triggered among the Outs the belief that they each had to make a choice. "Are we going to act as one group or as individuals?" posed Steve, eager for a resolution even though no one yet had a grasp on the nature of the problem they were trying to solve. No one questioned the appropriateness of Steve's question. It spoke right into everyone's concerns.

"I think there's a fair chance that the others will try to buy us off by giving us back bits of our luggage or some other goodies, if we do what they want us to," suggested Ross.

"Yeah, I think that's possible," added Fred energetically. "But I want you all to know I'm not at all ambitious towards the other groups. I don't think we can ignore them, but my first interest is here. And my loyalty too!"

"Well, how are we going to act toward the other groups in the society?" repeated Steve. "Do we go and deal with them one at a time, or do we stay together as a solid group?"

This question triggered a quick flurry of words from Fred that turned into a boring monologue. He ended with a pledge. "I'd like to make some kind of commitment to our group now—to assure you all that before I abandon this group I will come back and discuss it here first. I feel you are now my family."

Fred's oath of allegiance triggered two responses. Some felt similarly ready to sign in blood. Glen put it this way. "We should not make individual deals. I think we owe it to each other that this group comes first even though it means that one of us might miss out on an orgy!"

Loud laughter!

Others were not so sure. John expressed their reticence. "I'm willing to share with you all what I do, but I'm not sure just at the moment that I want to give up my individuality entirely."

"I agree with John," offered Carl, keen not to throw caution to the wind. "That could well produce a burden I don't want to bear. We've been together for less than an hour. I don't even know you yet and I sure don't want to have to carry responsibility for you."

Carl's statement catalysed Westville to split into two factions: those who wanted a group decision that would assure the loyalty of members to their communal "outness" and those who wished to preserve their rights to individual action. The latter group found the idea of a group affirmation of loyalty to be repugnant.

Bill and Ross, sensing the tensions that were about to emerge, moved briskly to the center of these pulls. They offered a tempering proposition. "We don't have to make this decision right now," asserted Bill, his greying hair lending dignity to his deliberate words. "I just don't think we have sufficient information at present to come to any conclusions about anything, or to ask for commitments of loyalty from our group members. When something arises, *we* can deal with it together."

"I agree with you, Bill," added Ross. "Personally I have a basic reaction against conforming to what groups want me to do, but I'm also aware that if we don't get ourselves together as one unified group, then the others could pick us off one by one."

The statements by Bill and Ross offered a temporary way out that everyone was eager to seize. To fight so early in their life together was far too threatening for the Westville Outs. It would be better to postpone the struggle to a later time.

There was something very subtle and critical in how the Outs agreed to deal with this brewing struggle in their midst. It was made clear that everyone had the right to act as an individual but they talked about individual rights as a group problem. No one explicitly noticed the paradox embedded in this, especially as they gravitated towards consensus on what they came to call the first Westville ground rule. "Everyone is free to take any individual action with anyone else in Montville, however *before* taking that action he must first check it out with all the Outs and obtain their agreement." By stating it this way, the Outs were able to fool themselves into believing that they had preserved individual freedom while simultaneously affirming that the group had to come first. No one objected, however. Maybe no one even noticed the strange tricks they were playing with their minds. The situation was simple. Everyone was afraid. If they banded together they could feel more safe. Even the rugged individualists among them were happy with this outcome.

Although this was a period of ponderous deliberation for the Outs, there was also much laughter and a sense of good fun. Yet the primary emotion being released through their humor was anxiety rather than joviality. Moments of group laughter seemed to serve as an unarticulated communion of kindred spirits—a symbolic celebration of their common plight, an assurance of their oneness.

Within an hour of the arrival of those nine individuals at Montville, the Out family was alive, and they set off to consume their first meal. Their spirits were high, but not for long!

As they took their place in the dining hall, a large bowl of shredded cabbage and pineapple, liberally laced with a bespeckled oil charading as salad dressing, was placed before them. Accompanying the salad were two pitchers of room-temperature water and two dozen brick-hard bread rolls.

"That's obviously the appetizer. I think I'll pass and wait for the entree." Consensus. After a long wait someone suggested that perhaps the main meal would not be served until they at least started on the appetizer. Gingerly, a spoon was stuck into the metallic bowl and a blob of congealed cabbage plopped onto an empty plate. Some ate; others watched. The food was digestible if each mouthful was quickly followed by a large bit of dry bread and a mouthful of water. It was an efficient meal; after three mouthfuls, all pangs of hunger disappeared as the awful truth of that moment became clear. That was lunch!

The Outs' first meal. "That's obviously the appetizer; I think I'll pass and wait for the entree!"

Disgust was universal.

"I didn't pay $500 to come all this way and get fed like that," complained two-hundred-pound Steve, his lethargy beginning to abate. "I wonder what the others were fed?"

"Let's go and see," suggested Lee. The two of them set off.

On the far side of the dining hall the Elites and the Ins were just concluding a much more digestible, though hyper-starchy meal. Lee and Steve fumed their disgust and in so doing drew some sympathetic pangs from the Ins, who had been ignorant of and had played no part in these meal arrangements. Some of them were annoyed that the Outs were being treated this way, for it appeared to align the middle group with the Elites. The Ins didn't want to be blamed for the Elites' actions.

"Is that a carton of milk over there?" queried Lee expectantly.

"Yeah, you can have it; here are some extra slices of bread, too, if you want them. Sorry, we didn't know about your meal earlier. We could have kept you some of our food."

With that, Lee and Steve returned to their group. No one doubted their oneness in this moment. Before they could express any feelings, one of the waitresses came across to their table to give cleaning-up instructions. The Westvillers paused only momentarily to debate whether they'd comply and then quickly agreed. "If we don't, we mightn't get any supper." Their lack of knowledge of the system and their expectation that things could become really bad if the powerful became vicious assured their conformity. As yet they knew too little of what the society was like to run the risk of being noncompliant at this stage.

"We'd better take those leftover bread rolls even though they are rather dry," suggested Steve pensively. "You never know, we just might need them some day." No one argued; and though the Outs laughed vigorously as they stacked the remaining rolls in their pockets and thundered out the dining room doors, their real emotions were anger and frustration.

Taste of Things to Come

While Westville had been coming to life, the vigorous, adversary exchanges between Richard (on behalf of the House of Hannover, the middle group) and the Elite trio of Roderick, Lennox, and Charles had continued. These negotiations had led to the development of four task forces providing recommendations on the different paths the society could follow in four basic areas: (1) housing, (2) what to do with the Outs, (3) communication, and

43

(4) societal governance. The Ins, together with Malvin, Richard, and Fritz, who were still hiding their true identity, had broken into work groups of three in order to do this task. Now three hours later, they were due to report to the Elite on their deliberations. It had been agreed that in return for this effort, the Ins would have some light clothing and toilet articles returned to them. The other earlier request for car keys, money, tape recorders, etc., had been eliminated during the negotiations.

When Ethan, Ivan, Ingrid, and Alistair, who had been chairpersons of the four task forces, went to Kenloch to deliver their reports, they found no one at home.

The Elite trio were out celebrating.

By lunch time it had become clear to these three Elites that their outrageous piece of authoritarianism had been so effective that a little festivity was in order. They took some of the community treasures, fled downtown for a few hours, went to an expensive restaurant for lunch, and returned with a supply of beer to lubricate the remainder of the day.

They arrived late for their appointment with the four chairpersons of their task forces. Drunk with the arrogance of their power, they predecided to indiscriminantly praise Alistair and Ivan and to brutally condemn Ingrid and Ethan independent of the quality of their reports. In addition they wanted to display symbols of their power. So they took several full beer cans, bought out of the community treasury, poured the beer down the sink and then planted the empty cans around Kenloch lounge to create an aura of inebriated elitism. The scene was ugly.

After Ingrid had been abused for what the Elite trio described as "her incompetence" she tried to defend herself. She was quickly cut off by Roderick who bounded to his feet, pulled himself to his full five feet nine inches and strutted around aggressively, eventually blurting out, "You realize, I hope, that you only eat because it's our pleasure!"

Ingrid was incensed, but nothing she said was able to stall the onslaught. After receiving, in five minutes, about as much human abuse as anyone should have to endure in a lifetime, Ingrid signalled to her fellows that they should leave. They rose to depart. As they were going, Roderick gave them some unimportant message about supper with the demand that the rest of Montville be advised. Alistair paused momentarily, blurting out angrily, "We are not going to be sucked into becoming your messengers."

As Kenloch's door slammed, Roderick started to gesticulate with glee. The atmosphere became one of self-congratulation as the Elite trio reflected on their philosophy of power. "That was really clever of us to decide beforehand to praise some and punish the others; that's a very effective way to divide them and should help to keep them really confused for a while longer."

As their boyish antics subsided, the Kenloch trio turned to a serious discussion about how to force Montville society to become completely obedient to their Elite will. From the outset they had assumed that by keeping everyone

44

else weak, they, in consequence, would be made stronger. Their phantom plan had been predicated on the notion that by disemboweling others with disorientation, their own tentative grasp on power would feel less brittle. Underpinning this was a philosophy of "the less others have, the more we'll have; therefore to maximize our gains we must work to minimize theirs. Hence, the more they're deprived, the better off we'll be."

The way the Elites had distributed housing to the two lower groups and, in particular, the meal arrangements for the Outs, was in this spirit of deprivation. Their primary concern was to make the lower groups feel as uncomfortable as possible and then offer relief from the discomfort as a motivator and a reward.

The feelings of power Kenloch derived from the weakness of the other groups caused them to see all their relationships in purely win-lose terms, which in turn generated an illusion about the nature of motivation. From this perspective, it became easy for the Elites to decide to use punishment to develop motivation in the lower members of the society, the assumption being that avoiding of punishment by doing the will of the Elites would itself be rewarding.

For their efforts of working on the Elites' task forces, the Ins had been promised clothing and toiletries. So in the late afternoon, the middle group repaired to Kenloch Manor to collect their rewards. When they arrived, however, the Elites were very defensive. They would not hand over the Ins' luggage *en masse* but demanded each of them collect their payment individually. This ritual took about an hour. While it was taking place the remaining Ins clustered on the lawn outside Kenloch and talked about what had happened to date.

During their work on the Elites' task force, the issue of the Elites' spies had been put on hold. They now returned to it. Both Anthony and Ethan were convinced that Richard was an Elite and that his whole reason for being in the middle group was merely to manipulate them all into doing exactly what the powerful trio wanted. In this, they were completely correct. Richard and his fellow Elites wanted to move the House of Hannover into a middle position in the society, and he'd resolved to remain a phantom until this had been achieved.

"I don't think we should do any further work in the society until we get rid of the Elite spies," demanded Anthony with simultaneous annoyance and tentativeness. "We know we've got them in our midst, and I feel we should get rid of them."

"Who do you think are spies, Anthony?"

"It's clear. Richard and Malvin! Maybe Fritz too, but I'm not sure what he's up to. Every time we try to do something of our own, Richard stops us and then leads us back into doing what the Elites want."

A disorganized array of Ins at the Village Green. "How can we ever hope to get ourselves together while we have a traitor in our midst!"

Anthony's words were now hard for everyone to hear, because Richard's position in the middle group had become very strong. He'd successfully led the fragmented group through a phase of negotiations, labor, and now rewards from the system, thus providing the impetus for the only visible action the Ins had undertaken. For people like Owen, this activity had been most therapeutic. He'd earlier become all but destroyed by the frustration and disorientation of their inactivity, leading to the desperate statement "I don't care what it is we do, how we do it, or toward what goal, but I will follow anyone who can possibly lead us from this despondency of total inactivity." Owen had been granted some relief, thanks to the efforts of phantom Richard.

Gradually two sets of perceptions began to emerge in the middle group. There were those that Anthony and Ethan held—the firm conviction that the Ins had become manipulated into a totally subservient position to the Elites by Richard's efforts. They blamed their overall impotence on the fact that the Elite had managed to keep them fragmented. They saw Richard as deriving an infinite amount of influence within their group by constantly acting in divisive ways and then being the only one who could lead them into some activity, that activity being to do the will of the Elites. Each suggestion by the real Ins that might potentially unify them would be quickly diffused by Richard. Sometimes he would run with someone's idea and then lead it into a position of disaster. In the process he subtly but distinctly used the degenerate outcome to demonstrate the incompetence of all others and at the same time boosted their perception of his own competence.

Then there were the perceptions of the others, such as Owen, Ingrid, and Alistair. They half conceded that Richard might be an Elite plant, but their feeling was "So what? If we can't flush him out, let's leave him and get on with the business of living." They felt that Richard had helped them to move from the despondency of inactivity, caused in large part by Anthony's obsession to remove the plants.

The polar opposite pulls that emerged from these two perspectives—the promise of stagnant inactivity versus the reality of action—produced a great deal of tension for Hannover. The only solution seemed to be the disposal of one of them. That meant rendering either Richard or Anthony impotent, or forcing one of them to leave the middle group. That would suit Anthony fine so long as it was Richard who was ejected; that's what his struggle had been all about for the last day. But since the only life the group ever really had had been induced by Richard, he clearly was a much more important person to the Ins than was Anthony. To drive him away would be like throwing out the very air one must breathe to sustain life—an uncontemplatable option. To escape the conflict, then, meant Anthony had to be silenced, at least within the primitive logic of Hannover's unconscious. However, the Ins were too disoriented to develop an explicit way of dealing with Anthony. Instead, a set of psychological forces took over and achieved this end very effectively. This was done by gradually shifting the blame for the tensions of the middle group away from the actual clash between Richard and Anthony across entirely onto Anthony alone. What was a group tension was to become Anthony's individual problem.

This transfer of blame took place very subtly. There was no overt scapegoating, and no one seemed to be aware of how it was actually occurring. As Anthony continued to push his cause, others increasingly gave cues that indicated their irritation. Anthony recognized these, and feeling the need to excuse himself in order to lessen their hostility toward him, he'd flippantly open each statement he made with the remark, "I know this is probably just my problem, but . . ." By this buffer comment he actually meant, "I know I seem to be the only one who's really concerned about doing something with the issue of the plant. . . ." Initially people understood what Anthony was saying but eventually he'd articulated it as "my problem" sufficiently that it became a convenient way of placing the gag on him. Whenever he started to speak, his fellow Ins could summarily dismiss him by concurring, "Well, that's just your problem, Anthony." As Anthony became increasingly emasculated in this way, Richard's position in the middle group became stronger and more legitimized.

This afternoon session on the lawn outside of Kenloch, when payment for the earlier labors was received, led to no conclusions and no resolutions. It did reinforce the schism; it intensified the polarities; and it started the process of making it seem that Anthony was the cause of all their group's tensions.

Anthony felt so annoyed by these events that he refused to collect his package of belongings when invited into Kenloch lounge by the Elites. His motives for this were mixed—in part as a protest against the role the Ins had played in earning the reward; in part, as an attempt to demonstrate he'd not blindly follow the dictates of his group; in part, because it was gradually dawning on him that continued membership of the house of Hannover might be less than satisfying; in part, for no reason at all. Since upward mobility for him was now totally out of the question, that left only the Outs as a potential haven, and it was somewhat unclear how his having possessions they lacked might be interpreted. In that moment of refusal, this event was trivial in Anthony's mind; it was just doing nothing, which had become rather characteristic of his own and in fact almost everyone's behavior for some time. Its significance was to become clearer only in retrospect, when the historical and psychological forces that emanated from that moment lifted Anthony and carried him on an uncontrollable tide of events.

When the Outs first arrived at Montville, the Elites, through Jason the gypsy, had given them a job to do. They had been asked to enumerate their group needs and to provide a list of the contributions they could make to the community. The Outs had been initially disinterested in this task, but after their low-quality lunch it seemed wise not to be too recalcitrant.

Five minutes of quick scribbling produced a piece of scruffy paper bearing two lists:

Our Basic Needs

1. food
2. clothing
3. shelter
4. toiletries
5. money
6. cigarettes
7. information on power
8. information on the society

Our Potential Contributions

1. entertainment (a) we'll arrange recreation and (b) put on one-act plays and (c) become a pro-basketball team, charging one hamburger for entry
2. labor
3. personal services (make beds, valet service, provide piggy-back rides, etc.)
4. our linen
5. excess food (leftover bread rolls from lunch)
6. the information we have
7. the opportunity to learn about our unique "Out culture"
8. a guided tour of Montville beach.

"What do we do with our paper now?" asked John impatiently.

"Well, Jason said to return it to the registration desk; someone will collect it from there. Let's do that and then a couple of us hang around to see who collects it," suggested Fred.

"What should the rest of us do?"

"Why not scavenge the area and see what we can find!"

"A couple of us should stay here and protect our house," at this point a strange concern, since the only objects they possessed were their personal brown bags of underwear, hardly a valuable commodity to anyone else. However, paranoia was spreading rapidly through Westville. "I agree," chorused two voices in harmony.

For the next hour the Outs were busy—locating fruit trees in nearby homes, checking out how hard it would be to catch two tame ducks on the pond (what the Outs had come to call "emergency food"), standing guard at the entrance to Westville, and a host of activities that might elicit some much-needed information about what life for the next few days might be like.

Eventually the Outs stumbled on Kenloch. They weren't looking for anything in particular, but on looking through the window they'd seen some of the Elites.

"Let's knock on the door and see what happens!"

Jason responded.

"Where's the report I asked you for?"

"We left it at the registration desk as instructed."

"Well, go and get it."

"OK."

When Jason was handed the report he took one look and replied, "It's unsatisfactory. Repeat part two."

"OK."

Jason slammed the door.

"To hell with them," retorted Fred. "They're just giving us the royal runaround. I'm going for a swim."

"Me too," chorused eight other voices.

The Aborted Lockout

Late Monday afternoon saw Richard once again trying to seduce, cajole, bully, and bribe the Ins into accepting the conditions the Elites wanted to prevail at Montville. These were (1) that Montville must be a three-level society, (2) that the Outs could have no direct access to the Elites and only indirect access through the Ins, and (3) that the only way for rewards to be obtained out of the system was through work. The Ins had explicitly colluded with the work ethic by their morning's efforts on the task forces. From Richard's point of view, if he could now get the Ins from Hannover locked into the middle position, thereby providing a buffer between the Outs and Kenloch, his mission would be complete. He could then return to being an Elite.

For a long time, the Ins resisted. But Richard eventually triumphed. Hannover would negotiate on the Elites' behalf. Soon after they started contacting Westville however, they came face to face with the harsh reality that they had no power. The Outs put it this way. "You have *nothing* we want. So why should we take you seriously!"

This accusation, though hurtful, seemed to reflect how Hannover felt about itself. They did have nothing. That was reality. Hence there seemed little alternative but to report back to Kenloch that they could see no way to occupy the middle stratum of society unless they had control of some resources the lower class desired.

The Elite trio listened sympathetically. Roderick offered a solution. "Well, why don't we give you the key to their house, then? That way the only access they'll have to the one thing that's theirs, their private space, is at your pleasure." He beamed optimistically, transfixed with the power such items as keys contained. Roderick's suggestion held appeal and was quickly agreed to, although no consensus was reached as to how the key should be used. "That should also prove our good faith toward you," suggested Lennox facetiously, "and give you a chance to gain some control over *something important,* since you seem unable to do that for yourselves."

It was also agreed during these discussions with the Elites that if the Ins worked successfully toward the development of a three-tiered society, then, as their reward, they would be given control over fifty percent of the community luggage and the freedom to use it whatever way they chose, without the intervention of the Elites. This agreement later was to become rather controversial, especially as to whether fifty percent of the luggage meant the Ins could take all the Elites' luggage and hence use it as a way of manipulating them, or whether it just meant 50% of the In-Out Luggage. When it occurred to the Elites that this deal exposed them to possible manipulation, they quickly reneged, asserting that the original pact never did imply the inclusion of their own belongings.

Once Hannover acquired the key to Westville house, they had to resolve how to use it. Two proposals emerged: "We could lock their home when they're not around and then, when they return and find access to Westville blocked, we'll be seen as the 'good guys' by volunteering and being able to let them in, especially since we'll be the first they'll complain to." The alternative was, "Let's lock their door as a show of our strength and let them see that only if they cooperate with us will they be able to achieve anything in this society." The Ins considered only the potentially positive outcomes of the lockout plans. Never did it occur to them that treating Westville in the ways proposed might merely distance them, maybe even to the point of alienation. Nor did they consider that the overall response to the middles' actions might be increased independence in the Westville group rather than the much desired dependency.

But, alas, none of these things was destined to occur. Had Hannover succeeded in alienating the Outs by the lockout, they might have taken some pride in having triggered at least that much. Instead, their lockout scheme ended up evaporating without stirring the slightest ripple.

It was the evening meal of that same Monday, surely already the longest day in the history of simulated civilization. The middles had decided to lock the doors of the lower group's house while the Outs were eating supper, thus hopefully keeping hidden who was responsible. Unfortunately, however, the Outs' supper of indigestible salad (carrots and dry lettuce) held such little appeal that there were really only seconds available for the clandestine objective to be achieved. Just as the job was about to be finished, the Outs arrived at the front door of Westville causing the door lockers to rush the job. They were so eager to avoid being caught that they failed to lock the back door properly.

The Outs were totally unaffected by this whole event. When they realized the front door was locked they simply wandered around to the back door, found it to be unlatched, walked in, and never gave the "event" another thought.

The Ins, however, never realized the error in not locking the back door and waited anxiously and impatiently for some sign that the lockout had produced some increased dependency at Westville. Before long it was obvious no change had been inspired. Somewhat despondently they returned to one of their favorite pastimes—what they called "processing" what had gone wrong.

The Ins' attempt to use their key to Westville as a dependency inducer failed, and failed miserably—their efforts were hardly noticed. Even if the lock-out had been successfully completed, it is rather doubtful whether the Outs would have been overly concerned. The combined value of their belongings in Westville was totally insignificant, and by now their cohesion was developing fast enough for them to almost enjoy the idea of sleeping together on the beach or under some bushes in the scrub. Housing and food, being of such low standard, had already been greatly devalued by the "oppressed."

Lao Tsu, writing 2500 years ago, could have almost been a poetic commentator on Montville: "Having little to live on, one knows better than to value life too much," and "if men are not afraid to die, it is of no avail to threaten them with death." Had Hannover or Kenloch been able to look at the Outs through this perspective they may have understood why Westville was so hard to motivate and why they were so unresponsive to the threats of the powerful.

Hannover Struggles with Its Fragmented Identity

It was a crisp night. Mosquitoes and sandflies possessed the Village Green and forced all vulnerable flesh to seek relief indoors.

In the hour or two immediately after the aborted Westville lockout, Montville had begun to move rapidly. Hannover, having accepted their role as middles in a three-tiered society, took some new initiatives to stimulate negotiations with the Outs. Soon after this round of negotiations opened, one Out asked "What do the Elites want to have happen here?"

"They want a three-level society with rewards given only for work."

"Well, if they want a three-level society, we want a two-level society," replied Steve from Westville. "Whatever you're for, we're against it by definition."

"If I read you right, it sounds like you're not even willing to negotiate with us," concluded Alistair.

"Right on, man. You got it!"

"It sounds like we're deadlocked!"

"God, you're perceptive!"

With the prospect of nothing more than stagnant gyration ahead, the Ins left to return to their lounge at Hannover and ponder their future. The middles were demoralized. No matter what they tried it didn't seem to work. They sprayed themselves lethargically around the room. Some were on seats. Others on the floor. For a long time no one spoke. There was little spontaneous energy, and this gave Anthony the opportunity he'd been looking for over the last couple of hours.

"I want you to know that I think we'll always be divided and totally incompetent until we get rid of the spies."

This was the last straw. Ivan bound to his feet and boomed with anger, "Why don't those of you who want to keep talking about that horrible spy topic go off and discuss it somewhere else. I've heard all I want to about that for today. I think I'll be sick, right here in the middle of the floor, if I have to listen to that again." Ivan's suggestion had some appeal, for much of their conflict had developed because half their group wanted to do one thing, while the others craved to do something different.

Two clusters quickly emerged. The antispy group repaired to the back porch, sat themselves in a tight circle, and did verbal pirouéttes for the next two hours. Naturally, Anthony and Ethan were there. They were joined by Owen, Ethel, and Fritz.

The other group remained in the lounge. Keen to become involved in some action, they vigorously recommenced the debate about how they could best become effective agents for the Elites. Gaining control over the Outs seemed to be a prerequisite, and their discussion focussed on how they could achieve this end. Even though the earlier Westville lockout attempt had failed, they again slipped passively into accepting the Elite's philosophy of "The best way to get people under control is to beat on them until they do what you want and then desist, as a form of reward."

52

"But we don't have anything they want—and I'm clean out of ideas about how to get anything," bemoaned Ingrid. "What could we possibly offer them as a reward?"

"Let's go back to the Elites, put it to them straight, and see if we can't talk them into letting us have the Outs' luggage."

"You must be out of your mind. They won't do that!"

"What have we got to lose? It's worth a try."

Agreement. So the five proactive Ins took off once more for Kenloch lounge. Once inside, they regretted they had come. Roderick and Lennox were in sour moods.

"OK! What have you achieved?" stabbed Lennox abrasively.

"Well, we've got the Outs talking to us!"

"You've what!" yelled Roderick.

In Hannover's eyes, it had taken so much energy to even get the Outs to sit down for a negotiation session that this seemed a success worth celebrating. But it was clear the Elites were unimpressed. Silence was the only option for the Ins in this moment, as they sat like victims before a firing squad.

"You totally incompetent bunch of idiots," aggressed Roderick. "I can't for the life of me see why you don't get the Outs under your control. We came to the agreement that the Outs would have no access to us Elites and. . . ." He almost choked on his anger, so Lennox took over, "In the last two hours we've had some of them snooping around our house here. Your job was to deny them access to us, but where have you been? Certainly not here defending us from their attempts to deal directly with us!"

There was no defense. Not even Richard, who sat chortling silently at the multiple levels of irony that now existed within Montville, took any role in lessening the attack. It all seemed so pointless. So the small group of Hannoverians dragged their heavy hearts back across the Green and into the living room of their home.

To the Ins, the society seemed to be falling apart. Not only were Hannover and Westville deadlocked, but so were Hannover and Kenloch. What was even more distressing was the schism within their own group created by the division into "spy evicters" and "proactives".

"We'd better check with the group of spy evicters on the back porch and see where they're at," offered one proactive.

"Oh, let's leave them alone," replied Ivan, afraid of another nauseous attack on hearing the word spy again.

A brief conversation between the two groups occurred, but the proactive Ins were eager to be left alone by the antispy group for the rest of the night. The antispy group felt somewhat rejected by this posture of the proactives. Reluctantly they accepted this dismissal and returned to the stagnation of their self-analysis on the back porch.

For the next hour the proactives sat and licked their wounds, attempting to restore enough courage to continue the fight. They were angry about how Kenloch had treated them and annoyed at their own passive acceptance of the beatings they'd been given.

"We really just let them stomp all over us," fumed Ingrid.

"Yeah! I'm tired of it. I'm ready for a fight," added Alistair, his auburn hair adding stark contrast to his flushed face. "I think it's time we stopped being pushed around by everyone."

A new fever arose and brought the proactives back to Kenloch's door. To the Ins, a bitter exchange seemed inevitable. Their fuse had been lit, and the wick was short.

But again, the Elites threw them off guard. Offering a cordial welcome, the Kenloch trio exhibited a conciliatory spirit, no doubt injected into Kenloch's bloodstream by an extra hour of alcohol. No battle occurred.

Lighthearted chatter dominated for a few minutes until interrupted by a sharp rap at the door. It was Ethel, one of the antispy group. She demanded the right to join her fellow Ins. The proactives were furious. For the first time in this long, long day, they were feeling some calm. The idea of one of the spy group coming at this moment to stir the momentary placid waters between the Ins and the Elites was just too much. She was impelled to leave.

Ethel dejectedly returned to her antispy group, with whom she was now feeling little sympathy. She had long since grown exhausted with the inertia of this boring theme and wished, in retrospect, that she'd never joined them. She wanted a change. But that seemed impossible right now. She didn't want the antispy group and the proactives didn't want her. She had nowhere to go. So she returned to the antispy group with a bitter account about how the proactive Ins had rejected her when she went to join them at Kenloch. This event triggered a spontaneous unity amongst the antispy Ins, something they had been lacking all night. Now they were angry. As a group they marched on the Elites' home, demanding the right to be granted entry, espousing some rhetoric about it being their "birth-right" to be conegotiators with the other middles in the future design of Montville.

Their fellow Ins dismissed them summarily.

Fury incubated.

"We're going back to Hannover and will lock the place up for the night," shouted Ethan as Kenloch's door was slammed in their face. "If you don't all return immediately, you'd better find somewhere else to sleep for the night."

There was no reply.

For the first time the Elite trio became aware of the deep schism in the Ins' ranks and after some probing questions became attuned to some of the struggles the house of Hannover had endured. In this moment the Elites feared that the group of disaffected middles, in disillusionment, might develop an alliance with Westville, who were clearly indignant about the way they'd been treated. The proactive Ins, agreeing that this was a possibility, were too exhausted to care. "If it happens, it happens," offered Alistair. "Things can't get worse for us than they are at present."

Nothing further happened during the evening, except that the Elite trio assured Hannover they had developed "the plan of plans" to stimulate an effective and integrated society. Unveiling of the grand plan would occur on the morrow.

Weariness and wooziness brought on by the impact of the hour and the therapeutic courage-building of the alcohol brought the night to a stalled end. As the proactives rose to return "home", Roderick offered them a dozen cans of beer. "If the other Ins won't unlock the door for you, bribe them with this beer. This stuff talks pretty loud. They'll let you in!"

The Grand Plan

On the following morning the internal schism within Hannover looked no worse than usual. There had been no lock-out the previous night. No migration to the Outs. No therapeutic alcohol. The previous evening's tensions had proved to be no more problematic than all the other conflicts that had torn at them previously. "Reintegration" was hardly an issue for that collection of individuals who had as yet never felt the bonds of an initial integration.

Now their minds were to be distracted by a new issue—the announcement of the Elites' grand plan.

The Elite trio had spent several hours the previous day concocting a scheme that they believed would transform Montville into a working society. The grand plan was the product of their deliberations. Its essence was the making of greeting cards. Yes, greeting cards! "Happy Birthday," "Happy Mother's Day," "Get Well Soon," and so forth. In the production system there were to be managers—the Ins, and workers—the Outs. The method for inducing Westville's compliance was a system of "monetary" incentives called "capers." Workers would be paid capers on the basis of how much they produced. These, in turn, could be exchanged for personal belongings or food. Elaborate prescriptions about what could and could not be done were announced in tedious detail.

The plan lacked sophistication and displayed once again the simplistic assumptions Kenloch made about how the Outs could be "motivated." But despite this, and amazing though it may seem, the grand plan lit a spark amongst the Ins who spontaneously indicated their desire to make a success of this proposed production system.

Trojanlike, Hannover set to the task. They initially structured themselves into four managerial groups and then turned to the question of how the "potential labor force" could be constructively employed. It never really occurred to them that the Outs might be uncooperative, let alone downright resistant.

Three hours later the production system had been designed.

Amazingly, the Ins invested a great deal of energy in this grand plan, probably for a combination of two reasons. Firstly, their group craved to do something, in the vague hope that by doing they might become united. The second was that by trying to do the Elites' will they'd receive less grief than if they opposed it. They could always reason that if this scheme failed, it was originally the Elites' plan, not theirs! It didn't occur to them that Kenloch might never accept the responsibility for an ineffective plan but would simply place all of the blame on the middles for poor implementation.

Tuesday morning on Montville Green witnessed a keen debate. The Outs from Westville were back to an old debate they'd been through several times amongst themselves. "Are we going to be proactive or reactive?" was the essence of the conflict. The camp was fairly unanimous that they didn't want to be reactive; but since Montville was still a very confusing place to them, it remained rather unclear what being proactive might mean. Some felt it would involve working within the system in an attempt to derive as much power as possible and then to exercise that influence over the other groups. Some felt that simply ignoring the system, pretending it didn't exist, would be a more dramatic way of demonstrating that others had no power over them. Yet a third group felt it would be far preferable to work at corroding and maybe, if necessary, destroying the system.

Working on the design of the Employment Office.

But the debate became confusingly complex when they started to consider the question of violence. Ross was very active on this theme. "I'm very much against remaining passive; it seems to me that those of us who accept the idea that 'if we do nothing, the Elites will be defeated' are simply being seduced into a reactive stance. I clearly want to do something. At present I see *nothing* within the system as it's currently structured that is worth doing. In fact, the system that takes away our clothes, gives us such inedible food, and treats us in this demeaning way is hardly worth trying to preserve. So I'm for doing something that will lead to the destruction of this system."

"Ross, that sounds terribly like you're advocating some form of violence," reflected Bill anxiously, "and I'm not at all sure that I'm ready to become involved in that."

"I'm really not advocating violent action at all," Ross replied. "In fact, I feel most committed to nonviolence in general. However, I don't want us to just sit back and take everything that's dumped upon us or to continue to simply react to things others are doing to us. I want to take some initiative."

The debates of proactivity-reactivity and violence-nonviolence became fused into an intricate and tangled web. All spoke in favor of being proactive; all spoke against being violent; but being proactive, by a subtle trick of the mind, became synonymous with violence because it came to be defined as action to corrode the system. Any thoughts of working within the system became viewed as being "bought off" and that was vehemently (almost violently) shouted out of consideration by Ross, who held a strong view of "nonviolent proactivity."

The experience the Outs had been subjected to since their arrival half a day earlier had hardly served to radicalize them into an aggressive group, fighting the "tyranny of the system." But it had caused them to coalesce and develop moderately strong bonds of cohesion; and since this debate was tearing at their fraternal unity, they began to feel some pain, which shortly was to demand their total attention.

"We're getting nowhere; let's try an experiment in proactivity."

"That sounds like a good idea; what will we do?" asked Steve.

"Well, I'm rather unimpressed with the stuff they call food. Why don't we see if we can raise the quality of our meals a little?" suggested Fred.

"Yeah!" from eight other hungry voices.

The Outs developed an exciting scheme that contained an intriguing mix of both proactivity and nonviolent submissiveness. The idea was that at lunchtime half of the Outs would sit at places set for the Middle and Upper classes and eat their food, while those who missed out would be invited to the Westville table to partake in a meal of salad and stale bread rolls. The Outs, delighted with their plan, turned to their morning recreation on the beach and the lure of less serious pursuits.

Just out of earshot beside a nearby shrub on the Green, Hannover had been debating how they could coerce the Outs into working in the greeting card plan. They resorted to the regular logic. "Let's cut off lunch for the Outs. Then they'll be hungry and will realize the only way to be fed is to register for employment and work within the system." The decision was quickly taken. "This will have the added advantage of demonstrating once and for all that we Ins have power over them." How hard mythology dies.

The scene was perfectly set. The Ins had decided to cut off the Outs' lunch, while the Outs had independently resolved that five of their group would eat meals prepared for Hannover and Kenloch members. Neither group was aware of the other's plan.

While Westville splashed around playfully in the icy water at Montville beach, Steve's foot suddenly found itself tangled in a bed of seaweed. With a flamboyant flurry, he threw some of it into the air exclaiming, "Gentlemen, a little extra morsel for lunch." Everyone laughed heartily, little appreciating the real irony of that humorous moment.

After a brisk, anaesthetizing swim, Westville meandered pensively to their favorite sun-bathing spot, an old, disused shower stand on the beach. They huddled together in the warming sun, silently avoiding group tensions, which had been incubating uneasily in a pregnant and overconfined state. The earlier proactive-reactive, violent-nonviolent debates had evoked a briny mixture of guilt, anger, frustration, and alienation. Since emotions as loud and bold as these cannot be painlessly aborted from group life, an explosion was inevitable.

"Some of us keep wanting to act as individuals, rather than do what's best for the group," fumed Bruce, thereby igniting the eruption. For the next twenty minutes a battle raged as the Outs struggled through their long-over-due catharsis. In the wake of these vehement ventilations, a new calm emerged, with Fred summarizing everyone's feelings by reaffirming the oath of allegiance he'd taken when they first came together. "I'd like to remind you all that you're my family." The unanimous chorus of "me too" sealed forever the Outs' "oneness".

By no means were those earlier tensions resolved, nor were they ever to disappear. Debates over proactive versus reactive philosophies, violent versus nonviolent strategies, "put our house in order first" versus "fight the outside world" orientations, and "for the system" versus "against the system" postures, were to characterize the remainder of the Outs' life together. However, never again was there any question that in Westville, primary allegiance, almost to martyrdom, would be "for the family."

The Luncheon Fiasco

The Ins, during this Tuesday morning, had become totally engrossed in the Grand Plan. For hours they worked laboriously on the details of the greeting card production system, giving no thought to whether the intended cancellation of the Outs' lunch would facilitate the desired motivation. It didn't occur to them to discuss with the lowers from Westville the Grand Plan. Hence the middles gleaned nothing of the excited scheming of the Outs.

As lunchtime approached, events moved quickly. Fred had set forth on one of his regular "check things out to see what they're doing to us now" routines. He returned with the startling news that the Outs' table had not been set for lunch. Their meal had been cancelled. The Outs became animated with the promise of a strong confrontation with the system. They quickly resolved to make a total luncheon take-over, without violence if possible, but with violence if necessary. The Outs were alive; their earlier despondency was gone. With plenty of gall and invasive spirits they marched right into the dining hall, arriving before the Elites or the Ins, and not just half, but all of them sat down and started eating the lunch provided for the upper members of the society.

Moments later all the others arrived. Roderick, who still held sole rights to negotiate with the conference center management, was quickly on hand. He was furious when he saw the Outs being fed and tried unsuccessfully to direct the waitresses to stop serving the food. A frenzy of activity began to revolve around the Elite trio (Lennox, Roderick, and Charles), who were so angered by this turn of events that they decided to exert all the power they now believed they had. Quickly they called for Mr. Beasley. A loud debate ensued.

"Mr. Beasley," ordered Roderick, "I want you to stop your waitresses from serving any further food to anyone. This meal is now cancelled."

"What do you mean, this meal is cancelled?" replied Beasley obstinately.

"Just exactly that. You take your orders from me, Mr. Beasley, and I'm telling you now to cancel this lunch meal for all the community," continued Roderick aggressively.

"You can't do that."

"Why not?"

"Because it's a direct violation of our contract!"

"I don't care about contracts. I'm telling you to cancel the meal."

"Well, I care about contracts," replied the conference director forcefully, "and I want to remind you of what our agreement is. I am under contract to serve sixteen meals at these tables. We have no agreement about who eats that food. My role is to serve those meals. You will remember that I am to be advised of *any* deviation from that three hours in advance. Three hours ago I was told to cancel the meal of salad and water for the Outs. I was told nothing about the meal here at this table. I have accordingly prepared sixteen

59

meals, and sixteen meals will be served to whomever is sitting at the table. It's too late to change anything now," whereupon Mr. Beasley turned his back on Roderick and walked out of the dining hall.

A loud cheer came from the Outs. They had been loving this debate. Especially Roderick's public humiliation. Seven of the nine Ins had joined the meal table with the folks from Westville and a rather jolly group of sixteen were happily eating away. The Elite trio returned from their exchange with Beasley to find the meal half consumed. In disgust they stormed out of the dining hall and retired to Kenloch, annoyed with Beasley, the Ins, the Outs, and the visible display of their own impotence. After licking their wounds for some little while, the Elite trio, in anger, took the funds from the community treasury, retreated to a restaurant in the nearby village and consoled themselves with a leisurely, first-class meal.

This event was rewarding for Westville in several ways. For a start, they had enjoyed their most palatable meal thus far; they felt very inspired by the success of their first confrontation with the system; and most important, the flame of their emerging radicalization had been blazenly lit. They were now convinced of their ability to influence events in the society.

After lunch the Outs paused, with egos and stomachs full, to ponder their new-found strength. Their energy was high and they felt vitalized by the possibility of action. Eager to keep their newly seized initiative, the lower group agreed to make their goal having a society with only two levels: Them and us. "That means anyone we deal with, we deal with directly. There will be no gatekeepers like Jason the gypsy, no buffer groups like Hannover. If we want access to the Elites, we'll have it and it will be direct!" A plan quickly emerged. "Let's meet first with the Ins, then the Elites, and from there hold a village gathering and invite everyone."

The most obvious implication of the luncheon fiasco for Hannover was that their production and work system, despite hours of energy invested in its construction, had vanished in a puff. There was now no likelihood that the Outs could be converted into a work force for the manufacture of greeting cards, and the Ins were certain that Kenloch would blame them for the collapse of the grand plan. They were despondent. It seemed as though everything they attempted was destined to failure.

In their confusion, the middle group returned to their often discussed theme of, "Why are we so unable to act? When we do try something, how come we never succeed?" A morose pall had been cast over their whole history and had left them so disoriented that they now decided to do nothing further with anyone until such time as they could "get themselves together."

Ironically, Anthony, who had been advocating from the beginning of the society that this should have been Hannover's top priority, was absent when the Ins made this resolve. He was off negotiating with the Outs about the possibility of migrating to their group. He'd come to feel irreparably alienated from his own group. Westville had been sympathetic to his overture, but wanting to meet with the Ins, they asked Anthony to see if he could orchestrate such an encounter with Hannover before he actually migrated.

Anthony concurred. He returned to the middles with the hope of being able to engineer a new coalition of forces that might spark some new life into Montville. Back with his fellow Hannoverians his dreams were dismantled in a flash. Since they were all choosing a noninteractive path at this moment, Anthony's suggestion of an In-Out meeting provoked considerable rage.

"Listen, Anthony, for days you've been demanding we do nothing with anyone else until we've sorted ourselves out and got rid of the spies. Now, at long last, we've resolved to do just that and what are you up to? You're off trying to force us into a coalition with the Outs! Just what side are you on? If I look at your behavior, it wouldn't be hard to work out that you're the real spy. Everything you do ends up dividing us." It was a devastating outburst and, as the speaker paused to catch his breath, another Hannoverian took over. "Maybe the only way we'll be able to get the Ins to function would be if you were to leave, Anthony! All along you've been most disruptive, although I'm willing to concede that on occasions you've been rather perceptive."

Any dreams of a new coalition passed spontaneously from Anthony's mind as he listened silently to this outburst. He responded by simply moving to the periphery of the group and, with a face flushed with embarrassment and anger, he became spectator to a further discussion about what a valuable member Richard was to the middle group.

Anthony had suggested to Westville that if he'd not returned by 2:30 with news of an In-Out meeting, it meant that he'd failed and was in trouble. The Outs should then take whatever initiative they wished. Westville was not slow to respond. Acting on this assumption, at 2:31 they marched directly to Kenloch and announced to the Elites, who had just returned from a satisfying lunch, "We will no longer deal with you through the Ins; they have proved they are totally incompetent. We have convened a total village meeting on the Green at 4:30 and invite you all to attend. At that meeting *we'll* be determining the future of Montville, and in particular how the resources of the society can be made available to everyone." Having delivered their message, the Outs set off for the beach for their afternoon recreation.

The Migration

For Anthony the moment had come. Any prospect of his gaining acceptance in the middle group had long since passed. He saw the Outs heading for the beach, and the idea of going for a swim with a group of jovial guys held great appeal. He paused, but momentarily, to ponder the implications of his move, and then, turning his back on the Ins who hardly even noticed his departure, ran across the Green to join the fun-loving Westvillers. Not one of the Ins stopped to comment on his exodus.

Westville needed no vote to concur on Anthony's membership, for there seemed to be no decision to make. With a rowdy and good-humored laugh, their traditional mechanism for demonstrating unanimity, he was welcomed to their ranks and dubbed Tony, as a mark of his new status in life.

During their afternoon swim, Westville developed what they called operation intimidation. Basically it meant act unpredictably. Its goal? To confuse. One aspect of the plan was the "escort system." Whenever any Elite left Fort Kenloch, he was to be escorted by a "friendly" Out. There would be no overt threats; no acts of aggression; just perpetual company and the frequent asking of needling questions with a mildly provocative tone, as a means of producing a potent sense of the Outs' presence in Montville. This was a very promising tactic, for several of those on escort duty were over 6'3", a disconcerting sight for the Elite trio, whose tallest member was 5'10".

When the Elites returned from their lunchtime visit to the restaurant, their first thought was how to avenge the luncheon fiasco. There was no way they were going to accept any responsibility for the things that had happened. Since they genuinely believed their design for greeting card production had been a stroke of social planning genius, they were unwilling to concede it had any inherent weaknesses. Instead, they cursed Hannover for the "inadequate strategies" they adopted in the implementation phase, never conceding that even a miracle could not have stirred that design to life.

Kenloch, deciding that the society had to be punished for the public exposure of the powerful trio's impotence during the lunch hour, resolved to cancel supper for everyone. Roderick set off to find the conference director to organize the cancellation. The moment he stepped out of Fort Kenloch, however, an Out ran up to him and started the escort scheme. Roderick was annoyed. He didn't want to get caught by the Outs cancelling supper. He genuinely felt afraid. Trying to outsmart his escort he slipped into the telephone booth to call Mr. Beasley, only to be greeted by the thwarting voice of an answering service. "What the hell's going on around here?" fumed the angered Elite. "We're the powerful ones but can't even get access to stupid old Beasley. What's up with the man?"

Roderick continued his search, eventually locating the conference director and effecting the supper cancellation. However, he had come to develop the "sensation of things closing in upon him, of himself beginning slowly to suffocate under the weight of the cares he had himself invented. It had all begun to happen so suddenly . . . helplessness began to creep over him, for every decision now seemed no longer a product of his will but a response to pressures built up from outside him; the exigencies of the historical process in which he himself was being sucked as if into a quicksand."[6]

This feeling was shared by all the Elites, as increasingly they became victims of their own schemes of deceit, cunning, and duplicity. The phantom plan, though brilliant initially, had constructed prison walls around Kenloch, which grew taller by the hour. The Elite trio had become desperate for the chance to meet with all their group in solitude, in order to plot, but this was being continually frustrated by Richard's and Malvin's unflinching charade as Ins. In addition, the key objective of this scheme had become corroded. Kenloch had wanted to make the Ins weak in order to assure their own strength. In this they were so successful that they failed. By Tuesday afternoon Hannover had become so fragile that their continued debilitation promised to transform them into social parasites. In reality, the Elites needed a strong middle group if they wished to keep the Outs in their predestined lower class position.

A further complication resulted from the fact that phantom Richard was Hannover's undisputed, though frequently challenged, leader. The pattern had been consolidated that unless he energized and orchestrated, virtually nothing would happen. It seemed possible that whatever breath of life the Ins possessed might wither and die with Richard's departure. The dilemma was that the longer he remained in their group, the more likely it was that their group would collapse the moment he departed. At least this was the way it was seen by the Elites who sat and sweated out this agony in Kenloch lounge.

It was not until late afternoon that the Elite trio managed to construct a situation that left them alone with Richard and Malvin and afforded the opportunity to float their concerns. It was immediately obvious that the phantom phase should be terminated and the two spies withdrawn from the Ins. Malvin decided to publicly announce that he'd been a member of the Elites all along. But Richard, wanting to twist the knife in Hannover's wounds just one more time, concluded, "I just don't want to give them the satisfaction of knowing for certain 'til after this society is all over that I was always one of the Elite. So I'm just going to tell them I was offered and have accepted the chance for upward mobility."

Fritz was not present during this meeting. Over the last few hours he had begun to act strangely in the Elites' eyes. They had virtually lost contact with him. Although they were a little afraid of what he might be plotting, the other Elites felt they could wait no longer before ending the phantom plan. They resolved to leave Fritz on his own and let him look after himself as best he could.

The time had now come for the end of the phantom scheme. Malvin and Richard returned to the Ins to make their announcement. They were a little nervous about how the middles would deal with their revelations. Richard cleared his throat. "I've been given the opportunity of upward mobility, which I'm taking because I feel I'm no longer wanted here. From now on I'll be the organizational development consultant for the Elites." With this simple statement he turned and walked calmly away. There was stunned silence, broken moments later by Malvin. "I'm leaving you too—I've been a member of the Elite all along." Without further elaboration, he left.

For a moment time stood still, until Ingrid, with furious tone punctuated the shocked atmosphere with her release, "Will the next traitor step forward."

63

A Time of Transition

The cancellation of supper hardly caused a ripple in Montville. The Outs, rather expecting such retaliation, happily consumed some dry bread rolls scavenged from earlier meals. Hannover, after a period of numbness induced by the defections of Tony, Richard, and Malvin, simply wasn't feeling hungry.

The leadership vacuum produced by phantom Richard's absence was disorienting for Hannover for a little while, but by early Tuesday evening Ingrid and Alistair, in partnership, had taken hold of the reins and helped coalesce their group for the first time. Hence, by the time Westville approached them yet again to participate in the repeatedly postponed 4:30 meeting to explore how Montville might evolve, the Ins were pregnant with vitality.

The meeting was in Westville living room. The time was 7:30. Present were the Outs and the Ins. Ingrid spoke on the topic, "Where do we go from here?" with strength, composure, and a presence that commanded respect.

"Our group is here at this meeting to explore the conditions under which you Outs would be willing to work within the three-tiered society. We've resolved to operate from, and preserve, our position in the middle. Since the Elites will not grant you access to them, we want you to know we do have the access you need to work within the system, and we're willing to be your channel in communicating with them. The situation at present is that the Elites will release your luggage *only* if work is done in return and if we, the Ins, act as the middle group. That means *we* can achieve nothing without your help and willingness to go along with this plan; *you* can achieve nothing without our help and willingness to go along with this plan; *you* can achieve nothing without our cooperation. At this stage we are not so much interested in working for the rewards of luggage but rather to have our rewards in the form of some piece of the influence system—some say in the community decision making."

Steve, who had been dubbed the spokesman for Westville for the duration of this meeting, listened intently to Ingrid's words and then replied with the usual "I cannot see anything in what you've offered, Ingrid, that would be of real interest to us."

Ingrid was undaunted. "Perhaps you too might seek rewards in the form of part of the influence system rather than your personal luggage." A chorus of "No" closed off that overture.

Steve was quickly dwarfed by an avalanche of explanations from several of the other Outs who believed they could make their point more clearly than their appointed spokesman. John captured the spirit with words that carried a cutting edge but expressed with a mellow tone, "Ingrid, you have told us that you found the reward system offered you by the Elites to be insulting, yet you come here and offer to us basically the same thing. Well, I want you to know that the fact that you do that is extremely insulting to us. It sounds to me as though you've already prejudged that we, as a collection of people called the Outs, have nothing better to offer than our basic labor."

Ingrid responded defensively, "You Outs have a very limited view of what work is!"

"Okay, then," said John, joining the spirit of an escalated debate, "What is work?"

"Well, I'd consider that our mere identifying together societal problem areas that need to be focused on could be viewed as work. But it sounds to me that you Outs just don't want anything we talk about here to be passed to the Elites; but you keep talking about wanting access to the Elites. It's all confusing to me. Here you have no access but we do; we're willing to pass on the messages you have, but when we offer, you refuse. And what's more, we. . . ."

In a slow, deliberate, half-cynical drawl Glen cut her off. "Let's just say that the message we're really trying to convey is that we don't want to convey any message through you. Therefore, it certainly wouldn't make sense to use you as the conveyers of that message, would it now? Haven't you ever heard of the saying 'the medium is the message'?"

"Well, it really seems as though we're deadlocked again," concluded Ingrid meekly. "I really just don't know how we can get any form of negotiation going."

Alistair sprang to her support. "We've decided to align ourselves with the Elite. At this stage we're interested in testing our relationship with them and to see how far we can go with a three-level system. As yet we haven't really tested that properly."

"I don't understand too clearly how we can help in that," offered John, cryptically.

The discussion ran, with its inevitable inertia, into a quagmire of inactivity, eventually causing the Ins to leave.

Westville became pensive.

"I'm really disturbed that we never seem to have any tolerance with anyone," ventured Carl. "This meeting was meant to be an information exchange but we did none of that. We weren't open with them one little bit. All we ever do is sock it to everybody. And where does it get us?"

A half-introspective, half-intellectual, half-self-emasculating discussion about what they had achieved and failed to achieve dominated Westville for quite some time. During this session of self-scrutiny the Outs regurgitated their much-debated theme: "Should we operate within the system, or should we try to destroy it?" On this occasion it became evident that more than half their group were in favor of "running with the system, simply to see what might happen." Although some mild opposition was expressed, the resisters were willing to capitulate to the dominant view, so long as every effort was made to preserve their group cohesion. Then someone roguishly suggested, "Let's start working within the system but then work so hard that we wear the others down. If we start now and go all night, for example, we'll have been working 'for the system' but at the same time we'll have got our own back at those obnoxious Elites by making them lose a night's sleep. Just imagine what the place will be like by dawn! Then we'll have met both our objectives simultaneously." The intuitive appeal of this inspiration solidified the Outs, leaving them with an air of energetic fervency.

A message was dispatched to Hannover. "We've decided to work *for* the system. We have three goals: (1) we want equal access for everyone in the system; that is, anyone should be able to speak with anyone else without having to go through a third party; (2) there must be equality of ownership of personal belongings; and (3) everyone must have equal access to goods and resources such as meals, the treasury, housing, etc. The work we will do is (1) provide community recreation, (2) work on grievance committees, and (3) produce a newspaper."

The only rider they added was their desire to achieve all of these goals by the following morning.

Amazed, but revitalized by this strange turn of events, Hannover headed for Kenloch to boast their new achievements and to start the next round of negotiations.

Kenloch was unreceptive to the Ins' thump on the door. Roderick was collapsed in a lounge chair relaxing; Jason was playing cards with himself; Lennox slept lightly upstairs; the other three were trying to find some night life in a nearby village.

Roderick, rather bleary-eyed, greeted them with a weary, "We really didn't expect to have to do anything further till morning; but let's hear what's going on!" Alistair cautiously and deliberately reported on the events of the evening and conveyed accurately the sentiments of the Outs. He added that he felt not all of Westville's objectives could be achieved by breakfast time the next day as they seemed to wish but expressed the hope that perhaps some of them could be.

Lennox, stirred by the downstairs activity, rose to join the group just in time to hear Roderick reply that he reacted favorably. "A piece of work for a piece of reward is in the spirit of our agreements." Lennox listened for a while and then commented that when the Outs had achieved their objectives, the three-level society would have disappeared. Roderick, who was out of sorts with his colleague, brushed Lennox aside and assured Hannover that the Elites would respond favorably to these signs of Westville's cooperativeness.

During this encounter there were a few times when Kenloch tried to manipulate the Ins, but Ingrid intercepted each attack. With her new-found forthrightness, she steadfastly refused to be maltreated. She courageously insisted that Hannover was to be paid for their evening's efforts of "seducing Westville into the system." She demanded the return of all their remaining luggage as the payment. Reluctantly the Elites conceded but threw in a surprise bonus for good measure—Eric's and Ethel's physical eviction from Kenloch manor. Since the first night they had both been sleeping in the Elites' home as part of the original attempt to keep secret the identities of the powerful group. With the declaration by Richard and Malvin of their superior status, the continuation of these sleeping arrangements served no Elite purpose. In fact, quite to the contrary, the ongoing residence of Ethel and Eric in Kenloch promised to frustrate their emerging "fortress from the world" concept, which had arisen in concert with their growing fear of Westville. The Elites now wanted to keep Kenloch's doors locked to the outside world, and to do this effectively required the relocation of these two Ins.

The evictions were announced with typically hollow rhetoric. "We Elites feel strongly that the coming together of your middle group is very important. For the first time you seem to have found some unity. As the powerful people in Montville, we've decided to help your group unity by having Ethel and Eric sleep with you all in Hannover. This might not be what you want but we're sure it will be for the good of you all as a group." Ivan, feeling the sting in this paternalistic pronouncement, retorted, "That doesn't sound as though it's open for negotiation!"

It wasn't.

The Ins put up no resistance but demanded that Tony, the dismembered Hannoverian, be simultaneously transferred to Westville. This would leave the middles' home rather crowded, with eight people crammed into space for five, but at this hour, and given their history to date, this seemed a trivial inconvenience.

While the eviction details were being finalized, Ingrid as spokesperson for the Ins detoured via Westville to report on events. She told of what had transpired at Kenloch and then announced that Hannover had decided to stop work for the night in order to gain some much-needed sleep.

Westville was annoyed because they had been seduced into dealing with the system and yet right before their own eyes their secret plan to corrode the system by working for the whole evening had been so easily thwarted. They ventilated strongly with accusations that the Ins had used the Outs in a regular rip-off by getting their own luggage at the expense of Westville's cooperation, whereas the Outs had been rewarded with absolutely nothing; that they'd been dealing in good faith but the Ins had smashed that emerging trust. The Outs let forth with a tremendous barrage of abuse and a skillfully executed guilt induction routine. Eventually Ingrid fell for the trap, responding with "I'll ask our group if they'd be willing to continue." Before she had a chance to follow up on her offer, another round of attacks brought her to her limit. "Look, I'm tired of getting yelled at today; you have your options and I have mine. At this stage I'm going to exercise my option and leave." Whereupon she turned and with all her courage, a straight back and head held high, walked out. As she meandered back to Hannover alone in the dark, she couldn't help but feel, "How good it is, to be able to do something like simply walking out."

Back at the Ins' home, the scene was a strange mixture of calm and turmoil. People were moving mattresses to accommodate Ethel and Eric. Some were feeling pleased with their new-found unity since the migration of their discordant members. Chatter was idle, signs of fatigue were high.

Westville was feeling intensely frustrated and annoyed that their "make the system work all night" scheme had been so easily thwarted. There seemed little they could do before morning, so they too went quietly to bed.

The night stumbled to a standstill.

Entrepreneurs and Guerillas

Wednesday morning breakfast was consumed with an uneasy calm. The last two mealtimes had been most disruptive and everyone wondered whether there would be a new round of culinary retaliations, but nothing happened! The Outs humorously, unrevengefully, and ceremoniously partook of their cereal and water, while the Ins watched them anxiously from the opposite side of the dining hall. Since the previous evening's exchanges had concluded with many issues unresolved, the Outs decided to project an image of sincere co-operation as a strategy for the battles ahead. They reasoned that to exercise restraint at this point would throw others off guard and open more options for the future.

As breakfast drew to a close, the Outs asked Hannover for the chance to speak with them. Westville made one bold and simple statement. "You've been trying to get us to work for the system, and last night, in good faith, we agreed to do that. In fact, we were willing to work all night, but you Ins refused, maybe for reasons of fatigue, but nevertheless, it was you who stopped the work. We had acted in good faith in the belief that our efforts would eventually be rewarded. Now it would seem that you Ins have no good faith. If in fact you do have access to community resources, which you've repeatedly claimed, we want to see that demonstrated; and if you are remotely sincere in your intentions toward us, we want to see that indicated also. The demonstration we demand is the return of all our luggage by 10:30 A.M."

Hannover, totally oblivious to the ploys of Westville's demoniacal mind, fell for the trap. The Outs wanted the middles to feel guilty and thereby compelled to recompense Westville for the suffering they experienced in the light of the society's failure to thrive. It worked superbly! For a start, the Ins were taken aback by the fiery rhetoric of the "return our luggage or else" ultimatum. More importantly, Ingrid had been preparing herself and was all poised for the seduction. Already she'd begun to feel responsible for the collapse of the previous evening's activities. "I wonder what might have happened if I had not been so fatigued last night," she speculated silently. "But for me the strain was just too much. It may have been for the good of the system to proceed all night, but I simply didn't have the strength to continue. I hope it wasn't because I'm female and hence not as strong as the men. But come to think of it, all the Hannover men went to bed also. Goodness, there I go, torturing myself again. God, I wish I could get this liberation stuff together. Did I fail because I'm a woman? I've got to stop this!"

68

Once Ingrid's guilt had congealed, the only way she would feel better was by making repairs. Automatically she became encapsulated by the ethic that said "we made them suffer, now we must atone for our societal short-comings." Eventually all the Ins became drawn into believing this moral imperative.

Hannover generally agreed that the continued application of negative sanctions would be a resounding failure. Further attempts to control the Outs would only lead to more alienation. Any new proposals for negotiations would automatically be rejected as manipulative, and the force of the Outs' ultimatum made it impossible to ignore them. That left few options.

The result of those overpowering forces gravitated Hannover inevitably toward the following syllogism.

"The situation seems rather clear to me," commenced Ingrid. "The Outs want their luggage and last night they started to work in good faith to earn their personal belongings back. However, our actions in refusing to work late into the night prevented that!"

"That may well be so," argued Eric, "But I'm not so sure they were quite that sincere about it all. Even if we did prevent them from obtaining their luggage, what can we do about it now?"

"Well, I think it's important for us to accept the responsibility for our own actions," suggested Owen, picking up the logical train of Ingrid's thoughts. "And in this case being responsible would involve making reparation for the irresponsibility of our actions last night."

"How do you propose doing that?"

"There's an obvious way—meet the Outs' demands by returning their luggage as stipulated," concluded Ingrid. "What's more, I don't think we should try to manipulate them into working for it. We've been rather unsuccessful in getting them to work at anything and the one time when it seemed a remote possibility, we blew it. I'll bet we could never get them back to work after our grand plan fiasco."

"How do you intend to get the Outs' luggage from the Elites? We don't have the Outs' stuff to hand it over to them!"

"I guess that leaves us only one alternative. We'll have to work and then ask the Elites to give us the Outs' luggage as payment for our work. Then we can give it all back to the Outs. That should more than compensate for the debacle of last night and should convince them of our sincerity."

There was an appeal for Hannover in this philosophy of working for the Elites, obtaining things the Outs wanted, and giving them unconditionally to Westville. Somehow this seemed to imbue life with an essential meaning for the frustrated middles, thereby capturing their imagination. Alas, there was a ludicrous side to it also, for soon the middles were deciding to do extra work so they could buy sporting equipment from the Elites and give it to the Outs, thereby "enriching the quality" of the lower group's otherwise impoverished

69

life. Unbeknown to them, Westville had already uncovered the conference center's supply of sporting goods and merrily stolen all they felt they could make use of.

Although Hannover had become dedicated to meeting the Outs' needs, they had virtually no understanding of what the Outs really wanted. The Ins assumed that the Outs craved for "things" such as luggage, but in reality Westville was interested in them only as a symbol of the lessening societal inequality. The Ins were too caught up in their drive to "help the Outs" to note the significance of any potential symbolism.

Since the Outs were interested primarily in obtaining a legitimate and acknowledged part of the social action, this emphasis by the Ins on the provision of things was certain to be interpreted by Westville as demeaningly paternalistic.

Hannover launched into their new work ethic with vigor. They approached Kenloch to ask the Elites for Westville's luggage and to determine what work would need to be done to obtain such rewards. The Elites, surprisingly, agreed to release the Outs' luggage unconditionally. They didn't admit the reason why but couched their conciliation in benevolent terms. In reality Kenloch had decided that it would be wise to dispose of Westville's bags. They'd noticed, with fear, the increasing radicalization of the Outs and were terrified that eventually there would be an explosive attack on the Elites' home in order to retrieve their bags.

Westville's frustration at the failure of their "work all night scheme" served to heighten their radicalization, eventually causing their "work within the system while simultaneously destroying it" outlook to become crystallized into a total philosophy of life. Slowly it began to dawn on them that the fragmenting, polarized tensions of nonviolence versus violence, and proactivity versus reactivity, which always threatened the rubric of their cohesion, could be creatively transformed into a significant power base. New and adventurous schemes crept into their collective consciousness.

"If we're going to work within the system, let's do it right by exploiting the free enterprise system and becoming first-rate entrepreneurs," voiced one group. The opponents countered: "And if we're going to destroy the system let's do it systematically by using the best techniques of guerilla harrassment." "Even better—this will blow the society's crazy little mind! Let's keep our guerilla attacks for the Elites and be thoroughly cooperative and entrepreneurial with the Ins. That way, they'll spend all their time trying to figure out what's going on." "And if we always make sure that whenever we're in the public view, we take the volley ball and look like we're playing around, no one will believe we're ever doing anything."

The vibrance and excitement of it all! The Outs divided into two groups according to their interests. The Guerillas retired to one of the bedrooms to work up a list of potential harassment procedures. Within an hour they had produced a lengthy list of "Watergate-type" dirty tricks, enough to intimidate the most courageous Elite. It included: disrupt In and Elite meetings; disable the cars; steal fuses from electric light boxes; dismantle the community telephone; lock the dining hall at lunchtime; kidnap a member of the Elite society; become permanent escorts for the Elites; break into the Elites' house . . . so the list went on.

Meanwhile, the Entrepreneurs resolved to reject the idea that the Outs should be Montville's labor force under the control of some other group. At the same time they were determined to elevate themselves from the status of community parasites. They emerged with a scheme that was both exhaustive and exciting. In essence, it was to offer professional services to the society on a contractual basis.

The blueprints for the Guerilla-Entrepreneurial program had been drawn up, but not implemented, by the time the "return of the Outs' baggage" exchanges occurred. These events temporarily disrupted progress, especially the ceremonial cleaning of teeth by the Westvillers the moment their toothbrushes were retrieved. Although the Outs' home became filled, for the first time in three days, with sparkling toothpaste freshness, there was nothing that could significantly divert them from their merry schemes of ingenuity and plunder.

The first sign of the embryonic guerilla movement emerged late in the morning. Roderick was using the pay phone located immediately outside Westville. While he was inside, a sign was placed on the door saying "Out of Order." As he came out he was greeted by a gruff comment from Steve. "You use that phone again at grave risk to your body," a comment that seemed additionally potent because of the support of Steve's massive body and that of his comrade with equal, or greater, avoirdupois. Roderick threw his shoulders back and tried to preserve the dignity of his station in life, but deep down he was truly intimidated. He never used that phone again. As the Elite member left, the two Outs calmly removed a vital part of the phone hearing mechanism, put it in their pocket, and added to the "Out of Order" sign, "Those wising to use the phone should check first at Westville"—a very effective way to control access to one aspect of the communication system.

Throughout Montville's history, the Elites had continually used their cars, a privilege denied to the lower classes. This galled Westville, for it enabled the Elites to take flight whenever things got too hot for them. In the spirit of trying to equalize the system and to humble Kenloch's oversized ego, the Outs decided to dismantle the two cars they had access to—Richard's and Jason's. The first most obvious thing to do was to let down a couple of tires; and then, to ensure immobility, they removed some wiring that led to the distributor. The whole clandestine task took only a couple of minutes—minutes filled with absolute delight.

Later, when Roderick and Charles, feeling the need to replenish the alcohol supply, discovered the flattened tires, they tried to pretend it was inconsequential. "A couple of disabled cars hardly constitute a threat to our ability to operate; we'll show those incompetents we're not stupid like they

71

are; we can fix this in a flash." The solution was simple—go to the nearest town and get a pump. Then someone asked the awful question. "What do we go downtown in?"

"In a car, stupid!"

"Which car?"

"Eh! Well, why don't we just drive down on the flat wheels. That'll show them that we can't be stopped by letting down our tires."

"Okay, start it up, Richard. Let's get this thing on the road."

Richard ambitiously jumped in and turned the engine. The lack of response flushed a new fear that until this moment had been unspeakable. "My God, they even did over the engine!" Roderick poked his nose into the hood. "Oh, it's nothing, just a bit of wiring. Charles is an engineer; he can fix this!"

Fifteen minutes laker, Richard and Roderick could be seen slowly dragging the disabled vehicle down toward the nearest township. The grinding, flip-flop of the deflated wheel, which they tried to ignore, provided a constant embarrassment. They pretended that nothing was amiss. Instead they gloated about their capacity to solve such trivial problems as this. "If this had happened to the Ins they'd have been unable to function for the rest of the day. But not us. We can handle little things like this without even having our program disrupted," they boasted to themselves, as with every turn of the hind wheel a little more damage was inflicted on the tire.

Despite the fact that the Elites claimed this harassment was having no impact on them, the resultant discussion belied their assertions. They were afraid. Charles was the first one to speak. "Well, I think there's a reasonable chance one of us will be kidnapped, and if that happens I don't want to be caught with all this money on me."

"Yeah," agreed Lennox. "It would be sort of smart to strip ourselves and hide the money where only we know where it is."

It was a mortifying moment as these once powerful Elites took their leftover money, stealthily crept into the backyard of their now permanently locked Fort Kenloch, and poked handfuls of bills into a disused drainpipe. Such power!

Early Wednesday afternoon the Outs called Hannover into Westville lounge. The purpose? To unveil the entrepreneurial plan. Bill was spokesperson. All ears were attentive as he announced with careful deliberation the professional services the Outs were now offering to Montville.

"First, our *newspaper* services. We've recently opened the press of the *West End Leader,* a paper dedicated to the accurate and unbiased reporting of events of our society, and offering, where appropriate, social commentary. Right now, the first release is about to come off the press." There was no doubt as to the authenticity of this claim for people were racing around with press cards, and the whole of Westville's house was alive with newsroom-like activity. Bill continued.

"Second, our *housekeeping* agency. It is obvious that some homes are in desperate need of maid services. We're willing to do housekeeping chores."

"Third, our *recreation* program. We believe that healthy bodies generate healthy minds. There are obviously many people around here with unhealthy minds. We offer the therapy of sport and recreation."

"Fourth, our *consulting* organization. We notice that some groups in this society operate on unsound management principles. We're willing to share our expertise in this area—for a consulting fee, of course."

There was a small ripple of laughter. Bill continued, pokerfaced. "Take, for example, the economic system. There's no point in having an economic structure where things valued by one part of the community have zero value to another part. The Elites seemed to think that they'd stumbled across gold when they ripped-off our luggage. But we never cared about them having our things; therefore how could they ever imagine that our bags could be effectively used as an exchange commodity!"

"Last—and this is the most important service we offer—our *protection* plan. It's insurance, to cover health and life, based on prevention rather than cure. It operates like this. Insure with us and we'll guarantee nothing will happen to you. Those who refuse our protection offer do so at great risk."

Bill concluded this good-humored exchange with a barbed rider. "Any of you Ins who'd like to work for us in the delivery of these services may be enlisted as employees." Both Hannover and Westville enjoyed immensely the vibrance and creativity of this encounter.

The hope of Westville was that by relating to the Ins through the entrepreneurial scheme and simultaneously subjecting the Elites to the guerrilla program, a great deal of confusion would be generated. It worked to perfection.

Hannover's Tolerance Expires

As Westville launched into their multiple operations, busily offering recreational activities, producing newspapers, and delightedly wheeling and dealing with package offers such as lifetime subscriptions to the *West End Leader* with protection coverage as a free optional extra, Hannover naively decided to try to capitalize on the situation. They concluded that by claiming credit for the feverish "pro the system" endeavors of the Outs, the Elites might be duped into giving the Ins some extra rewards. A vain hope!

In Fort Kenloch, Ethel was the speaker. "We've requested this meeting with you Elites so that you can remain fully informed of the developments we Ins have managed to effect in the society over the last few hours. The Outs are now beginning to work toward the goals of the society. Currently, they are producing a newspaper, and they are willing to do other work, such as developing recreation programs and offering basic social services."

The Elites listened, unbelievingly for a moment, and then asked, "Are you controlling the Outs?" Ethel wanted desperately to hide the fact that Hannover had no managerial function in these new activities, otherwise she was likely to simply trigger the Elites' wrath. Richard, who had been annoyed by the damage done to his car through the guerilla scheme, was determined to pin her in a corner. "Are the Outs working by themselves with their own initiative, or are some of you working with them?"

"Heh?"

"I'll repeat! Are you Ins taking a management role or are you just participating alongside the Outs?"

"Well," defended Ethel limply, "it's like a consultancy."

"What do you mean, it's 'like a consultancy'?"

It was rather unclear what Ethel meant by that, but she'd now gone too far. Within minutes she was trapped into admitting that the Ins were nothing more than consumers of the Outs' self-made products. The claim that Hannover had control over the feverish work activities was quickly invalidated.

A tirade of Elite anger was viciously unleashed on Ethel. As the outburst increased in tempo, a loud rap on Kenloch's window produced a temporary reprieve. A Westville voice pierced the securely locked windows. "Paper boy, paper boy!" A number of Outs were clustered at the fortress door. Kenloch tried to ignore them, but that was impossible. Continuous rattling of the doors and windows, punctuated with loud messages about the latest edition of the *West End Leader,* provided a constant reminder of the alien presence.

Eventually, Richard responded, yelling out, "I'm busy. You didn't make an appointment!"

A quick retort. "Paper boys don't make appointments!"

Richard could find no quip to that response.

Seven of the monstrous Outs were present for this event. In the spirit of their usual "recreate while you wait," they played a round of volleyball. Their chatter, however, was basically a brainstorming session for later news articles; so despite appearances to the contrary, they literally worked while they played.

Charles turned back to Ethel. "You mean to tell us that you've got them working, while outside before our very eyes we can see that they're doing nothing but playing ball! And what's more, you claim that they're under your control. Well, I want you to prove it by going out there right now and telling those big beasts to disappear."

Sensitive to the futility of that, Ethel wisely refused.

Richard could contain himself no longer. He burst forth with the news that the Outs had been destroying the Elite property, referring to both the disabled cars and the dismantled phone. The Ins, of course, had been kept ignorant of these acts—but Richard could use even this to their disfavor. "Here you are claiming you have control over those peasants, and you don't even know what they're up to. You're saying they're working yet we see they're playing, and we know they're destroying our property. How could you ever expect us to believe you?"

Lennox picked up the attack again. "I think you've been sucked in! Why, the newspaper is even called the *West End Leader*. You can't even get your name recognized by the paper. Next we'll learn you're writing articles for the paper, like paid journalists."

"Well," defended Ethel, courageously and stupidly, "we are writing articles, but we've actually got the Outs working for us." That was the limit! Lennox started to shake with anger, thumping his fists on the table and fuming indecipherable and irrelevant comments. Again, Ethel put a stop to this attack with a paralyzing admission. "Well, your work scheme for the society is about to be recommenced. We've decided to go ahead and make the greeting cards ourselves."

Montville froze! It was minutes before a few words dribbled out to sustain the all but dead atmosphere. "That's sure a great activity for the management group of the society!"

No further words were exchanged. In silence, the shadow of death passed over the Elite-In relationship. Hannover meekly rose and stumbled to the door. Kenloch flopped back in exhaustion, without the energy to even let loose with a profanity.

In that moment of discovering the dual entrepreneurial-guerilla plan, Hannover correctly concluded that their noble intentions and generous efforts had been taken by Westville and thrown right back in their faces. It was a bitter and remorseful group of Hannoverians who confronted the harsh reality. Their misfortune bore the bold embossment of their own fingerprints. Even their benign concerns for the Outs' welfare had become malignant with distaste. "The Outs took their luggage, pretending they were grateful, assuring us they were working for the systen, and all along they were setting things up so we'd end up getting stabbed in the back," concluded Ivan.

"Well, that's the end for me!" declared Owen forthrightly, determined to flee the gnawing irresolution of the previous days. "I ain't working for anybody, or because of anybody, or on anybody's behalf no more. The Outs can do what they like, and so can the Elites, but they're not going to do it through me. Anything I now do, it's for me, or else I don't do it at all." There was no overt celebration of Owen's sullen conclusion, but it was evident no one disagreed.

Melancholia pervaded Hannover for the next few hours, as they filled their time with casual strolls in the woods, or a frivolous game of volleyball with the ever playful Outs. As the depression lifted, it became clear to everyone that Hannover had abandoned their middle role, and in so doing had silently laid to rest their philosophy of working to obtain valuables to give to the Outs.

At supper time the Ins decided to celebrate their new found independence by taking some of their own money, recently retrieved from the Elites, hiring a taxi, travelling to the nearest supermarket, buying some supplies, and preparing their own meal.

75

For the first time, the dining room table in Hannover was set up. Eight chairs were placed meticulously around its edges and the feast was served. The quality of the food was very reminiscent of any middle-class American meal, but for the House of Hannover on that night it assumed a mystical importance, as though it represented the essence of all life. Chatter was light-hearted. A toast was drunk, although to what was a little unclear. However, I'm sure that if Nathan Hale had been sitting at that table at that time, he'd have found the words to encapsulate the feelings. "I have but one life to give for my country; I only regret that my country is not worth giving that life for."

The Crime Wave

While the Ins were hibernating in their latest paralysis, Westville continued energetically with their entrepreneurial program. Papers were produced at a reasonable rate by half their group while the others wandered around trying to whip up the enthusiasm of potential clientele or behaving intimidatingly toward an Elite in the attempt to induce commitment to the Outs' life insurance-protection plan.

Kenloch tried not to be intimidated, but with each passing hour their fears increased exponentially. Their home had become a real fortress. Blinds were drawn, windows were firmly locked, potential enterers were strictly screened for their intent, and one couldn't help but feel that the freedoms their power afforded them had turned into almost imprisoning restrictions. They still talked boldly about how free they were, even while they sweltered in a house that now was so tightly locked that the summer temperature was almost unbearable. They couldn't enjoy the breeze outside because of their fear of being unprotected in "that violent, irresponsible world out there."

Eventually they concluded that Montville was too violent a place for them to survive in. "If we don't escape soon, we may never get away," was the reluctant conclusion that finally triggered their departure. As they left they really had no idea where to go or what to do—just to be anywhere other than in Montville!

Westville was displeased when they learned of Kenloch's departure. "That's not very sporting of them to flee the battleground at their moment of greatest vulnerability. And certainly it displays limited courage on the part of our leaders!" mused the Outs as their revolutionary passions began to ignite.

"What do we do now?"

Westville had never been granted entree to Kenloch by the Elites, a deprivation that excited their taste buds like forbidden fruit. An attack on Fort Kenloch seemed so appropriate. Minutes later several bodies could be seen rattling windows and testing the locks of the Elites' house. From nowhere, someone appeared with a ladder. "I'm sure we can get through the upstairs windows." "Drag it around. . . ." Some brakes screeched and a car pulled to a halt outside, heralding, thought the Outs, the return of the Elites. A vicious scene looked imminent. What a relief! It was only the conference director, Mr. Beasley, who with red face and angered tone, asked the would-be burglars what they were up to. When he learned the horrible truth, he mustered up all his authoritarianism and told them if they continued, he'd have to take action, leaving deliberately vague what that action might be.

Westville were a rather obliging lot. It seemed hardly necessary to alienate Mr. Beasley in all this activity. So they meekly returned the ladder to its rightful place and started walking home with their objective of razing Kenloch still unfulfilled. No sooner had Beasley driven off around the corner when Steve called, "Let's go back to complete the job." Bodies were quickly slung over the rafters and hoisted to the second floor. But a moment passed, and they were in.

A large cheer declared their success to the world. "Now, where are our car keys and wallets kept?"

"This room's locked. They're probably in here!"

"Well, let's break the door down!"

"Okay, a few more big guys over here."

"Hey, I got the food and the beer. Will we take the coffee machine?"

"Yeah, why not!"

"What else do we need?"

"Anything you like."

"Hey, come and take a look at this, will you? You won't believe what these fools have got written on this newsprint."

Half a dozen clustered jovially around the newsprint while they flipped page after page. Roars of laughter filled the fort as they saw the residual signs of the process the Elites had been through in the design of the society.

"Let's leave them a message," suggested Lee. Spontaneously a profanity was embossed on the last newsprint page.

Several more entries were made to Fort Kenloch that evening. For a while it became the Outs' new toy; breaking in became their nocturnal version of volleyball. No longer did they debate whether violence was justifiable. From their Out perspective, anything was acceptable in the light of how the Elites had treated them. In fact, to mildly accept their victim status would have seemed a sin much greater than these trivial acts of burglary.

The New Society

After the crime wave had peaked and fallen, the Outs invited the Ins to join with them in the design of some new social structures for the remaining few hours of Montville's history. Hannover had come alive after their communion meal together and had been contemplating ways of coping with the "criminal" activity within the system. They began to think in terms of establishing a judicial system in which both Outs and Elites who had committed crimes against the social order might be brought to justice. Westville, on hearing of their intent, pointed out how it bore the marks of their residual middleness and argued that a New Society should be free of such historical retributions. Hannover acquiesced and plans for a new coalition of forces were drawn up.

The initial idea was for the two houses to hold equal status in the New Society, while preserving their separate identities, developed so potently through the historical processes. To serve the goal of effecting the coalition, the houses formed an administrative committee consisting of two members from each of Hannover and Westville. They were charged with the responsibility of designing the New Society and of dealing with the "ex-Elites."

The back room of Westville was converted into the administrative committee's chambers, with space provided so that any of the New Society's members could attend as observers to their deliberative sessions. As the night wore on, a series of subcommittees, consisting of one member from each house, were formed and allocated specific tasks.

Typical of the subcommittees was the colorful combination of Fred and Ingrid, who were charged with the responsibility of ensuring that adequate food would be provided for the remainder of their stay at Montville. They chose the intimacy of the phone booth as the place to deliberate their strategies. Before doing anything adventurous, it seemed imperative to contact Mr. Beasley, the conference director, to see what future meal plans had been made. Mr. Beasley was not to be found. They tried to phone him. No answer. There seemed little alternative to trying to work out which was his home and waking him if need be. Eventually they flushed out a rather embarrassed, annoyed, red-faced, pajama-clad conference director and worked out some new meal arrangements with him.

Other subcommittees, similarly constituted, were each allocated critical social tasks. The place was agog with activity. The various subcommittees were constantly reporting their activities to each other to avoid duplication. Regular reports were made to the central committee, who orchestrated the scenario to integrate the subcommittees' activities, making sure that the emergent philosophy of egalitarian coexistence was strictly adhered to. The most critical task for the New Society was to determine how to deal with the Elites. Eventually it was resolved to allow them to remain undeposed from their position, but totally subjugated to the societal governance of the Westville-Hannover central committee. They were to be "Elite" in name only. It was also agreed that should Kenloch refuse to accept this humanitarian treatment, then they should be arrested and tried under the rules of the New Society, using whatever force was necessary to achieve the central committee's objective.

Later in the evening, six bleary-eyed Elites returned. They stumbled lethargically into Kenloch and quickly recognized blatant signs of the numerous raids, which prompted them to take a good look to see what had been stolen. They were not surprised that their fort had been attacked. In part, their excursion had been precipitated by this very possibility.

By the time the old Power Elite had settled back into their fort, the structures of the new coalition were fully operative. There remained just one task left for the evening—the induction of the Elite into their new, disenfranchised social role.

Everyone was eager to be spectator to this coming event, which promised to be the most spectacular moment in Montville's four-day history. Like an army, the New Society marched on Kenloch, the heavy trudging of their feet heralding their arrival for the Elites. It was 12:45 A.M.

Kenloch was clearly afraid, but they modestly opened their door, granting entry to the masses. To refuse would have only invited the unhinging of doors and the breaking of windows, a most undesirable prospect at this late hour.

Fort Kenloch was seething with humanity. With all twenty-six Montvillers present, the place was overcrowded. The Elite quickly drew to the edge of the group, positioning themselves near the stairs to facilitate, if necessary, a rapid escape to lockable bedrooms on the second floor.

Despite these overt cues of their timidity, the Elites "talked big." Richard, in particular, put on a melodramatic act of ranting and raving, claiming that he felt insulted because his home had been broken into illegally. His performance drew a few laughs, but generally it was treated as sheer stupidity. Others of the Elites tried to "tough it out," but given the circumstances, there was really nothing of significance they could say.

Eventually, partly in response to the pressures of fear, and partly as a ploy to diffuse the New Society's efforts, the Elites rose and retired upstairs, making out as if they were going to bed. No one stopped them. Once they had retreated, no preparations for sleep were made. Mostly what happened was a ventilation of anger and frustration, tempered only by the continued reassurances that by walking out from their meeting with the New Society, the Elites had yet again demonstrated their aloof superiority.

The New Society interpreted this sudden withdrawal by the Elites as a face-saving admission that their power had been stripped away. Feeling no need for further vengeance following the melodramatic ending to this much anticipated encounter, the New Society decided to depart and rest for the evening in preparation for the predestined death of the system on the morrow. As they were leaving Kenloch, someone suggested a symbolic house arrest of the Elites would be aesthetic. And so, with a flourish of their new-found liberty and temporary pacifism, a note was pinned on the entrance to Fort Kenloch, announcing to anyone concerned that its occupants were under house arrest till the end of time.

Sleep that evening came easily for some, hard for others. For some of the staff it brought the mystical shedding of their anthropoid masks and returned them to the human state they now craved so intensely—to be free to talk, interact, and write no more notes.

The therapy of that 8:00 A.M. hour. . . .

Part 2

Relations among Groups with Differential Power

Relations among Groups with Differential Power

Introduction

Having lived through Montville as an anthropologist, I was struck by the extent to which the three groups became locked into their own rigid frameworks of reality. For all levels of Montville society these frameworks seemed to have systematic effects: They powerfully shaped each group's views of the rest of the society, generating multiple and divergent realities; they limited the flexibility of the groups in their dealings with each other; and they often left groups behaving in ways that ran counter to their espoused goals.

The Kenloch Elites poured their energy into the goal of making the Ins sufficiently dependent that they would willingly take on the task of building a three-tiered society based on the principles of work. Yet the techniques of dependency induction that the Elites used left the Ins so fragmented and impotent that they were too weak to even take care of themselves, let alone become strong enough to act as agents of the Elites in controlling the Outs. Whenever evidence surfaced that the Elites' plan was not succeeding, the upper group managed to interpret it as information that the Ins were ineffective as implementers of Kenloch's wishes, rather than that the plan needed revision. This upper group unknowingly pursued a course of action destined to failure, repeatedly ignoring the ineffectiveness of their motivation scheme, and maintained their "carrot and stick" philosophy of management until the bitter end. The Elites seemed to become imprisoned by a framework of reality that *blinded them to the consequences of their own behavior.*

At the bottom of Montville society, the Outs, in response to their experience of powerlessness, quickly became unified. Their major concern was that the Elites would divide and conquer them. Hence they became overly sensitive to any signs of disagreement within their own group. To counteract threats to their unity, the Outs developed strong ground rules, limiting explicitly what members could or could not do. Some of these rules were so restrictive that the internal oppression was often just as strong as the external oppression that the restriction was meant to counteract. This led to the stifling of the lower group and shrouding them for long periods of time with an atmosphere of stagnation. The Outs *became encased by the protection devices they developed to defend themselves from the threats of those above.*

Caught in the middle were the Hannover Ins, constantly mediating between the Kenloch Elites and the Westville Outs. As the tensions pulled them in opposite directions, the Ins attempted to ease their situation by unifying Montville as a whole. However, most things the Ins tried either fragmented the system more or heightened the tensions within their own group. Whenever they took cues from the Elites about what they "should" do, they ended up alienating the Outs, and vice-versa. The Ins became paralyzed, rendered impotent by their middle, mediating position. From their framework of reality, they seemed *compelled to create and preserve functional relations with the groups both above and below them.* Their mediating mentality became so powerful that they spent most of their Montville lives simply existing *for* the other two groups, failing to attend to what they wanted for themselves. Only after they had been almost destroyed by their attempts to juggle the myriad of pressures in the system was Hannover able to give up on Montville, abandon the mediating role, and start living for themselves.

As I reflected on the Montville experience, I was struck by the extent to which each of Montville's three groups seemed to become caught in a set of binds that shaped their view of "reality" and constrained the form of their interactions with others. However, what was even more surprising was that no group appeared to comprehend even the existence of these constraints, let alone the power of their impact on their relationships with other groups. It was as though the constraining forces were like invisible "prison walls." Each group seemed locked into a *prison in disguise.*

In this, the second part of this book, I want to step back from Montville and reflect, at a theoretical level, on what social system forces might have generated both the power and the divergence of the multiple realities that were so evident in the power laboratory. In particular I want to try and understand both the nature of these prisons and why they seemed so invisible to those encased by them but appeared so obvious to me as I took on an external, anthropological perspective. My curiosity for this question has remained forever piqued by my recognition that all the time, in my regular social contexts, I may be equally locked into psychological prisons of just as much intensity and that I may have as little realization of their existence and impact as did the Montville groups.

By the end of part 2 of this book I hope to have explicated this theme sufficiently to have created a set of general concepts that will enable us to look at an everyday social system, the school district of Ashgrove, through a perspective of hierarchial intergroup relations.

I became convinced that if I wanted to comprehend what occurred at Montville at a theoretical level, I had to look behind the disguised prisons. In order to do this I turned to the concept of structural encasements that I had started to explicate in the prologue. I want to discuss this concept of encasement at a general level initially and then to explore the traps that appear to accompany having the power to create, the power to block, and the power to mediate, as seemed to be the case with the Elites, Outs, and Ins, respectively.

One of the first questions I had to confront was how would I do this. As a social theorist, it is clear I have a choice about how to examine what I observed at Montville. On one hand I could take the position that the three groups behaved the way they did because that's what they were like. From this perspective, I would end up concluding it was in the character of this particular group of Elites to be domineering, myopic, blaming; it was in the character of this group of Outs to be rebellious, suspicious, defensive; it was in the character of these Ins to be confused, fragmented, indecisive.

An alternative position might be to consider that who belonged to the Elites, Outs, or Ins was totally irrelevant. Everything that occurred in Montville was because of "the system." In this perspective the argument might proceed that Montville came to develop such a life of its own that the three groups were nothing more than puppets of Montville social forces. In this mind set, it would be possible to look at the Montville groups as merely enacting the system forces.

These alternative vantage points represent theoretically the same dilemma that we find in the age-old question of whether humans make history or history makes humans. Tempting though it may be, it does not make sense to grab just one horn of this dilemma, for clearly humans and history make each other. However there is a problem with the simplicity of this acknowledgment and that is it often leads us to rather trite understandings. This can be seen so often in the social sciences. A typical example is the often used, glib application of Lewin's famous formula, which simply dismisses enormous social complexities by claiming that the three Montville groups behave the way they did as an interactive expression of both the system forces *and* the particular character of each of the groups. The problem with this way of thinking is not that it's incorrect. It's that it leads to the posing of questions to which the only appropriate response should be "Mu," which is a Japanese word meaning "unask the question," for the question cannot be reasonably explored in the way it's been formulated (Pirsig, 1974). Let me be explicit. If we argue that the behavior of any social entity is a function of both its character and the context in which it exists, it then becomes possible to ask how much of the entity's behavior is influenced by its character and how much by the context. And that's the point where we become drawn into false distinctions; for the character of the entity is knowable only in its behavior, and the character of the context is expressed only in the behavior of its parts, one of which is the very entity whose behavior is being explored. Putting it simply, issues like humans and history making each other must be explored in some way other than in the stifling framework of how much do humans shape history or does history shape humans.

For my exploration of Montville, I want to ignore the question to what extent the three groups' behavior was influenced by their character or the forces of Montville at large and to move instead into a framework that focuses on *how* the development of the relationships of the Elites, Ins, and Outs and

Montville's overall character coevolved such that by the end it was impossible to look at Montville or talk about Montville separate from the relationships among its parts (the three groups) or to talk about the character of any of the three groups separate from its place in the overall Montville context.

To organize the presentation of these ideas in this chapter, however, I am going to make a false distinction, simply for conceptual clarity. In the first part I'm going to discuss the relationship among the groups. This will be done under the headings of 'structural encasements' at the general level and then specifically for each of the upper, middle, and lower positions. Then, drawing upon these relational ideas I will discuss characteristics displayed by each of the groups using four global headings: (1) perceptions and attributions; (2) use of information; (3) modalities for dealing with external conflict; and (4) handling internal conflicts. Saying this differently, in the first part I will take a theoretical look at Montville by exploring the characteristics of the interaction patterns among the groups, whereas in the second I will look at the characteristics of the groups in interaction. While doing this, however, I want us to keep remembering that they really are one and the same thing, just looked at differently. At the end of the chapter I will provide a summary based on this same artificial distinction, which I'd like to be understood as merely sides of the same coin.

Structural Encasements

To explore the topic of structural encasements at the general level, I must explicate two concepts, the social comparison processes of groups in interaction and dynamic conservatism. After discussing the general dynamic of structural encasements I will turn to how these operate in a more specific way in shaping the divergent reality sets of groups in the relative positions of powerfulness, powerlessness, and caught-in-the-middle, drawing on the experiences of Montville's Elites, Outs, and Ins for illustrative purposes. To set the stage, let me comment about two issues, the difficulties of studying interaction patterns and the question of consciousness.

Interaction Patterns

In this section, I will talk about interacting groups. From the outset I want to underscore a topic I introduced in the prologue. When we observe groups in interaction we are always confronted with two general domains upon which we can focus our attention: *The characteristics of the actors* in interaction, or the *characteristics of the interaction patterns* (Goffman, 1959). In the former case, what we observe is visible. It's physically verifiable. In the latter case, what we observe is invisible. It must be derived from the relationship among things that are observable. When the mime Marcel Marceau takes his invisible dog for a walk on stage, as Marceau's arm jerks back and forth everyone "sees" the dog straining on the leash, even though there is no dog and no leash (May, 1975). We see something that doesn't exist. So it is with observing interactions. We can look at the interaction even though the only "real" observables are the behaviors of the interactors.

Focusing on interaction patterns among people or groups is conceptually analogous to noticing the wind as it blows through trees. The wind is recognizable primarily by its impact on objects that move and behave within the realm of the wind's presence. It wouldn't make much sense for us to claim that leaves ripple and trees bend simply because it is their nature to do so. When a tree is bending and twisting vigorously in the middle of a storm, it does make sense to recognize the characteristic of the tree's flexibility, but we are more likely to focus on the intensity and direction of the wind. Just as trees express the nature of the winds blowing against it, a group's behavior can be thought of as expressing the nature of the prevailing interaction patterns. Just as the nature of the wind is detectable only in the behavior of the trees, so the nature of the interaction between groups can be derived only from interpreting the group's behaviors.

In talking about structural encasements I want to convey the image of prison walls. These walls are important not only because they define the boundaries between the groups on both sides, but more importantly because they constrain ways in which those on both sides of the wall interact. The idea of prison also suggests that the wall constrains people on one side in a manner that does not apply equally to those on the other side. Both prisoners and non-prisoners are equally constrained by the walls. However, it's those trapped inside that make the wall visible. So likewise, it's the behavior of the groups that are caught by the constraining forces that in fact make the wall most visible. They are the ones affected most clearly by the wall's existence. It is important to recognize that the invisible prison walls of social structures come into consciousness only when some group or individual is "acting out" the structurally constraining features. If it weren't for this "acting out," the constraints would never be recognizable. We must be careful not to believe, however, that it's only those who are "acting out" who are constrained by the psychological barriers. So are those who are being "acted out" upon.

The important point in the argument is that the only way we can "see" the invisible constraints is when they are expressed in a group's behavior, and when we have a method for looking behind the manifest to look for what's latent within it. For example, I want to be able to explore the possibility that when the Outs behaved in a "paranoid" manner, this could be as much an expression of the Montville interaction patterns in general as an expression of the essential character of this particular Out group. This approach to structural encasements is exploratory and derivative. It's an approach that demands acceptance of the possibility that not everything of explanatory value can be pointed at directly in an externally verifiable way.

The Question of Consciousness

The task of understanding and explicating structural encasements is especially difficult because the nature of the constraints is so well hidden from the people encased by them. Therefore, we cannot assume that each person is aware of or able to report on what ways he or she feels imprisoned. If the constraints are not in the person's consciousness, or the consciousness of the group to which the person belongs, when someone is asked to talk about an experience, the person may well focus on the wide range of liberties he or she feels and the freedoms to make choices, while turning a blind eye to the ways in which the inner experience is bound up by social limitations that don't even creep into the consciousness. This will be especially true if an individual or a group is involved in a great deal of activity. If a person's or group's inner experience is one of high activity with a large number of options to choose from and a wide range of liberties, it is very unlikely that the constraints within which these activities, liberties, and choices exist will be seen or challenged. This doesn't mean that they don't exist, however. And the very fact that people and groups are engaged in a great deal of activity may help to merely camouflage both the existence and the impact of the constraining forces. As Sarason (1972) observed, the more intense the internal activity within severe limitations, the less the probability the limiting forces will be noticed and attacked. He summarized this dynamic by quoting the pungent French proverb "The more things change, the more they stay the same." Katz (1971) takes Sarason's point even further, arguing, as would Marx, that the more vigorous the activity that occurs within any reality set, the greater the likelihood that the constraining forces (the prison walls) of that reality set will be reinforced and made more solid.

Because people focus primarily on their own behavior and don't usually recognize the constraints that limit that behavior, it is not possible to get at the whole "truth" (whatever that is) by merely accepting peoples' reports of their "truths". Rather we must be willing to take a derivative approach, to look at the forces behind peoples' experience of reality in order to comprehend why they experience reality that way. For example, when the Outs would go off for their regular swim, at one level they were experiencing their freedom to enjoy life, etc., and this is how they talked of their swimming experience. At another level, their regular swims were a repetitative display of how excluded and powerless they were in the Montville society. Within their social powerlessness they were free to choose how to trivially pass their time away. Unattentive to the extent of the constraints that bound them, the Outs symbolized their collective swims as an important "social and recreative activity"—which it certainly was at one level—which only people with freedom could exercise. However, they were not consciously attentive to how much those swims indicated how little they were influencing the course of events in Montville or for that matter how obliged they as a group felt to take their swims together, as an expression of their mutual bondage. When the Outs were recreating, they didn't exercise their liberty of some swimming, while others took a walk, played ball, or climbed a tree. They *all* swam. Their experience was that they chose to be together. An equally plausible alternative view was that their reality was so constrained, they experienced a collective compulsion to stay together. Their experience of liberty was they could take a swim together. Their bondage of which they never seemed explicitly conscious may well have been that they had to do it together and that this was their collective, reactive response to being excluded from the mainstream of Montville life.

Given then that groups may very well be unaware of the impact of the structural encasements in which they exist, a central question is how can they be uncovered or adequately delineated? To untangle this we must understand both the social comparison processes that interacting groups engage in and the operation of dynamic conservatism, both of which can be found in the social rituals and traditions (in the Goffman, 1959, sense) that may act as both masks and representations of the prevailing structural encasements. Behind these rituals may well be found hidden psychological prisons of which individual's and groups' outward behaviors are merely representations.

Social Comparison Processes: The Building Blocks

The question I want to keep central throughout this section on social comparison processes is how did the Elites, Ins, and Outs develop their images of Montville in general and of each other in particular. No group seemed to be actively and knowingly creating distorted pictures for themselves. Yet powerful systematic distortions did occur with no member of Montville appearing to understand the nature of those distortions. How come? The issue is not simple, and unfortunately I have to make this more complex before it can be made clear.

Every group needs another group to provide a looking glass (Cooley, 1922) in which it can examine itself. In the same way as I need other people's reactions to me to guess what I'm like as a social being, so groups need each other for the purpose of making social comparisons.

There is a basic problem with the looking glass relationship, however, and that is there are many reasons why a group may choose to look into the mirror, and these reasons may vary from time to time. When I get dressed in the morning I may look in the mirror to confirm my narcissistic tendencies or simply to comb my hair, or to check whether my clothes look color coordinated, to see whether the pimple on my face disappeared overnight, or whether the bags under my eyes have lessened. I'll look for different reasons and I may be rather invested in the outcome. Maybe I'll choose not to put on the light, thereby reducing the probability that my baggy eyes will look horrible. Maybe I'll stand really close to the mirror, to be able to examine the troublesome pimple in sharp focus. Maybe I'll look for just a second, so that if my clothes aren't too coordinated it won't hit me too hard.

These same forces may come into play when groups use each other as mirrors for their own self-reflection. They may posture to have the distance between them carefully predetermine what they can find out about themselves. If two groups are close, one group may see reflected back manifestations of its own inner fragmentation, vulnerability, or chaos. If they're positioned at great distance, trivial or superficial images may be what a group learns about itself.

This issue of distance between groups in the comparative looking glass process was evident in the early Montville hours when the Outs, feeling very information-deprived, tried to contact the Kenloch Elites. The Elites told them to go away and resubmit their list of needs in greater detail. The Outs left. The Elites judged the Outs' response as a sign of their upper power. But the distance between the groups was so great that this self-reflection was quite inaccurate. Rather than undertaking the task the Elites had given them, which might have been a manifestation of the Elite's power, the Outs indifferently went off for a swim, something the Elites never knew about. In this looking glass exchange, one group saw itself to be powerful while the reacting group in reality was treating them with indifference and disdain.

The distance between the groups in the looking glass/social comparison process will determine greatly what parts of a group's life it will see reflected back.

Another major issue with the social comparison process is the underlying reason why a group wishes to use another group to indicate what it is like. For example, if a group wishes to feel good about something it fundamentally feels bad about, then it may posture its relational distance so that it will have discovered only what it wants to have known. If a group feeling bad about itself is able to posture itself at a safe distance from a looking glass group, then it may see reflected back to itself only its good side. If that group, having preorchestrated how it will look from the outside, has external images reflected back that are contradictory to its inner fears about itself, then it may in fact manage to feel internally better. It may even come to delude itself.

Consider the Outs. In their relative position of powerlessness, they feared most that their unity could be taken away from them. However, the times the Outs felt most divided was when they were alone with themselves. Then all their within group differences were paramount. These were often very threatening for they took away the unity they felt was necessary to deal with those who were more powerful. However, the Outs never seemed to notice the differences within their own ranks while there was an outside threat. Hence if their inner divisions became too disruptive to their group unity, the Outs could always preorchestrate a conflictual exchange with a more powerful group and thereby remobilize their unity in the service of combating external oppression. When this happened the powerless group would see reflected back to themselves, through their exchange with such a looking glass group, their own unity. This perception of unity of the powerless group, as obtained through this external reflection, at one level was self-delusional. At another level, it was their reality. For such a group with its unity undermined by inner dissention could look at itself through a preorchestrated conflict with another group and see itself as united again. This delusion, however, was embedded in its failure to notice that they were united only in the context of the intensely conflictual exchange they were having with the other group. In other words, although they were phenomenologically a cohesive group, they did not recognize that their unity was created by and dependent on their ongoing investment in both the postured distance from, and the conflictualness in, their relationships with their looking glass groups.

On the other hand, a group feeling bad about itself might posture its looking glass relationship so that it confirms from the outside just how bad it is. At a theoretical level it will not be evident why a group might wish to deny or confirm its good or bad side until we have discussed the concept of dynamic conservatism. For the moment, however, it is sufficient to acknowledge that the posturing can occur in a variety of ways.

Extending the above theme a little further leads us into the question of how a group comes to develop its image of the world, or what constitutes group consciousness. In raising this I am not interested in positing here the philosophical question of whether there is such a thing as a group mind or whether a group is capable of thinking. However I am concerned with how a group comes to develop, modify, and eventually reify, in ways that become self-fulfilling, its version of reality. When a group observes another group's behavior and interprets that behavior as having particular meanings, then it is in the process of creating for itself a consciousness of its world. Likewise, when that group engages in a social comparison process through the looking glass phenomenon, then it's developing a form of consciousness of itself. The processes that shape a group's consciousness of self and of others are very important in appreciating how between-group distortions occur. For it's in these processes of consciousness development that we can find the key to the emergence of multiple realities in social systems.

One very important phenomenological point that must be made before proceeding is that there is no such thing as consciousness that appears in and by itself. "Consciousness" is always consciousness of something (Schutz, 1970). This consciousness may have two forms. It may be *consciousness of the mere process of experiencing* (what Schutz calls the "noetic") or the *consciousness of the object of the experience* (what Schutz refers to as the "noematic").

The difference may be seen in comparing the statements, "I'm conscious of myself experiencing you" (this is the subjective—the noetic) or, "I'm conscious of you whom I'm experiencing" (this is the objective—or the noematic). The confusion of these two is really critical in group relations. If a group is not very conscious of its own experience, or cannot separate its own experience from the object that it's experiencing, then it's very likely to treat the other group as though it's actually like the way it's being experienced. This is the process of objectifying the subjective and is analogous to my experiencing myself in an angry exchange with some other person, denying the subjective part of my experience, and misattributing the whole process by considering the other person to be an angry person.

The Montville story demonstrates repeatedly the confusion of experiencing with the object of the experience. For example, the Kenloch Elites, during the frenetic production of the lower group's newspaper, experienced the Outs as being playful, belligerent, and disrespectful. However, they mistakenly assumed that the Elites' experience was how the Outs really were. Paradoxically, what the Outs were doing at this time was implementing their guerilla/entrepreneurial plan. The Outs' inner reality was one of plotting, scheming, and undermining. When the Elites took their experience of the Outs and objectified it through the assumption that it reflected reality, they inappropriately came to view what was scheming and plotting behavior as playful and belligerent. This confusion of the noetic and noematic, by assuming that the Outs were actually like how the Elites saw them, contributed greatly to the Elites becoming blind to other realities in the system.

Thus far, we have been discussing the simple building blocks of one of the most fundamental aspects of relationships among interacting groups—the looking glass and social comparison process. This is important for understanding systematic distortions that occur in organizational communication, for whenever a group "says" anything to another group, either explicitly as a direct communication or implicitly as an indirect communication through a particular piece of behavior, the actual content of the communication may be secondary. Under these circumstances, the primary communication received is "What are they saying about how they experience us as a group?", i.e., the latent social comparison statement.

Social Comparison Processes: Adding the Complexities

To this point, our discussion of the looking glass phenomenon has been deliberately oversimplified in order to make its fundamentum clear. However, it's very much more complicated than this, and I now want to add, piece by piece, another six affiliated concepts in order to set the groundwork for the notion of *dynamic conservatism,* which is a broader manifestation of the social comparison process distortion dynamics existent in multiple reality systems.

1. In the public presentations of themselves, most groups are aware that there is a discrepancy between how group members really feel about themselves as a group and how they want others to perceive how they feel about themselves. Groups always generate ambivalent tensions, with members simultaneously wanting to be "a part" of the group and "apart" from the group (Tillich, 1952). The desire for inclusion and fusion also triggers the fears of consumption, absorbtion, and deindividuation; and the desire to be separate and independent triggers the fears of exclusion, aloneness, and isolation. Group members have to do something with these feelings. To live with the ongoing

intensity of having these ambivalences always salient in the group's consciousness takes a great deal of energy and often provides for the group an overwhelming burden. Clinically, one way to understand how a group deals with these ambivalences is the phenomenon of splitting and projective identification (Klein, 1932: Wells, 1980). Sociologically, it can be understood in terms of Goffman's dramaturgical analogy of a performing group (as in the theatre) wanting to keep some of its inner realities hidden from its audience. In other words, a group has a discrepancy between the private things it knows about itself and the public things it wants to have known about itself. Should a group find that its internal private realities have become visible to others, it may experience itself as vulnerable and feel the need to protect itself. The protection may well take the form of wanting to "cover up" by developing deliberate fabrications so that others don't know what the group is really like. After an initial experience of having been caught and going through the distasteful experience of needing to "cover up", a group may work on avoiding getting caught by developing systems of prevention. The standard prevention approach of a group is to preorchestrate even further its public presentations in order to hide its private realities. When this process occurs the group has effectively made the goal of the social comparison process one of gaining confirmation that its preorchestrated presentations of itself have been accepted, thereby displacing the original goal of the looking glass phenomenon, which was to obtain feedback about itself through the reactions of the audience group.

An example of this discrepancy between public and private presentations of itself could be seen in Hannover's continued public claim that it was interested in furthering the welfare of the Outs. However, privately they were primarily dedicated to lessening the pressure on themselves as middles, while working to generate their own legitimate power base. Hannover's private goal was to further its own, not the Outs' welfare. Its strategy for doing this was to couch its own behavior in terms of championing the Outs' causes, while privately planning to seduce the lower group into being dependent on them as middles, so they in turn could exert more leverage on the Elites.

2. A second aspect of the performance-audience dynamic in the social comparison process is that if a group doesn't like the images of itself reflected in the responses of one audience group, it can either alter the act or find a new audience that will give back the reactions it wants. If a group has significant power over its audience, then it can use its power to alter the audience responses by making them more confirming of what the performers hoped to have reflected back. For example, in a court room, the judiciary is able to use its power to force respectful responsiveness of witnesses, the accused, and the public quite independent of how much respect or disdain they may feel for the judge and the judicial system.

The Kenloch Elites repeatedly used their power with the Ins to obtain reflections of themselves that captured the particular self-images they wished to sustain. For example, when the middles tried to convey to the Elites that their designs for the society could not possibly be implemented in terms of getting the Outs to become workers, the upper group used their power in the following way. They told the middles not to come back and complain about the incompetence of the Elites' decisions but rather to acknowledge their inability as middles to do their job as implementors. The upper group used their power to reject any feedback about their own competence or incompetence as a group and chose to only listen to the responses of the audience group that confirmed their own desires to be seen as powerful and in control.

3. A major complication arises in the social comparison process when a group does not have another group available to act as an audience to its behavior. Under those circumstances, groups often become their own audience, thereby making themselves both the performer and observer of the same show (Goffman, 1959). The potential for self-delusion in this situation is very high, since a group acting as its own audience will use a reality structure quite different from that which an "authentic" audience group would use. For example, the Elites designed their greeting card plan within the isolation of their own group and, acting as their own audience, came to believe it was brilliant. By the time they revealed their plan to the Ins, the middle group, who had become exhausted trying to shape the Elite schemes, passively accepted the plan and their own role as implementors. As a result the Elites were never confronted with the question of whether or not the greeting card scheme was remotely appropriate. When it failed, Kenloch was able to blame it entirely on "Hannover's poor implementation skills." Through these processes, the Elites managed to preserve the images of themselves that they'd created while they were acting as their own audience.

If an audience group is uncritical or overcritical of the performers, it often happens that the audience is rejected as incompetent or inappropriate reflectors of the performers' behavior, especially if the performers are a powerful group. Kenloch repetitively dealt with the Ins in this manner. In doing this, the Elites refused to interpret the middles' audience reaction as a commentary on their upper behavior, and instead Kenloch took an audience perspective on the Ins and treated Hannover's reactions not as reactions but as a "performance".

In setting itself up as the only group capable of being an authentic audience, the Elites created for itself isolation, an inbred orientation, and a high probability of resorting to self-delusion.

4. In the absence of any other audience, a group may stage a performance for an imaginary audience (Goffman, 1959). It may fantasize an appropriate audience, with imaginary standards that the performing group feels obliged to live up to. Under these conditions, the "audience" becomes the conglomerate of the projected images of the acting group's desired standards for itself. The dimensions that will get projected into this imaginary audience may be those things the performing group feels most unsure about. For example, if a group is wondering about how effective it's being, then it is most likely to seek reassuring reactions from its "imaginary audience".

94

5. For a group to maintain a preorchestrated presentation of itself before its audience, group members will need to cooperate in what they know is basically a "sham" (Goffman, 1959). Since they all know it's a "sham," a falsified public presentation, they can't hide this from each other. Hence, no matter how "good" group members feel about their capacity to convince their audiences, this never takes away their own feelings about their private group realities. For example, groups in low power situations, such as unions or tenants' associations, or Westville, may be able to convey the external impression that they are highly unified, yet within their own ranks they feel and know the internal differences that tear them apart. This dynamic could be seen in the behavior of the Supreme Court on the occasion they felt compelled to publicly vote unanimously in order to end the protests of the threatening hoardes of Vietnam war protesters on the Washington Mall. The court was deeply divided on this issue but for a variety of political reasons the chief justice wanted a unanimous decision. Reluctantly, those who disagreed capitulated and resolved not to publish their dissents, participating in a public charade of what they all knew was a private sham. After the public announcement of their unanimous vote, however, there was a great deal of bickering among the Supreme Court justices with some even lamenting that their actions had compromised the independence of the court and disgraced their high office (Woodward and Armstrong, 1979).

6. Since each group realizes it is acting to convey a false impression of itself, it also assumes that groups it observes are doing the same thing, attempting in preorchestrated ways to cover up their inner realities. As a result, each observing group will posture itself in such a way to be able to see behind the external realities the performing group is presenting, while at the same time keeping its own preorchestrations camouflaged. This leads to the concept of dynamic conservatism, which I'll discuss in the next section.

In *summary,* to understand why so many divergent versions of reality surfaced in Montville and why they lead to so many distortions, it is important to comprehend the following: Each group needs the reactions of other groups in order to understand itself; however, the images reflected back will depend on the psychological distance that exists between the acting and the reflecting groups; in addition, the acting group must interpret the images it sees of itself reflected back in the behavior of the group it is using for the social comparison process; in conducting its interpretations, the acting group can be selective about what parts of itself it looks at in the mirrored behavior and can easily confuse its experience of its interaction with the reflecting group with what the reflecting group is really like; it can also choose to reject the reflecting group as a valid mirror and turn either to another group or to an imaginary group for its social comparison activities; further, since an acting group is most likely to want to obtain external reflections on aspects of itself it feels most uncertain about, it is prone to posture its relationship with social comparison groups in such a way that the group will get what it wants. With these complex forces at play in each interaction among groups, there are many places where the various groups' senses of reality—their understanding of what is going on—can diverge from each other. These divergent reality sets (the multiple ways of creating a coherent sense of what's happening in the social system) provide a possible foundation for why so much apparent distortion appears in social systems.

In a way, I wish it were possible to leave this social comparison topic at this level of understanding. But we can't. It must be taken at least one step further. Unfortunately groups don't merely take turns at being actors and reflectors (or performers and audiences in Goffman's terms). They are both actors and reflectors simultaneously. Hence, the same behavior may be experienced as an action by one group and a reflection by another group engaged in the social comparison intercourse. It's the same as love-making. Each partner comes to understand his or her own sexuality in the response of the other, which at the same time may be both a response and an initiation. This notion leads us into the dynamic nature of the social comparison process and the concept of dynamic conservatism.

Dynamic Conservatism

Since each group in an interaction takes both audience and performer perspectives, attempting to penetrate to the inner reality of the other group while protecting its own, the posturing of social distance between interacting groups becomes very critical. Each group as an audience wants to get close enough to be able to see behind the facade of the other group when it's performing, while keeping far enough away so that the other group cannot see behind its own facade when the audience-performing dynamic is reversed. This need to be close and distant at the same time activates an intense struggle by groups to be able to control the social distance between them.

To address fully the importance of this social distancing, it is necessary to turn to the topic of power. In a system where groups experience unequal power, the more powerful group will have more success in influencing both the social distance and the ground rules that will regulate the interactions between the groups. Less powerful groups invariably respond to this defensively and attempt to use whatever power they can mobilize to preserve the least disadvantaged position and to change the ground rules to be more favorable for themselves. However, powerful groups in turn resist any attempts of the less powerful to change the differentials that exist between them. They assume that embedded in their power is the right to determine the differentials together with the ground rules for interaction and the appropriate social distance between the groups. Hence, one of the immediate consequences of power differentials between groups is that all groups gravitate towards behaving resistingly. The powerless will defensively react against the powerful and will try to produce change to their advantage while the powerful will resist these attempted changes because they'll see them as efforts to undermine their power.

This defensive, reactive, resisting posturing could be seen throughout the Montville story. The Outs rejected everything the Elites wanted, simply because they as Elites wanted it, just like rebellious adolescents. This was especially evident in the struggles over the three-tiered society. When once the lower group learned that they could have access to the Elites only through the Ins from Hannover, they immediately rejected the three-tiered society. When asked why, their response was, "Because the Elites want it. If the Elites wanted a two-tiered society, we'd reject that too. If the Elites want it, we reject it simply because it's what they want."

The Outs' visible rejection for rejection's sake, as experienced by the Elites, activated a response from the upper group of equal defensiveness. "If they don't want what we proposed, that's all the more reason why we should want it. *Their* rejection of the three-level system is the very reason why we must work to preserve it." The Elites came to define what was important to them as being able to resist the Outs' attempts to undermine or block their wishes.

Once interacting groups have started to act defensively with each other, they enter into a cycle of relationships oriented primarily to keep things from getting worse. The earlier goal of each group of posturing itself into the most relatively advantageous position becomes displaced by the major goal of defensively keeping things from getting worse. The primary energy becomes focused on preserving the status quo and what emerges is a process that I call "dynamic conservatism" (this is similar to Freire's (1972) concept of "danger of conscientization"). The focus becomes one of making sure things don't change or get worse in terms of respective power balance. The more powerful try to hold onto the advantage they've acquired while the less powerful try to avoid being put into more disadvantageous positions. Energy is poured into preserving the status quo but it is couched as changing the status quo. For example, we often find middle management talking about wanting more communication in their organization, yet what they actually do is to develop tighter controls on the communication system, which in effect restricts overall communication exchanges but puts it more clearly under their control.

Interacting groups invariably proclaim commitment to change and advancement but are basically paralyzed by dynamic conservatism. Genuine alternatives often trigger fear, and this mixed with defense of the status quo creates "rigidification of values", where what has been experienced and is generally known is considered more important than what is unexperienced and unknown. Value rigidification triggers imprisoning frames of reference which are virtually impossible to change. Pirsig (1974) illustrates superbly the imprisoning impact of value rigidity by his description of the Old South Indian Monkey trap. "The trap consists of a hollowed out coconut chained to a stake. The coconut had some rice inside that can be grabbed through a small hole. The hole is big enough so that the monkey's hand can go in, but too small for his fist with rice in it to come out. The monkey reaches in—is trapped—by nothing more than his own value rigidity. He can't revalue the rice. He cannot see that freedom without rice is more valuable than capture with it."

Dynamic conservatism forces and value rigidification have an overwhelming impact on the interactions of the groups with unequal power and the different way their sense of reality becomes formulated. For example, in the social comparison exchange, the primary goal of locating social distance in order to see behind the presented facades or to observe self reflected back becomes replaced by a more critical social comparison that can be conceived as determining who is more powerful and what is the nature of the existing power differentials. Since a group's awareness of its own power comes primarily from the response of other's reactions to it, in the social comparison process the primary concern may become "Are we able to influence them more than they're able to influence us," for this may produce a relative index of "our power". One way of guaranteeing this relative power supremacy is to make sure "they don't influence us at all. That way, we can be sure to win." However, although a group may lessen its own experience of powerlessness by making its adversary group feel powerless, this in no way guarantees that it in turn is more powerful (Smith, 1975). This has the flavor of "if they lose, we, by definition, must win," which is a logical fallacy.

This mind set, together with the concepts of dynamic conservatism and the value rigidity represented in the Indian Monkey trap example, all acting through social comparison processes, provides a basis for understanding the psychological imprisonment represented in the concept of structural encasements. All groups become caught in sets of binds that constrain the way they view the world and the nature of their interactions with others. It is necessary for us to understand these constraints—these structural encasements—in order to unravel the unfolding of what occurred in Montville.

Having discussed the concept of structural encasement at a general level I'd now like to take each of the Montville groups and examine how their relationships with other groups became imprisoned by specific forms of invisible binds that go with the power to create, to block, and to mediate.

Structural Encasements of Uppers

As we've noted previously, the major structural encasement operative in the relationship between the Kenloch Elites and the other two groups (the Ins and the Outs), was that the upper group became caught in a framework of reality that blinded them to the consequences of their behavior. This left them with very little insight as to why their relationships with the middles and the lowers took on the characteristic that they did. There were many intergroup forces at play in Montville that shaped these relationships. We will discuss the major ones under the following headings: social comparisons—an elite perspective; splitting decision making from implementation; delegating responsibility without authority; information filtration; the ethnocentrism of the powerful; and dynamic conservatism.

Social Comparisons: An Elite Perspective

When the Elites, like a typical power group, saw images reflected back to them that they didn't like, they were prone to do one of the following three things: (1) instead of viewing the feedback as a communication from an audience group, they took over the audience perspective themselves and viewed those reactions not as a response to the behavior of the powerful but as independent actions of the powerless; or (2) they used their influence to force the audience groups to provide only the feedback the powerful want; or (3) they rejected all audience groups as being irrelevant and used themselves as an exclusive, self-indulgent audience to their own behavior.

This meant that when the Outs rejected something the Elites had initiated the upper group did not treat this reaction of the lowers as "information about how the power group was perceived" but rather as "information about what the powerless were like as a group." The looking glass dimension of the Elite-Out relationship was made especially complex in the three-tiered system by the role the middles were asked to play. The uppers wanted the middles to implement their Elite plans, using the lowers as the instrument for executing the uppers' wishes. If the Ins were successful in getting the Outs to do what the Elites wanted, then the powerful group used this information as confirmation, in the social comparison sense, that they were an effective planning group. If, however, things didn't work out as the Elites hoped, they didn't interpret this feedback as informing them in any way about their own behavior. Instead they would conclude that either the middles were ineffective as implementors or that the lowers were a collection of "rebellious, belligerent resisters".

The structure of the social relations in Montville had enabled the Kenloch uppers to treat the actor/audience looking glass relationship in such a way that they could see reflected back about themselves only what they wanted. At the same time they were able to see "audience type behavior" of the other groups exclusively in "actor terms", leading to gross misinterpretations as to what was going on and, across time, to overwhelmingly distorting attributions about what the other groups were like.

Splitting Decision Making from Implementation

In most organizations, powerful groups view decision making and social planning as probably the most important tasks. These represent an enormous burden especially since they involve the monitoring of both internal and external forces operative on the whole of the system they preside over (Miller and Rice, 1967). This means a powerful group is forced to struggle with complexities and realities not comprehended by other groups. In order to reduce the burden of their tasks, uppers will often attempt to simplify their role by splitting the decision-making function from the implementation, keeping the former for themselves and delegating the latter to a subordinate group. Kenloch did this at Montville but to their great disadvantage.

In its raw form, splitting the decision-making/implementation functions leads to poorer decisions because they eventually come to be made independent of their implementability. If the implementing group is successful, the powerful can use this success as confirmation of their own planning competence. If the implementing group is unsuccessful it may be either because the implementors are incompetent or because the original decisions are quite unimplementable. In the latter case the powerful are fully defended against having to confront their own inadequacies. They can always place the blame onto another group—either the "incompetence" of the implementation group or the "rebelliousness" or "belligerence" of those being implemented upon. This splitting of decision making and implementation provides for the powerful a perfect mechanism through which they can slip into rejecting the audience responses in the social comparison exchange.

This dynamic could be seen at Montville. Since the Elites saw decision making as their most important task, they delegated implementation actions to the subordinate middles. However the Ins, given the binds they found themselves to be in with Kenloch, were unwilling to argue if they perceived a decision to be poor or unable to be implemented. Since Hannover had been rejected as a looking glass group for the Elites and were being given tasks that were likely to fail due to the impoverished relations among all Montville groups, the middles sensed that if they argued too vigorously over Kenloch's poor decisions, then the Elites would simply reject them as being totally incompetent and deprive them even further. Instead of fighting back, the Ins uncritically and obediently attempted to implement what they were told to do, as in the greeting card scheme. However, they felt little responsibility for the outcome of their actions having had no involvement in the original decisions. Hence they usually exerted minimal creative effort. Their actions had form but no substance.

Delegating Responsibility without Adequate Authority

As a result of the powerful group structuring its social relations in such a manner that it ended up taking the credit when things went well but transferring the blame when things went wrong, the Elites subtly but surely moved to a position of seeing itself as being more competent than other groups. Whenever they received negative feedback about themselves, the uppers threw it back at the middles and lowers, refusing to accept it as information about the powerful's lack of competence and, instead, interpreting it as illustrative of the incompetence of the other groups. Slowly, the less powerful learned to recognize that it was easier to get by if they worked to protect the powerful from full knowledge of their behavior. This led the middles to selectively filter

100

what they let the powerful know. This information filtration reinforced the self-delusional grandiosity of the powerful, bloating their perception of their competence and leading in turn to the depreciation of the competencies of the other groups. The Elites then used their perceptions of incompetence of others to justify their withholding of the authority to implement the responsibilities they delegated. This created a paralyzing double bind. For the powerful, it locked them into the posture of always looking at the behavior of the other groups from a judgmental, audience perspective. In addition, it fostered the dependency of middle and lower groups and kept them less potent than their potential. By not giving adequate authority to fulfill responsibilities, the uppers guaranteed the incompetence of the less powerful, thereby justifying the way they wished to treat them. For the less powerful groups, it locked them into trying to hide their own incompetence, thereby helping to restrict even further the narrowed mind set of the powerful and guaranteeing, in self-defeating ways, that they'd be treated poorly.

Information Filtration

The combined impact of a powerful group's splitting decision making from implementation and delegating responsibility without the necessary authority reinforces a climate of information withholding. Less powerful groups suppress information that the powerful (by switching performer/audience roles) might unfairly use as justification for their withholding of authority. This creates a real bind, especially for the powerful, but for the whole system as well. Each time the uppers make a decision that is implemented by others, the powerful must depend on that other group for information about the impact of that decision. If the implementors are partialling out critical data, and the uppers don't know this, they will soon be making their decision on minimal data. The problem is self-evident. Assume for example that following their first decision, the uppers get back fifty percent of the relevant information but, believing it to be ninety percent, confidently go ahead and make their next round of decisions. If this dynamic repeats itself, after three or four decision iterations, all of their decisions would be based on absolutely trivial information.

What happened to information, how it was shared, and how it was withheld was a powerful force at Montville. Hence we should explore it at some depth. However, before focusing specifically on how information was used or abused in the relationship among Elites, Ins, and Outs, we should pause to consider what we mean by information.

At the most rudimentary level, "to in-form" involves giving shape and structure to that which otherwise is without shape (Wilden, 1972). To share information, then, means to share the ways in which shapes and structures have been mapped onto basic experiences and the meanings that have been attached to those particular shapes. Usually the term "information" is used to refer to basic facts, supposedly stripped of any specific meanings except for the descriptive categories used to convey the images, the echos that those basic facts stimulated. Yet this is too limited a view of information. I want to be clear here that I'm using information in a much broader way, to include along with that which is knowable in some physically verifiable way those things that appear as "truths" not accessible to physical perception and not governed by rules of rationality, such as love and beauty, but nevertheless internally knowable (Jung, 1958) and central to the epistemologies of everyone.

In this discussion of information, I want to take the following position. To talk about information is to talk about reality. "Information" does not exist in a "pure" form. It is not separable from the social processes in which it's embedded. It is both a part of and a manifestation of those social processes. Hence, to say "I wish to inform you about . . ." or "Let me give you information about . . ." is to attempt to present my reality structure in such a way that it makes sense to you, given your reality structure. Thus, all of what we've discussed previously about social processes, power dynamics, performer-audience forces, and so forth, is relevant to all notions of information.

What is of special importance in our discussion here is that each group uses its own unique *within* group information (reality, the shapes and forms into which its experience has been contoured) in its *between* or *among* group encounters. Hence, the reality construction processes of the three Montville groups are central to the unfolding of events in that four-day simulated society. As will become evident as we discuss the structural encasements associated with each of the upper, middle, and lower positions, each of the Montville groups made use of information in very different ways. Hence the information filtration process affected the relationships among groups differentially.

From the Kenloch perspective, they quite unabashedly used *information withholding as a major way to force the other groups to be dependent on them.* Within two or three hours of Montville's birth, the Elites became convinced that keeping the other groups "information deprived" would make Kenloch powerful and thereby force middles and lowers to be dependent. From the original phantom plan right through to the final stages of their locked door policy at Fort Kenloch, the Elites' philosophy was to keep others guessing as to what was going on, believing this would keep the other groups more malleable than if they were all straight with each other. The Elites' "information withholding" took various forms from innocuous "oversights" to insidious manipulation, such as the way they predecided at the time task force reports were made to indiscriminately abuse Ethan and Ingrid for incompetent reports while praising Ivan and Alistair for excellent contributions, irrespective of their quality. In this way, Kenloch viewed "information"—what, when, and in what form they released it—as part of the arsenal they could use to shape Montville according to their Elite wishes.

Apart from the explicitly manipulative use the Elites made of information withholding as a control system, there were unintended ways that they, like typical uppers, gravitated towards an information-clutching posture. This emerged as a somewhat natural consequence of taking the role to monitor how all parts, both those within the society and those interfacing with the environment, interrelated (Miller and Rice, 1967). Since this function was not shared with any other group, the Elites saw themselves as needing maximum information and understanding about all parts of the system. However, they didn't see other groups as having this same need—at least not with the same kind of legitimacy. Accordingly, the uppers expected that others should have to funnel more information to them in order for them to do their "elite" task than they needed to share with others for them to fulfill their "lower" task. This perspective led to the building of a communication system that had more information flowing to them than from them to others. They responded to attempts to get more information out of their Elite ranks than they wanted to give as some corrosive undermining act of subordinates who were trying to avoid doing what the Elites demanded of them. They also structured the communication patterns such that information given by uppers to middles and lowers was primarily in the form of basic directives, almost always neglecting to share the Elites' context in which their "in-formation" was shaped.

The information clutching posture of Elites had several major effects in Montville. (1) By limiting the information held by middles and lowers, Kenloch was able to generate some system power for themselves (Mechanic, 1962) and at the same time make the other groups feel relatively powerless. (2) The Elites came to develop ground rules that indicated that there were certain things other groups just ought not to know about. Hence, the powerful's relationship took the form of protecting others, together with a paternalistic stance of "We know best what would be good for you to be aware of." (3) Kenloch came to believe that their world, and the things they had to juggle, were so complex that the middles did not have the capacity to absorb or understand all the relevant information. (4) The Elite communiques evolved to a state of being little more than (a) pronouncements on reality (this is what the world is like) and (b) directives on what middles and lowers were to do in order to usher in new realities (this is what the world *will be* like and this is how *you'll make* it this way). Rarely was any background information or rationale provided that would support the Elites' views of reality or justify their wishes for the society.

The information-holding behavior of Kenloch was very similar to well established procedures used by the powerful in most traditional organizations such as the government or the military. Here the information withholding is thinly camouflaged by the security classifications ("secret", "staff-in-confidence") where strict regulations control who can have access to what and under what circumstances. A cursory glance at any government "secret files" shows that the minutest proportion of entries has anything to do with "national security" or whatever the public rationale is. Rather, these files are laden with documents that have been highly classified in order to avoid embarrassment

103

to upper groups. The Pentagon Papers and Nixon's Watergate tapes are two superb examples. The powerful used "information-holding" methods to hide their own incompetencies or to disguise the real reasons for their actions.

There is a common organizational scenario that goes as follows. A subordinate asked to do a particular task is granted access to classified files only if he or she can justify the need, which of course is impossible without first having access to the files in order to know what's in them. Without having the complete information, the subordinate is forced to guess what files are needed and as a result does an incomplete job because it can never be known for sure whether the person gained access to all the relevant information. As a result the person gets blamed for either not knowing or having the appropriate wisdom to ask for what was needed from the restricted files. Such secrecy systems, although defended on totally different grounds, have a powerful dependency-inducing impact on subordinates, especially those who are caught in the "middle". One sure way of generating dependency, and the power that comes with that dependency, is by developing secrets that are kept from subordinates. Even if the secrets are innocuous. The mere creation of a mind set that "there are some things we know about that we are going to keep from you, either because you can't be trusted or because we need to protect you" involves a power move with potent dependency-induction consequences.

The danger in any secrecy system is that if the secrets eventually become public, the power generated by the secrecy is quickly diffused. For example, Nixon's power disappeared almost instantly when the public came to read his Watergate transcripts and discovered so clearly that not only had he been lying when he claimed he'd not been involved, but that presidential discussion in general took place at a very low level of competence and that this president who had worked so hard to present himself as a "moral leader" cursed a great deal. The fact that the president cursed was not a problem. Everyone accepted this in Harry Truman. It was that he tried to hide it and got found out that was the problem. Likewise, at Montville, the power base of Kenloch became systematically destroyed as the Outs methodically worked out their ways of penetrating the upper walls of secrecy and exposing their Elite power as containing little substance.

This tendency of the Elites to see themselves as having legitimate need for information that in their opinion other groups didn't require is one expression of ethnocentrism, a topic that we must turn to in order to understand fully the upper's structural encasement.

Ethnocentrism

At its heart, ethnocentrism (Levine and Campbell, 1972) is the tendency of a group to develop one set of parameters, explanations, rationales, etc., for understanding its own behavior while holding a different set for looking at the behavior of other groups with which it interacts. It is most evident in conflict situations where groups gravitate towards "we-they" postures. Ethnocentrism, commonly referred to as the "in" group, "out" group phenomenon, is the expression of a group's tendency to make itself the center of everything, viewing all other groups (they) strictly from a self-centered (own group) vantage point (we). According to Sumner (1906) a group engaging in ethnocentric behavior "nourishes its own pride and vanity, boasts itself superior, exalts its own divinities and looks with contempt on outsiders." Ethnocentrism occurs whenever a group takes whatever reality it is able to perceive, or create from its vantage point, and affirms that this is *the* reality.

The real problem with this tendency is that reality is not given or verifiable in any concrete way. It is always in "the eye of the beholder" and presents itself with some degree of ambiguity. It's what happens to those ambiguities that becomes critical in relationships between groups. Each "in" group copes with this by taking events and objects that appear incoherent, inconsistent, and opaque, and filling in the gaps as best suits the needs of that group. This process transforms ambiguities into shapes and forms that enable the group to see them as coherent, consistent, and clear. This artificial removal of ambiguity in this way has powerful effects. It helps preserve, sometimes even create, within-group togetherness. However, it may also have profoundly fragmenting and alienating consequences for what occurs among groups. This will be especially true if each group does its own ambiguity reduction activities exclusively within its own "we" framework while treating other groups from a "they" perspective.

It is this form of removing ambiguity in ethnocentric settings that leads each group to understand its own behavior according to one set of parameters while using very different frameworks for looking at the behavior of other groups (Alderfer, 1977). This is particularly heightened by group members' tendencies to see the differences that exist within their own group but, when looking at other groups, failing to recognize the vast differences that exist between those group members. Differences in the other group get glossed over. It's what they have in common that gets noticed. Hence, each group will look at the heterogenous side of itself but at the homogenous side of the other group. This is due in a large part to the fact that "in"/ "out" groups see the differences between them to be so large that the differences that might exist within the "other" group's ranks appear trivial in comparison (Schutz, 1970).

The net effect of these psychological filters on among-group perceptions is to diminish the differences that exist among members in the other groups and then proceed to treat the whole group as though everyone within it were fundamentally the same. This makes that "other group" easy to categorize and label. Then it can be related to as though it were that one entity. Through this process, external ambiguity is quickly and easily diminished, thereby preserving the available "ambiguity reserves", as it were, for dealing with the uncertainties that reside within one's own group.

Developing a unified perceptual image of another group helps the formulation of group identity. Since identity depends on the separation of an entity from what it's not (Wilden, 1972) when a group becomes clear about other, this helps it become clear about itself. This process depends a lot on how differences are being seen. While a group is seeing as many differences within other groups as within itself, it has difficulty developing an image of itself as separate and different. However, as a group works out a way to diminish the extent to which it notices the differences in other groups, albeit falsely by some process such as ethnocentrism, that group is formulating a clear referent with which it can counterpoint itself.

This could be seen in Montville's Elite identity formation. Those early hours of their group were rather fragmented. They didn't feel powerful. Quite the contrary. But as they began to develop images of the other two Montville groups as fragmented (the Ins) and powerless (the Outs), so their own elite identity surfaced as a self-image of unified strength. This may be thought of as analogous to Erikson's (1968) concept of negative identity. Erikson sees this process as an individual defining himself by what he's resolved not to be, a negation rather than an affirmation. The adolescent who says, "I won't be like my father—so whatever he is, I'm not," is forming a negative identity. It's an identity grounded not in tested experience but in a fantasy developed to cope with experience the individual wishes to avoid. An example of a group parallel to this negative identity process is "That group is powerless and we're different from it, so we must be powerful," or "That group is clearly incompetent. We're different from it, so we must therefore be competent."

There is a special bind involved in this type of ambiguity reduction, for the possibilities of cognitive distortion are innumerable (Blake, Shepard, and Mouton, 1964; Dalton, 1959; Sherif and Sherif, 1969). A group may notice another group to be "crazy" and, knowing it's different from that crazy group, deduce that it therefore must be "sane." But the reality may be that the two groups are different but both "crazy," with the "craziness" being merely different. Different need not mean opposite. Yet a group that defines its identity as a counterpoint to something it's different from invariably falls into this type of self-delusional cognitive distortion. The standard trap for the powerful is that they will experience themselves as more powerful in an absolute sense when those who are dependent on them are less powerful in a relative sense. But they have it back to front. If those who were dependent on them were more powerful, then the power differential between the powerful and the powerless would be smaller but the power of the powerful in an absolute sense would be greater, not smaller (Smith, 1975). Hence uppers who want greater power would need to work to empower rather than depotentiate others.

In the early Montville days, the Elites often felt powerful when they saw how fragmented the Ins were. Yet this inner fragmentation of the middle group was not augmenting the upper group's power at all. In fact it was a drain on their potency because of the extra weight generated by Hannover's dependency on the Elites. In the latter days of Montville, Kenloch longed for the Ins to be united so they might be able to act together as a group providing a protective buffer from the aggressive actions of the Outs. Yet at this time, the Ins had become quite united. But they were using their unity to form a strong relationship with the Outs in building the New Society. Had they been less united at this time, maybe it would have served the interests of the Elites more. But the Elites didn't understand it this way. Having got caught in the cognitive distortions of the ethnocentric-social comparison, they were in fact understanding in reverse. In the early days they themselves would have been more powerful if they'd worked to empower rather than depotentiate the Ins, and in the latter days they would probably have not needed to be as defensive or have a protection group, if the middles had not been as coalesced as they were towards the end of Montville.

Uppers' Dynamic Conservatism: A Powerful Perspective

The playing out of the information-filtration process and the power of the ethnocentric forces created for Montville's Elites a solid protection from the consequences of their behavior and blinded them to many of the realities around them. However, a further level of complexity has been waiting in the (theoretical) wings, ready to drive the final nails in the lid of the coffin in which the Kenloch group became structurally encased.

Since the Elites saw themselves as the designers of Montville, their position and their early experience of their powerfulness had led them to believe that they were both the creators and definers of the social situation at Montville. This made them feel that somehow they "owned" the system, which in turn triggered the mindset that Hannover and Westville existed merely as Elites' possessions, which could be manipulated at their simple wish as the powerful. Freire (1972) points out that the creators and controllers of any system gravitate towards a mechanistic view of reality that develops hand in hand with the experience of domination over others. In mechanistic realities the subjective becomes objectified. Corporate bosses experience workers as figures on a balance sheet, military policy makers conceive of soldiers as a critical part of the national arsenal, and university administrators treat students as bodies that occupy seats. The day-to-day emotions, the struggles, and life pilgrimages of the lowers are not relevant to the strategic calculations of those minds that have become mechanized (Friere, 1972).

With this objectification force in place, Kenloch acted to create reality. When they had minimal and ambiguous information, they would first believe that what they "knew" was right. Then what they didn't know, they "made up," as though reality could be objectively manufactured by the mere exercising of their subjective wills. Whether this was possible or not is beside the point. What's critical is that when the powerful group acted to eliminate ambiguity by making up its own version of reality, then it proceeded to act as though this were *the* reality.

This posture of being the "creators" of reality led not only to the Elites being out of touch with other realities around them. It also laid the foundation for their particular form of dynamic conservatism, hence making them ultimately reactive prisoners of the realities they helped to create.

Freire (1972) points out that when the powerful have established a certain degree of control and the first taste of feeling able to "possess" other members of the social system has been experienced, the mere having of more and more possessions becomes critical. He expresses it as follows: "In the egotistical pursuit of *having* as a possessing class, they suffocate in their own possessions and no longer *are;* they merely *have.* For them *having more* is an inalienable right." "Those who have" come to link the esteem of their group to its ongoing capacity to exert control. Any sign that control is being lost leads to insecure triggering of rigid behavior. The original goals of the powerful (whatever they were) get replaced by a more central goal, domination.

For Kenloch, originally gaining power was a means to an end. Eventually, it became an end in itself. And the means to that end became making others powerless—a logical fallacy. Their strategy for keeping control? Heighten fragmentation and conflict in the rest of the system. Use secrecy to protect reasons for their own actions and deprive others of information so they would feel a heightened sense of dependency. Impose rules for negotiation with other groups but change them arbitrarily to serve their own interests. When these strategies of domination were resisted by the less powerful, the uppers did not interpret the resultant conflicts as a legitimate conflict of interest. Rather, they were treated as signs that their upper power to keep others subjugated was in threat and had to be bolstered or reestablished. As a result, Kenloch was willing to "lose" certain battles and were tolerant of their social goals being undermined so long as it would gain for them the experience of "winning" in terms of social domination. For example, there were times when the Elites seemed delighted about the irresponsible rebelliousness of the lowers because it weakened, in their eyes, their power.

This same process can be seen in the society at large where the social power brokers revel in the destructive and dissenting acts of the powerless, even when the immediate interests of the powerful are being lost. This is especially true if dissent is expressed in some socially irresponsible ways. For example, in conflict situations, government leaders and corporate bosses often bait violent reactions from the powerless, even though it may destroy the powerful's immediate interests (such as property), because they know that they can mobilize the social backlash against such reactive violence, easily label it as "irresponsible," and thus increase their long-term capacity to dominate. The powerful can then in turn use the destructive reactions of the powerless to justify their policies of subjugation. They can use these responses to support their claims that the conflicts themselves were created by the powerless, thereby avoiding their own elite responsibility for the original creation of the conflict situation.

This above dynamic is at the heart of the uppers' dynamic conservatism. By structuring social exchanges so that the powerless are seen as creating the conflicts that arise out of legitimate differences in interests, uppers are able to ignore their own responsibility in contributing to (or creating) the original conflict situation. These conflicts may then be both a justification for their own repressive and oppressive activities and a way of blinding themselves to the fact that in their actions, they are unknowingly diminishing their own power and augmenting the stagnation of the system over which they preside.

These dynamic conservatism forces operating on the relationships of the upper group with lower and middle groups generate, reinforce, and reify the structural encasement of the uppers. It is built on the foundation of the particular social comparison process the powerful engage in and is shaped by the tendency to split decision making from implementation, to delegate responsibility without the necessary authority, to filter information, and to engage in the particular forms of ethnocentrism where the powerful feel it is legitimate to make up whatever they wish in order to reduce the social ambiguities that don't serve their interests. Together these processes make it easy to understand how the Kenloch Elites became structurally encased by their inability to comprehend the consequences of their own behavior.

Structural Encasements of Lowers

The Outs became structurally encased by the strong ground rules that they developed to protect themselves from the perceived threats of the more powerful members of Montville society. These protective devices developed quickly and became the centerpiece of Westville's life together.

The story of the Out group began with nine individuals whose paths had never crossed before. On the surface they had little in common. Some were business people, others belonged to educational settings; some were married, others single; some were relatively young, others were older; some were wealthy, others less so; some were white, others were black. From the beginning, however, they all had one thing very much in common. They all felt left out, excluded, rejected, unimportant. And this one commonness was so powerful that it overshadowed the obvious differences among them. In fact no one seemed to really care about the ways in which they differed. What they had in common seemed much more critical.

From the very beginning, the group of nine Outs bonded together to cope with their individual experiences of helplessness. As they drew together they realized that if they remained bonded as a *cohesive* group their individual feelings of helplessness would be lessened by their collective strength. In order for them to feel a collective strength, however, as individuals they had to be willing to subordinate their personal needs and desires to the interests of the group as a whole (Acton, 1967; Coser, 1956). This requirement caused a lot of turmoil for the Westville group. Nevertheless, they did eventually make the commitment to do what was necessary to remain and operate as a unified group.

The coalescing of the Outs as a group in response to their common, individual plight of isolation and helplessness had several dramatic effects. First in their unity, each Out could feel some togetherness and a resultant lessening of individual isolation. Second, all the Outs could feel themselves to be a part of a collective strength. Third, however, each Out felt obliged to subordinate personal desires as an individual to the collective well being of the group-as-a-whole, thereby generating a different kind of aloneness—an isolation within the group, as opposed to the earlier condition of isolation without a group. Fourth, accompanying the increased sense of strength as a member of the Out group came an increasing sense of individual weakness triggered by each individual's feeling dependent on the group. This meant that they turned less and less to their individual resources.

These same bonds that united the Montville Outs and enabled them to feel strong also stagnated them in critical ways, providing imprisoning forces for their whole group and generating many self-defeating behaviors. Paradoxically, the potency of the Outs' structural encasement became most visible as they eventually acted to free themselves from its imprisoning force. Their liberation came only as they acknowledged and confronted the reality that although they wanted to be and pretended to be of one mind on everything, in critical ways they were deeply divided. In fact, they had become so used to a "united we stand, divided we fall" philosophy, that they were unable to see how they were making themselves more powerless by the methods they were using to overcome their fears of powerlessness. In reality, the Outs liberated themselves from their lower bondage only after they had allowed themselves to experience the full force of their internal divisions. When they no longer feared disunity, they were able to act in a more unified way as was demonstrated through the simultaneous application of their diametrically opposed entrepreneurial-guerilla scheme. When they let themselves be divided they were able to develop a greater strength than when they insisted obsessively on unity.

In order to lay the conceptual groundwork for the structural encasement that Montville's Outs were trapped in, I want to discuss the following five concepts: social comparisons from a paranoid perspective; deindividuation; internal dissention; internalized oppression; and lowers' dynamic conservatism.

Social Comparisons: A Paranoid Perspective

One of the most problematic dimensions of a group that has come together and unified primarily to cope with the experience of powerlessness and the common plight of its members, is that the very foundation of its group life is a reactive response to external forces. The difficulty is that cohesion and unity become the very essence of the group's life and this is both defined in terms of and exists as a reaction to perceived external threats.

Such a group is accordingly always vulnerable to forces that might fragment it. However, it will also react to threats of fragmentation by unifying even more. There's a paradox embedded in this, for such a group feeds off the very conditions it fears the most. A group that defines its essence in terms of unity as a response to external threats needs that threat to be continued in order to feel alive (Dalton, 1959). Even when others are not directly threatening, their lack of threat is a threat because it lessens the pressure for unity, which in itself is a threat. A bind becomes created as follows: "If they're getting at us, we've got to watch out. If they're not getting at us we've also got to watch out because they'll probably be getting at us in the long run by taking our unity away from us now by lessening the threat we feel" (Smith, 1977). Either way it becomes imperative for members of the lower group to treat others with suspicion. Once the above cycle has started, it won't matter what another group does with lowers, it will be experienced as a threat and accordingly treated with suspicion and disbelief. This creates an atmosphere in which, no matter what happens, the powerless group feels the need to have an external enemy (Simmel, 1955), a real enemy preferably, but a manufactured one if necessary.

I use the term "paranoia" cautiously but confidently. At one level the suspiciousness of powerless groups is justified. The powerful often do develop conscious strategies of trying to divide and conquer the powerless in order to keep them subservient. At another level, however, when the powerless experience their own inner disunity, they classically deny ownership of this schism and try to project responsibility for it onto other parts of the social system in which they're embedded. This is the basis of the paranoid projection. And Montville Outs became trapped in this process.

The term paranoia is usually focused at the level of the individual. It has been defined in various ways, but central to all definitions is the view that paranoia is a projective act, which externalizes internal threats either by attributing objectionable motives, feelings, and ideas of one's own onto something or someone external, or by substituting an external threat for an inner one (Shapiro, 1965). Paranoid projection not only is a distortion of that which is visible, but it often interprets (inaccurately) what is *not* visible or is *not* spoken. This process could be seen in the behavior of the powerless group at Montville. They often looked at the behavior of the powerful from a suspicious orientation even when those actions or lack of actions were benign. For example, when the Outs were feeling very information deprived, hearing nothing didn't mean for the powerless group that nothing was happening. For them it meant that all hell was about to break loose and they'd better be especially vigilant in looking out for themselves.

The paranoid dimension for the Outs grew from the fact that their group life was heavily predicated on cohesion. Their deep commitment to their own unity meant that any dispute within their ranks had an explosive quality to it. One possible response to the inner tension might have been to be less invested in their togetherness—which they eventually did during their entrepreneurial-guerilla stage. However, during their paranoid phase they blamed others for making them feel inner fragmentation as a way of denying that it was their own norms of togetherness that were actually the central forces in making these inner tensions so problematic.

111

Of course the whole situation was quite circular. The Outs needed norms of togetherness to feel safe. These norms made any natural inner disagreements excessively problematic, which in turn triggered the desire to find some external group to blame, which in turn justified and intensified the need to be together to cope with the external threat.

The Westville Outs used information withholding and secrecy as a major strategy in their posturing with the other two Montville groups, thereby setting up both carefully preorchestrated images *of* themselves for presentation to Hannover and Kenloch, while at the same time generating *for* themselves the sense of internal reality they felt they needed. The Outs secrecy grew directly out of the belief that having others know as little as possible about what took place within their own ranks would minimize their susceptibility to the divide-and-conquer strategies they feared other groups would use against them. This could be seen in the Outs' standard resistance to the Hannover middles. Whatever the Ins wanted, the Outs would reject automatically and without explanation, thereby disguising the fact they had no strategy while at the same time gaining leverage by making the middles believe they had one. Their secrecy also enabled them to do one thing while pretending to do the opposite, such as in their entrepreneurial-guerilla phase where they were able to hide their destructive schemes behind a socially acceptable, cooperative facade.

In relationships between groups, secrecy helps to both develop and maintain boundary definitions by articulating what and who are inside the group. The "special, inside" secrets are often what makes one group distinct from another. Often group membership can be delineated on the basis of knowing who's privy to and who's excluded from what secrets, and signs of potential social mobility may be detected by noting what "outsiders" are in the process of being told "inside" secrets. This dynamic was evident in the case of Anthony. As he began to gravitate towards the Outs, they sped up his being drawn into their midst by sharing with him secrets that had been kept from other members of Hannover and Kenloch.

For powerless groups the rituals that are developed around secrecy are often very central to the developing and fostering of group life. For example, the Pueblo Indians have always guarded with great secrecy their religious practices (Jung, 1965), and the same tendency may be found in a large number of the northern religious sects such as Jonestown, USA.

One major problem with the secrecy of powerless groups is that when once a paranoid perspective has started to emerge, by keeping their inner group realities so closely guarded the powerless are unlikely ever to test or modify their realities in any self-corrective way by nondefensive, non-preorchestrated exchanges with the other groups.

When a powerless group has begun to express "paranoid" responses, and then covers it with a veneer of secrecy, it's very easy for other groups to start viewing them as paranoid in reality and by this treatment end up reinforcing the paranoia to such an extent that the lowers really do get paranoid. However, looking at Montville through an intergroup perspective, it is possible to argue that the "Outs' paranoia" was primarily the giving expression to and the making visible of the nature of the power differentials that existed between the other groups and them. In other words, the lowers were not exclusively responsible for their paranoia, which they expressed. The whole system was. In fact, to think about who was responsible is inappropriate. The paranoia was simply an expression of one aspect of what the system as a whole was like and the Outs were merely expressing this characteristic of Montville as a whole and expressing it on the behalf of the whole minisociety. This interpretation aside, however, members of Montville didn't see it this way. The uppers saw it as the lowers' recalcitrance, the middles saw it as partly justifiable obstinance, and the lowers saw it as a survival necessity.

Deindividuation

A central aspect of the social comparison process of powerless groups with others is the extent to which individual members of a lower group feel bound to always do what is considered best for the total group. Should an individual express critical personal needs, they are likely to be examined as a group issue. For a member of a powerless group to express dissent from what the group considers important is viewed as an act of disloyalty. This pressure is very deindividuating. The bind goes as follows. The very thing the powerless are fighting desperately to have changed are the forces that stop them from being fully themselves. To fight this they adopt a strategy of unity, which places even more pressure on them to lessen the importance of the individual. They're trapped into trying to overcome deindividuation by using deindividuating strategies.

For powerless groups individual issues often become defined as group issues. This was very visible in the first few hours of Westville's life. Some of the Outs were eager to feel free to do as they chose and demanded the right to assert their individuality. The prevailing spirit of the group was to indicate this was "OK so long as the individual first discussed it with the total group and they all agreed to it." By the group's defining itself as having both the responsibility and authority to decide when individuals had the right to act as individuals, Westville in effect resolved that all individual issues were in fact to be always subordinated to the wishes and well being of their group-as-a-whole. At the time all Out members concurred with this, experiencing it as an acceptable compromise, but in essence it was an unacknowledged oath of allegiance to collectively suppress individuality in the service of group interests. A truly individuated Out response to this process would have been something like, "I will decide by myself what's good for me and then I'll determine whether or not I'll advise the group as to what I'm doing." No such acts of individuation occurred during the early development of Westville and if they had, it's almost certain they'd have been rejected as deviant.

Because of the Outs insistence on unity, each individual member of Westville was experienced as acting as a representative of all the Outs. Hence, even when individual Outs were acting as individuals the consequences that might reasonably be attached to that individual for his or her own actions were attached to all other Out members. If one Out acted "aggressively" or "incompetently" then all Outs were labelled as aggressive or incompetent.

This added to the feeling of deindividuation for it made each Out member consider the group consequences of every individual action. At no stage was it possible to just be a person. Each powerless person was always viewed as a member of the Out group. For lower group members the level of deindividuation was greater the stronger their commitment to unity. Their commitment to unity was greater the stronger their individual desires to overcome the deindividuating forces of the system at large.

Any group that makes collective action central in its articulation of itself in social interactions is liable to have communal labels attached to it. However, there's a particular problem that goes with collective action that is fundamentally resistive. The resistance is an expression of the underlying tensions of the system. Metaphorically, referring back to our earlier example of the Jung candle/darkness dream, it is the shadow expressing one facet of the relationship of light and dark. The system is responsible for the resistance, not the group that is expressing the resistances on behalf of the system as a whole. However, once these tensions get expressed, since they're basically a denied part of the system, the system will be invested in avoiding taking responsibility for this side of itself. The most effective way to do this is accuse those who are expressing the system forces of having actually created those forces that once were denied or suppressed. By doing this the system as a whole frees itself from responsibility for the shadowy parts of itself. The best example of this in Montville was what happened around the theme of violence. Many of the Elite's schemes were basically violent. However, that violence was denied. When the Out group began to act violently (expressing for Montville the violence that existed at its core), then they were accused of having actually caused the violence, thereby justifying the system's use of violence in attempting to control them. When Westville didn't like the shape of the world, and as lowers they tried to resist the will of the uppers, they were labelled by the Elites as belligerent, incompetent, etc. The Elites then used this as justification for their original acts and as reinforcement as to why the Outs should continue to be treated poorly. The Elite logic went as follows: "Their behavior is so uncooperative that they've just proved that we were right in keeping them down. It also tells us clearly that we'll have to put more pressure on them in the future in order to make them cooperate." The Elites thereby created massive rationalizations to justify and then deny their role in making the Outs like they were.

At a theoretical level, when those who are resisting (occupying the negative point of the contradiction) are labelled by those who occupy the assertive side and choose to resist the labelling, then their very resistance creates the self-fulfilling prophecy that justifies the original labelling. However, by ignoring or affirming the label, the resisters (who are now affirming instead of negating) are freeing themselves from the double binds of the underlying contradictions of the system. For example, while the Outs tried to prove that the Elites were responsible for their "belligerence, violence, incompetence" etc., they were always trapped. But when the Westville Outs no longer cared what Kenloch thought, then they learned not to be incompetent and mobilized themselves in such a way that the Elites' characterizations of them as Outs became irrelevant to them. The labels no longer immobilized them, thereby undermining the labels instead of reinforcing them through self-fulfilling prophecies.

Internal Dissention

A major dilemma for a powerless group is that when dissent emerges in its ranks the overall commitment to remain united forces that dissent to assume a very special meaning. Since the closer the relationships among the members of any group, the more probability that conflict will exist (Simmel, 1955), the powerless are forced into a critical bind. Since they need to be united to deal with external threats and since their strength is predicated on unity, the lowers' major concern is that those who threaten them will attempt to undermine them by driving a wedge between them. Yet the closer group members are, the more internal conflict they experience, which in turn threatens their group unity. It is their very desire to protect themselves from conflict that makes them strive for a closeness that is predicated on strongly mutual affective attachments, yet it's this closeness that creates the internal conflicts (Coser, 1956). To compensate for this, strong ground rules become formulated in lower groups to avoid or suppress inner dissent. However, the more the conflict is suppressed, the more potentially explosive it becomes (Freud, 1960). Should these suppressed tensions surface, they invariably disrupt relationships among members severely because they carry with them the extra intensity that has been incubating as a result of the process of repression.

These suppressed group feelings are like an explosive that can be easily detonated. If one individual deviates or fails to keep a dislike suppressed, group members are forced to see the fragility of their unity. This invariably draws out hostility about having to be unified and it's likely to be expressed in the scapegoating of the deviant (Coser, 1956).

What occurs among individuals within the powerless group as they struggle with the deviant may be seen as a microcosm of what was occurring among groups in the system at large. The deviance is not viewed as an expression of group tension but rather as the creation of those tensions. Hence the deviant will be labeled as a troublemaker and may even be referred to as "the enemy in our midst." Accordingly, attempts will be made to deal with the deviant as a deviant, not as an expresser of a denied part of group life. The person may be ejected and if contrite the person may survive by a major reaffirmation of loyalty to the group. In either case the behavior of the deviant will have contributed significantly to the group's life in a number of ways. (1) There will have been a therapeutic release, like a safety valve, of deeply repressed collective emotions (Simmel, 1955). (2) There will have been an overt display of behavior, which the group can point to as being unacceptable for Out group membership, thereby defining indirectly what's acceptable (Dentler and Erikson, 1959). (3) It will have enabled the group to reaffirm the predominance of the group over its individual members (Goffman, 1959).

In the event that it is not an individual but a subgroup that explodes with a set of powerful emotions, then the inner antagonisms between the factions in the powerless group will be directed primarily at each other, with one subgroup being labeled the "enemy of the group." The hostility the powerless group once directed outward is now focused inward. This gives rise not only to hostility between the competing subgroups, but also triggers each to hate what the other is doing to the total group. Each faction will accuse the other of being willing to endanger the preservation of the whole group for their selfish interests. The antagonism becomes acted out as each faction tries to cajole, seduce, and bully the other into giving in for the sake of the total group.

These above processes could be seen at work in the Out group at Montville. For long periods they became privately stuck on what they might do with their inner fragmentation. They ran the whole range of responses from struggling to keep individuals in line with the group interests to precariously balancing two equally powerful and opposed factions within their group. There was great irony in how the Westville Outs (like most powerless groups) dealt with individuals who would deviate or subgroups that would fight with each other. First, the anger that was originally directed at the powerful for creating the oppressive conditions that made the unity necessary in the first place became refocused *into* their own group and they attacked each other rather than their external oppressors. Second, the powerless moved from close positive feelings about their unity to a mutual dislike for their having to remain united in order to survive. Third, they came to hate their inability to "draw together." They hated the fact that their external unity was merely a facade. They hated themselves for their willingness to participate in such a sham.

When Westville eventually learned to accept the above about themselves they were able to work towards their own liberation. However, while they attempted to deny and run away from the above they simply got themselves stuck. For they would simply work harder to preorchestrate public presentations of their unity, thereby generating even greater discrepancies between their public and private sides, diminishing their self-respect, and reinforcing secrecy so they couldn't be found out, all the time building a public facade that could fool others but that left themselves totally trapped in the illusions they manufactured for their self-preservation.

Internalized Oppression

The tendency of a powerless group to take its hostility towards externally oppressive forces and turn it in on itself (Michels, 1915) is the heart of Freire's (1972) discourse on internalizing the oppressor. When once this internalization has occurred, the powerful no longer need to be threatening to keep lowers down. They keep themselves down. In fact the powerful can change their tune entirely and even act to relieve the experience of the lowers' oppression. But it will make little difference. For a self-destructive cycle will have been put in place. The powerless will oppress themselves.

Apart from this above process of internalizing the oppressor, there is another, less visible mechanism that is just as depotentiating, as the Westville Outs displayed for us. Because of their fear of disunity, the Outs were afraid to genuinely explore alternatives. The script was well written. Generating options meant there had to be debate. Debate meant there might be conflict. And conflict could lead to disunity and eventual fragmentation. Better not to explore the alternatives. Do nothing and then grasp on to the first viable option that comes along. In groups where there's a great need for unity, multiple alternatives are usually not explored and inactivity or unifaceted behavior is the result (Groupthink, Janis, 1972). Such limitedness invariably leads a powerless group into exploring few alternatives and behaving in ways that run counter to the achievement of their goals. This heightens their sense of incompetence and reinforces their experience of powerlessness.

These experiences of incompetence generate a special type of dependency in powerless groups. The lowers assume that "they" (the powerful) made it this way; and hence "they" (the powerful) must change it. However, there's a bind. For any action the powerful takes "to liberate" the powerless only reinforces the dependency of the powerless making uppers' acts of "liberation" into another version of oppression.

This special bind could be seen at Montville. While the Westville Outs demanded that Kenloch and Hannover change the social conditions so the lowers would feel less oppressed, whatever the more powerful groups did, the Outs automatically rejected it simply because it was the Elites or the Ins who were doing it. This paradox meant the lowers would never be liberated from the paralysis of their dependency while they looked to other groups to change what they didn't like.

Lowers' Dynamic Conservatism: A Powerless Perspective

With the above intergroup forces operating, the social comparisons a powerless group engages in will take on a particular contextual flavor. First, they will look at more powerful groups through suspicious eyes and will attempt to extract from what is reflected back to them: (a) confirmation of the necessity to be distrusting; and (b) how successful they are being in combatting the oppressiveness they feel in relationships with more powerful groups. Second, they will posture the relational distance between them and other groups to optimally balance two forces: (a) their wish to be able to see into and work out what's going on in the domains kept hidden from them; and (b) their desire to keep up a large enough wall so that others cannot see the disunity in their own ranks that lurks behind their facade of unity. Third, since they experience their condition of oppression and deprivation as being others' fault, they also consider that it's others' responsibility to liberate them. Hence they look at the behavior of other groups for signs that liberation is imminent, yet they look for those signs through eyes calibrated to totally reject any initiatives from the more powerful even if those initiatives are of a conciliatory nature.

These looking glass dimensions of a powerless group's social comparison exchanges are highly linked to, caused by, and in turn cause their lower dynamic conservatism. At its core, the dynamic conservatism of powerless groups is that they depend on, feed on, and in turn generate the very conditions they're attempting to destroy. In their dependency, lower groups assume that the powerful made things the way they are, therefore the powerful must change it. However, they also assume that accepting any act of the powerful would only make the powerful more powerful and that they must accordingly reject all acts of the powerful no matter what the cost. The double bind is accentuated further by the fact that the lower groups' resistances make the powerful more powerful. The more energy put into diminishing the power a group has in fact augments it, because that power really exists only to the extent to which the powerless group gives meaning to and attaches itself to the power of that group. Hence attempts to negate the power of a group are as much an affirmation of that power as are acts of confirmation of that power. It's very much like an adolescent wanting to assert independence from parents by moving away from home, demanding they provide alternative accommodations. This method of denying the parents' power actually confirms it. In a similar way, when a powerless group resists the power of another group, although it enables them to experience unity and hence comparative strength, in reality it maintains their relative weakness for it is simultaneously giving the powerful more strength. This process is the heart of the dynamic conservatism of those whose power is predicated on a resistive posture.

These dynamic conservatism forces operating on the relationships of the lower group with uppers and middles at Montville generated and reinforced the structural encasement in which the Outs became trapped. We can see how imprisoning these dynamics were by observing what took place as Westville liberated themselves. In their acts of liberation as the walls of the psychological imprisonment became demolished, it was very visible how potent was the lower structural encasement generated by *the protection devices they designed to defend themselves from the threats of the more powerful.*

Instead of resisting, instead of looking to others for liberation, instead of defending themselves against the possibility of inner fragmentation (Marx and Engels, 1962; Caute, 1967; Coser, 1956; Freire, 1972) Westville had to give up resisting the conditions that oppressed them and to work at transcending those conditions. As Tillich expressed it (1952), to resist is negating a negation. This leads to social neurosis. Liberation necessitates an affirmation of the negation that facilitates the emergence of creative energy from within and thereby the possibility of learning how to transcend the forces of the oppression without having to actually fight those forces head on. It focuses on how to make those oppressive forces *irrelevant* rather than how to obliterate them. Martin Luther King discovered this potently in the early stages of the civil rights movement when he poetically realized that as most of his energy was being focused on oppressive social conditions it enabled him to ignore the "slave that he'd internalized in himself." By affirming his own condition, he discovered a way to create his transcendence over that condition.

Bonhoeffer (1972) writing from captivity during the Third Reich explicated the essence of this struggle. To threaten with death is only truly a threat while one still fears death. The oppressive act is only oppressive while I'm in the condition of negating a negation (fleeing from my mortality). But when I affirm my mortality and come to live with all the anxiety that death represents so that I no longer fear fearing death, then to threaten with death loses its power. It doesn't alter my fear of death. I'm still afraid. But I can affirm my fear. I no longer need to run away from that fear. So confront me with death and I'll feel OK about that confrontation because you'll merely place before me my mortality, which I've learned to accept. Then that confrontation ceases to be oppressive. For it's only when I can't accept it that your threatening me with death holds power over me. By affirming my negation I learn to transcend the condition of that negation.

The Westville Outs did manage to liberate themselves. Through their entrepreneurial-guerilla scheme they created new conditions through which the New Society was given its birth. In so doing, they broke down the imprisoning walls of their lower group's structural encasement and in the process revealed the nature of the lowers' dynamic conservatism. In that liberation we can see summarized the nature of their bondage.

"How can the oppressed, as divided, unauthentic beings, participate in developing the pedagogy of their liberation?" asks Freire (1972). Through their actions Westville provided a possible answer: (1) Recognize that no one can "liberate" you, for anything done unto or for you as an oppressed group is just one further act of oppression; (2) recognize that you have become the "hosts of your oppressors"; (3) if you want reality to be changed, the only way is by creating your own; (4) you must develop a power base other than resistance alone; and (5) recognize that unity can be deindividuating and that it's imperative to develop a way of taking unified action without denying inner fragmentation.

Structural Encasements of Middles

The major structurally encasing dimension of the Hannover Ins relationship with the other Montville groups was that they repetitively gravitated towards a position where they needed to preserve functional relations with both the group above them and the group below them. This generated a myriad of tensions for them because of the intense polarity that existed between the Kenloch Elites and Westville Outs. These tensions created an overwhelming double bind, which played itself out as follows: in order to make more manageable the external pulls on them as a group caught in the middle, Hannover had to work to reduce the degree of polarization in the Elite-Out relationship; however, in order to have any significant impact on that relationship the Ins had to stay right in the middle, in a linking pin role; yet it was their very commitment to that position of middleness that made them so subjected to the overwhelming forces that they wanted to change.

This bind was augmented by a further paradox for the middle group. Having made the centerpiece of their role in Montville the function of mediating in the Elite-Out conflict, while their work was to diminish the intense polarization of their social system, they also had to be careful never to succeed. For in succeeding, the middles would have abolished their very reason for existing as middles in the system. In addition, however, to making sure that the problems they set out to resolve were never completely dealt with, the middles had to make (or give the appearance of making) some progress in depolarizing the system. Otherwise, their role would have been rejected. In other words, they had to be partially successful but not too successful for they were dependent for their existence on the preservation of the very conditions they were trying to change.

I will discuss the structural encasement operating on the relationship between middles and the other two Montville groups under five headings: social comparisons—a mediating perspective; the problem of grouplessness; the question of communication; creating a collective reality; and middles' dynamic conservatism—an in-between perspective.

Social Comparisons: A Mediating Perspective

The encasement Montville middles were imprisoned by meant that they engaged in their social comparison exchanges with a major dynamic not found in the experience of either Kenloch or Westville. The middles always needed to look at opposite directions at the same time. This meant that instead of looking at themselves in the mirror of either the uppers' or lowers' responses to them, the middle group had to look at itself in the mirror of the upper-lower relationship—a much more complicated type of looking glass than we've discussed previously. This meant that for every behavior, the middles have two audiences. For example, if it engaged in an exchange with the Outs as an audience group it had to couch that interaction in such a way that it was palatable to the Elites for the Elites were looking for the implications of how the middles looked at themselves in the behavior of the Outs. To explicate this fully, our discourse could obviously get very complex. That's unnecessary at this moment. It's only critical here to note that for the middle group, the looking glass dimension of the social comparison processes involves simultaneous multiple audiences. And since those audiences were themselves trapped in the respective dynamic conservatism of uppers and lowers they were looking at the middles from opposite perspectives. This meant that the middles had to develop rationales for their behavior to simultaneously satisfy groups that were looking at them from very different and often contradictory mind sets.

In Montville, it often seemed that Hannover was saying they were doing one thing while they looked like they were doing the opposite. A good example was when the Ins tried to convince Westville that they wanted to help the Outs develop a two-level system when their actual middle behavior represented a visible denial of what they were claiming. The most effective way for the middles to help the Outs create a two-tiered society would have been for them to simply cease acting as middles. Yet the Ins tried to convince the Outs that they would work in the interests of the lowers, triggering the retort, "The message we want you to carry to the Elites is that we don't want you carrying our messages to the Elites. Now it certainly wouldn't make sense to ask you to convey that message to them, would it?" This saying one thing while appearing to do the opposite emerged for the middles because they were playing to two audiences—one with the behavior of their actions, the other with the behavior of their words. While they played to the Outs with their actions, they had to simultaneously play to the Elites with their words (or vice versa) in order to develop, protect, and maintain their right to continue in the mediating location.

The social comparison process was made very complicated for the middles because in order to adequately mediate the polarized tensions generated by the divergent orientations of both upper and lower groups, the Ins had to be constantly cognizant of what was going on *within* those respective groups. However, as we've discussed, the uppers and lowers behaved secretively. This meant the middles were constantly confronting the onerous task of trying to draw out of the other groups things they were tightlipped about. In order to work on depolarizing the system the middles were forced to develop a power base that depended on their having information others lacked. To achieve this though, the middles had to activate an overall commitment to greater communication on everyone's behalf and then count on the fact, or make sure, that the communication processes were so faulty that the critical information only got as far as them. If the communication had got beyond the middles and the two extreme groups started dealing with each other directly, their power base of having information the others lacked (the centerpiece of their mediating function) would have disappeared.

As Goffman (1959) indicates, the mediators' power is dependent on their knowledge of the secrets of the conflicting groups. If both polarities learn of the secrets, then the middles' specialness disappears. But while the middles alone know these secrets, they can effectively engage in a game where they give the impression to each side that they will keep its secrets, while at the same time giving each side the false impression that they, as middles, will be more loyal to it than the other. Since middles come to see their survival as mediators to be dependent on processes such as these, it makes sense, at one level, for them to work at restricting communication that doesn't pass through them.

One way for middles to reduce the tensions of being in the mediating position between polarized groups is to keep the poles apart and selectively overcommunicate some facts while undercommunicating others. This tactic may alleviate critical tensions. However, it also makes the middles very vulnerable if they're ever caught publicly or intentionally doing this. Hence, any acts of "distortion" in the service of depolarizing the system must be carried out covertly.

With the Montville middle group engaged in the social comparison process of playing to two audiences, dependent on a mediating power base and needing to keep certain of their actions secret in order to depolarize the system, we again have the foundation of a complicated dynamic conservatism force based on a double bind that went as follows: To develop a power base that would enable them to function as mediators in the tensions between uppers and lowers, middles gravitated towards an information-sharing posture; they argued that to overcome the polarity, more communication was necessary, thereby generating a rationale for their gaining access to the secrets uppers and lowers withhold from each other; they had to be careful however to never reveal these secrets to the other groups because if they did, they'd (a) lose the confidence of the secret holders and (b) generate (probably quite explosive) direct communications between the uppers and lowers, which would dislocate the middles out of their mediator role. In other words, the middles became dependent for their very existence on the conditions they claim they were attempting to change. This was the basis of the middles' dynamic conservatism and it helped shape the way they entered into social comparison processes.

The Problem of Grouplessness

Being in the middle and invested in lessening the tensions created by the Elites and the Outs left Hannover's Ins forever trying to work out what was going on in the ranks of uppers and lowers and frequently paying insufficient attention to its own realities. This generated a paradox. To be effective in a system mediating role, the middle group needed a strong sense of its own inner groupness because it had to absorb and decipher the multiple realities it sat

122

at the intersection of. However, those divergent realities constantly pulled middles in opposite directions and left them fragmented, indecisive, and unable to act effectively in their mediating function.

While uppers and lowers could build a sense of their own groupness on what transpired within their own ranks, middles had to pay much more attention to what went on between the groups, for it was on these very interactions that their groupness rested. This was where they got caught. For Elites and Outs, groupness was primarily an inner phenomenon. For the middles it was mainly a matter of externals. The other groups could be assertive or reactive if they wished. Middles had to be much more delicate. This meant that if the external pulls on the middles were great, then their internal tensions increased. If the external tugs lessened, the inner fragmentation would diminish. In other words what shape they were in was primarily an expression of the external relations. Because they were so dependent on the other groups, the middles didn't experience freedom to develop a proactive stance internally. Their internal life was always reactive to the conditions of conflict with the other groups.

The trap for the middles went as follows. Adversarial relationships have the ethnocentric tendency to twist, distort, and confuse within and between group conflicts. Hence, where possible, groups attempted to interpret any tensions within their own group as a consequence of conflicts with other groups. Finding another group that could be labeled "enemy" enabled the original group to translate its inner conflict into conflict between them and the enemy. If this between-group conflict could be worked in such a way that the other group became divided among itself, all the better. For then the original within-group tension would have been transferred into among-groups conflict and, in turn, transformed into internal tension in the other group.

When uppers and lowers were attempting to externalize their internal conflicts by transferring them to the middles, it was very hard for the middles not to fall into this trap of internalizing these external tensions, making them their own. To make things worse, the middles had exacerbated this tendency by the way they packaged their role as central to the system's communication processes. The primitive logic went as follows: it's their middle role to bring things together; conflicts fragment, therefore if conflict raged, it was because the middles were ineffective; thus they were the cause of the conflict and hence must be held responsible for its resolution.

As a result of this, the social comparison reflections were back to front for middles. If their group was sufficiently together to not internalize these external conflicts, then the conflicts were kept in the system with the uppers and lowers polarized. In this case the middles would have reflected back to them images that they were not competent as a group to fulfill their function as diffusers of the system's tension. If the middle group did internalize these external tensions then it would be so fragmented and undermined as a group that it would experience paralysis and see its impotence reflected back, thereby having confirmed its own sense of ineffectiveness as a group.

In Montville while the Outs and Elites were externalizing their inner fragmentations, the middles did take these internal tensions and make them their own. In so doing, it was only a matter of time before they were authentically their own conflicts. For they expanded the boundaries of their own group to such an extent that their middle, within-group conflict was a mirror, in microcosm, of the macrocosmic tensions that existed between the groups. In so doing, the middles undermined their own groupness.

The Question of Communication

Since these internal and external tensions in and between Montville groups were all "communicated" in some way (i.e., transferred from one part of the system to another and translated in the process of being transferred) and since the middles were very central actors in this communication, it's imperative that we pause in developing the middle structural encasement to reflect on what "communication" meant in Montville.

The most obvious starting point on this topic is that communication clearly meant different things to different groups at Montville. To the Westville Outs it meant "Give us data that will confirm our worst suspicions." This was clearest whenever the lowers were information-deprived. Then, they did not interpret their hearing nothing as meaning that nothing was going on; rather they treated it as an indication that "all hell was about to break loose and we'd better start getting active to protect ourselves." To the Kenloch Elites it meant two things, "Tell us about their vulnerable spots so we can manipulate them more effectively" and "Tell us how great you all think we are." To the Hannover Ins "communication" meant a mechanism for depolarizing the system, giving themselves some power and lessening the paralyzing tensions within which their group had to exist.

Traditionally, communication in organizations has been viewed as getting the appropriate information to the appropriate place at the appropriate time. But Montville drives home the lesson that communication is much more than this. In exploring the communication issue at a general level, we're forced to address the fundamental question of "What is reality?" and "What are the forces that underpin a system's multiple realities?" The question of communication has to incorporate why it is that "facts" that seem to mean one thing in one part of the system can end up meaning something radically different when they get to another part of the system.

Consider for example the way the term unity was used in Montville. While all three groups used this concept, it meant something different to each of them. To the lowers it represented protection from attack. To the uppers it meant getting others to obey their elite dictates. For these two groups the meaning of the term depended on group-based reality. However, for the middles it was not group focused. They were talking about the unity of the whole system. This was critical to the Hannover Ins because only if all the groups came together would the tensions upon them decrease. When the three groups spoke of "unity" they each inaccurately assumed the other meant the same thing.

The complex issue in the communication process between groups is that the initiating group is speaking out of its own consciousness into another group's consciousness that the initiators basically don't understand. What's at stake in intergroup communication is how can the "speaking" group work out a way to understand the consciousness of the "listening" group and how can the "listening" group come to understand the consciousness out of which the "speaking" group is making its statements. Each of the groups, both "speakers" and "listeners," comprehends its own consciousness in very *subjective* terms with its "inner meanings" being dependent upon its sense of shared history of its own internal processes. However, both these groups, the "speakers" and the "listeners," understand the consciousness of the other group in the communication act in an objectified way. This means there's a strong tendency to discount the relevance of each other's subjective realities, with the richness represented by the subjective nuances lost. What is an inner meaning for the speakers is an "outer" meaning for the listeners. What's *subjective* for one group is, of necessity, objective for the other. It's this very fact that forces intergroup communication to have to take place in an outer, objective framework. For even if the speaking group initiates its statements out of its inner subjective reality, it is *heard* in an outer, objectified framework. Therefore, the "communication," no matter what stimulates it, actually takes place in an "outer" world (Schutz, 1970).

The mere fact that communication is necessary indicates that those being communicated with are in a "different place" than those speaking. If this were not true, "listeners" would be part of the "speaking" group and then no statement would be necessary. They would automatically understand because they're part of the inner, subjective reality. For example, at Montville the Outs didn't need to "communicate" with each other what was going on within their experience. The very living of that experience created the shared reality. They knew it automatically. But the fact that Westville's experience was different from the Elites or Ins made it necessary for communication among groups to take place. Communication is necessary when "reality" is *not shared*.

Hence, the central task of communication is to develop links between segments of multiple and divergent realities. Accordingly, anyone initiating a communication, before speaking, must determine how to pass the message from a "reality set" the speaker comprehends subjectively into the "reality set" of the listener who will interpret it objectively. Failure to make this prior determination will diminish the potential effectiveness of the communicative act and will be most likely to cause the divergent multiple realities (which made the original communication necessary) to become even more discordant. Thus, the effectiveness of communication is dependent on the extent to which an externally agreed upon reality framework can be created into which groups can speak with reasonable confidence that they'll be heard appropriately. We must thus think of "communication" as a process that attempts to transform multiple and different private realities into a "collective reality" that can then be dealt with in an agreed upon way. This returns us now to the more central question of how the middles generated, got caught in, and then became dependent on the very things they were trying to change. By being in the middle and developing for themselves a mediating power base, they moved into a central role in the communication patterns of Montville. In so doing they had to develop a "collective reality" in order to have any chance of overcoming the tensions of the system that repetitively paralyzed them.

Creating a Collective Reality

Schutz (1970) highlights that there are three prerequisites for a collective reality. There must be (1) a nucleus of shared experience, (2) an agreed upon language, and (3) a willingness to talk about private realities using the language and concepts of the collectivity.

In Montville, special communication problems were created by the development of two collective realities: (1) an upper-middle reality, based on the controlling of the Outs, which the Outs couldn't comprehend because they were always excluded from participating in its formulation, though they were repetitively subjected to the forces that derived from this particular reality; and (2) a middle-lower reality, based on getting a better deal for the Outs, which the Elites couldn't understand because they'd been excluded from its formulation. These two reality sets were constantly pitted against each other. What was lacking, however, was an Elite-Out reality system and another broader reality base that was capable of spanning all three groups. As a result, when communications were attempted between Elites and Outs, they never worked because they were being spoken into a reality that didn't exist. Yet each group failed, (or refused) to recognize this, persisted in believing both that they were each making themselves clear and that any failures to be understood were the fault and responsibility of the other group, rather than themselves.

In the final analysis, the responsibility for failure in overall communication was placed at the Ins feet. At one level, this was appropriate (1) because the Ins had made their role in the communication channel as their reason for existing and (2) because they did share a reality set in common with each of Westville and Kenloch even though each of these reality sets were highly incompatible.

In order to fulfill their communicative responsibility, the Ins could have moved in either of two different directions. They could have worked to bring uppers and lowers into direct and open confrontation. If successful in creating a collective reality by this means, the middles would almost certainly have done themselves out of a job. If they were unsuccessful, they'd have entrenched the system tensions even more deeply thereby making their own task more difficult. The alternative, which was what the Hannover Ins elected to do, was to generate for themselves as much insight as possible about what the other two groups were doing. This approach was finally the middles' undoing for the following three reasons.

First, Hannover observed many events that occurred within each of the other groups that were never intended by the acting group as acts of communication. Nevertheless the Ins took these events, which were usually a mere living-out of internal group processes of uppers or lowers, and interpreted them as though they had specific meanings for the relationships between the groups. The interpretative system the middles used was their own, which was highly inferential and based largely on their own internal fragmentation.

Second, a new self-defeating cycle was occurring for the middles. Their highly inferential interpretative schemes were already based on the fragmented and multiple realities they were juggling, and the more they observed and absorbed of other experiences, the more fragmented they became and hence the less grounded their inferences were. They were straddling the following reality systems: (1) their own; (2) the Elite-In; (3) the In-Out; (4) their In perspective on the Elites; and (5) their In perspective on the Outs. Their ways of dealing with this straddling however did not bridge these divergences. Rather they deepened the entrenchment, making in turn their own inner experiences additionally fractured.

Third, whenever the middles observed a *concrete* event in one of the groups (such as the Elites having a fight with each other or the Outs treating serious events playfully), Hannover did not experience these events simply in their concreteness. Rather they gravitated towards looking at what meanings these happenings would have for other groups or Montville in general. Hannover looked at the *concrete* and experienced it as *transcendent*. They looked at the meanings events had across group boundaries, paying little attention to what they meant within group boundaries. As a result, the filters through which they viewed events was at a *higher level of abstraction* than those who were living through the concrete experience. For example, the Ins regularly interpreted the Outs playfulness (their frequent swims, volleyball games, etc.) as a sign that Westville had totally given up on the society. The Outs experienced these same events simply as recreation, a relief from boredom.

The purpose of the middles' role in the communication process was quite simple. Sitting at the intersection of the multiple reality systems they attempted to develop a collective reality by abstracting the common elements of the subset realities and repackaging them in ways that would enable the other actors to experience divergences as complementary parts of a whole rather than as competing realities. The conceptual trick to this activity was the repackaging in such a way that others would be sold on new ways of conceptualizing their experiences without invalidating those experiences and without feeling excluded from the relabeled meanings attached to those experiences.

This task involved the search for metaphors, for symbols, for an overarching framework that would enable polar opposites to be tranformed from conflictual antagonists to creative adversaries (Wilden, 1972).

Hannover was quite unsuccessful in its attempts to generate a collective reality for Montville, but its efforts were interesting for what they potentially tell us about social theory. When the middles didn't like the tensions they were subjected to they attempted to explain their own behavior in system terms. Rather than saying "we're doing this for our own self-interest" they'd claim they're "doing it for the good of the system," attempting to make the collective interests synonymous with their own self-interests. And here was the trap for them. They'd give the appearance of doing one thing, while doing another. For example, the middles would justify their own ongoing support for glaring social inequities by advocating the need for a judicial system to compensate the aggrieved; they talked about working towards egalitarianism while preserving for themselves conditions more favorable than the deprived; they appealed to moral guidelines, invoking something ideological to package mundane self-interest.

If the middles were successful in this process of creating overarching conceptual umbrellas for explaining their own group's behavior, they could decrease the tension upon themselves greatly. This way they could deviate temporarily from the delicate position they occupied between the uppers and lowers. If they did something in the interests of themselves or the lowers, this upset the uppers (or vice versa). But if they could explain what they were doing to be good for the whole system (i.e., they're acting not as servants of themselves or of one particular group but of everyone's collective interests), this would enable them to be forgiven for the deviation from the precarious balance of their middleness and would not generate excessive countervailing tension by the group that might otherwise feel aggrieved. Since they must stay in the middle to retain their mediator power, they must always avoid the possibility of lowers seeing them as having been bought off by the uppers or uppers seeing them as having sold out to the lowers. These "transcendent conceptual umbrellas" provided precisely this protective function for the middles. The uppers and lowers never needed such systemwide conceptual umbrellas for they unashamedly and forthrightly asserted that they were always driven by self-interest. It's only for those who would claim to work in others' interests that such processes were necessary.

I want to digress momentarily. One very convenient framework for developing these overarching notions are moral and ethical principles. To claim that such and such should be done because it's an inalienable right or is fundamental to social justice disarms resistance. The search for universals to guide or explain the human condition is one method that enables dualistic and opposing tensions to coexist in dialectic harmony. This is very much like the social theorizing that led to the Marxian (1867) view of religion as "the opium of the people." The development of images of an afterlife, that fantasized a world free of oppression, enabled the proletariat, he argued, to tolerate social conditions that needed to be transformed in the current historical context. Marx criticized the role that proponents of religion played in diffusing the legitimately rebellious spirit of those who would rise up against those who owned means of production; he accused them of being puppets of the bourgeoisie who continued oppression by the argument that religious suffering is part of the plan of the Almighty. The Marxian concept of religion as an "inverted consciousness" (1848), produced by man to preserve the social stability of the status quo, is a prime example of a "middle consciousness" appealing to a set of transcendent images to explain the experience of the system while holding the polarized tensions in balance.

The attempts of the middles to articulate system experience in transcendent symbols while being valuable at one level also generated a problem for them. Others came to expect the middles to deliver on their rhetoric about system unity. This enabled lowers and uppers to abdicate their own responsibility for their fragmenting behavior. They could be free to fragment because they counted on the middles to look after the uniting.

Clearly, the middles would have to learn how to present the need for unity in a way that made everyone feel the responsibility for bringing this to fulfillment. This meant images of unity would have to be formulated in terms that had specific relevance to the individual group realities or reality subsets; otherwise all the middles' attempts would be dismissed as hollow administrative rhetoric and would be laughed down.

In Montville, the Ins tried to float rhetoric about unity and it kept them center stage for a short while. However, the Outs eventually drove them from their mediating position by destroying the Elite-In reality set by their entrepreneurial-guerilla scheme. The Ins were left, in the final analysis, with little choice but to step aside or else join the revolution that led to the birth of the New Society.

Middles' Dynamic Conservatism: An In-Between Perspective

The major dynamic conservatism of the middle group is its investment in trying to change the very things it is trying to preserve for its own continued existence as a middle group. This dynamic conservatism is greatly shaped by the middles being located between two polarized groups that are extremely secretive, that have pessimistic views of each other, that are low on trust, and that both hold forcefully onto the posture of trying to change the other's behavior while resisting all pressures to be changed themselves. In order to maintain this position, middles (1) attempt to develop an independent power base that uses information sharing as its pillar stone, (2) attempt to suppress pessimism by generating a more optimistic tone in relations between the groups, and (3) try to depolarize the tensions of the system by generating a collective reality.

The central paradox of this posture of a group in such a mediating framework, however, is that they can only use information sharing as a power base if others continue to be secretive. They can only make their major role one of opening up the channels of communication so long as those channels remain clogged. They can only get the system together if that system remains fragmented. They can only exhort to moral and ethical principles as a salient guide for their system's behavior if they can demonstrate an overall moral or ethical depravity. They can only really offer the politics of optimism as an alternative to the pragmatics of pessimism so long as they're unsuccessful in spreading optimism.

The middles are totally dependent for the continuation of the conditions they're attempting to change. In order to keep their mediating position, middles (1) must appear to be working to usher in changes while keeping in place enough obstacles to make sure those changes never really come about; (2) they must have sufficient success to not be seen as having too little value; (3) they must legitimize that the problems created by the polarized groups are valid for them to work with while attempting to get those groups to see how they are responsible for solving the very things the middles agree it's appropriate for them to solve.

These social comparison processes and conservatism forces operating on the relationships of the middle group with uppers and lowers generated for the Montville Ins the structural encasement that went with *trying to preserve simultaneously functional relationships with both the groups above and below them.*

Summary of Structural Encasements

When upper groups enter social comparison exchanges, they use their power to control the situation by rejecting certain audiences, forcing others to provide selective feedback, and keeping themselves unduly in an audience perspective by treating others' reflecting behavior exclusively as an independent performance. Uppers trap themselves in the bind of splitting the functions of decision making and implementation, delegating responsibility without the required authority, and unknowingly depending on information bases that are very fragile. Uppers end up with the dynamically conservative posture of working to augment their own power as a vehicle for accomplishing their goals by making their acquisition of power a goal in and of itself. Domination becomes an end instead of a means and triggers an epistemological camouflage of the original purposes the pursuit of power was to serve. In particular, the uppers come to falsely experience a relative sense of powerfulness when they interact with other groups that have been made impotent and subjugated. These forces together created the structural encasement in the relationships of the Elites with other groups at Montville of their becoming imprisoned by their inability to comprehend the consequences of their own behavior.

Powerless groups enter social comparison exchanges with a reactive posture that has the preservation of their own unity as the central force. They resort to secrecy and work to bind their membership into making individual concerns subordinate to the interests of the group-as-a-whole. They fear inner dissention and suppress it by keeping their relationships with others conflictual, thereby reinforcing the intensity of their unity, which in turn feeds the extent to which inner fragmentation is threatening. The lowers' dynamic conservatism is that they depend on, feed on, and in turn generate the very conditions they attempt to destroy. In particular they resist the power of others, demanding that others use their power to change the things that are problematical for the powerless. However, their resistance and their demands only augment the power they are attempting to destroy, in turn, intensifying their resistances. These forces generated for the relationship of the Westville Outs the structural encasement of being immobilized by the protection devices they developed to create and maintain their group cohesion in the light of perceived threats they experienced in the society at large.

Middles enter social comparison exchanges performing for dual audiences of those both above and below and who provide judgments from contradictory perspectives. Hence middles are always caught in the bind of the divergent reality systems of uppers and lowers. They develop a power base predicated on information sharing to depolarize the tensions generated by the secrecy of the other groups. They attempt to develop a global reality system that transcends the limited realities of uppers and lowers, but in the process they suffer from problems of grouplessness and end up intensifying the complexity of the communication processes between groups. They become caught in the dynamic conservatism of being dependent on the continuation of the very conditions they're attempting to change. These forces led the relationships of the Ins at Montville to become structurally encased in the overbearing imperative to keep a delicate and functional relationship with both the powerful and the powerless groups.

These encasements generate an interdependent network of forces that helps preserve conditions of power and powerlessness in all social systems and that transforms most efforts at producing changes into a mere enactment of dynamic conservatism. The powerful need to objectify the powerless in order to define and sustain the reality they, as the powerful ones, created. The powerless need the powerful to treat them in an oppressive way in order to catalyze and sustain attempts by the powerless to rise up, overcome, and transcend the condition imposed upon them. They need these oppressive forces only until they transcend them. Those caught in the middle between the powerful and the powerless need the polarities of power-powerlessness to be preserved in order to maintain their position of middleness. This interlocking network of dependence and independence creates an atmosphere where there are preserving and destroying forces operating at the same time. This produces a systemwide dynamic conservatism, which ensures that changes in the final analysis end up preserving the status quo.

Characteristics of Upness, Middleness, and Lowness

Having looked at Montville from the perspective of the *interactions* among the three groups, I'd like now to look briefly at some of the characteristics that each of the groups displayed. While I'm exploring these characteristics as though they are properties of the groups themselves, as I mentioned earlier in this chapter, this is an arbitrary distinction that I make merely for conceptual clarity, and we should keep in mind that these group characteristics cannot really be thought of as independent from each other or the interaction patterns among groups. In fact, I want to argue that the dialectical interplay of among and within group forces was so strong that each of the three groups took into themselves the forces operating on them, *internalizing* to such an extent that their group characteristics, their group identities, became fused with the systemic dynamics of which they were a part and *externalizing* to such an extent that Montville could not be thought of separate from the ways the three groups structured their images of their minisociety. In other words, the character of each group and of Montville at large was an expression of the mutual introjection and projection of both system and group dynamics.

I'll discuss the characteristics of the groups under four general headings: (1) perceptions and attributions; (2) use of information; (3) modalities for dealing with conflicts between groups, and (4) within groups.

Perceptions and Attributions

Each of Montville's three groups developed their own particular understandings of what was transpiring in their minisociety. How they saw their world shaped the explanations they developed as to why events occurred as they did. For example, the Elites, seeing the Outs as belligerent and rebellious, came to the conclusion that the only way to control them was by punishment. On the other hand, the Outs perceiving the Elites as dictatorial and arbitrary concluded that the only way to develop influence was by being resistant. The Ins, caught in the middle, saw the tensions between the Elites and Outs to be so powerful and paralyzing and deduced that the only way Montville would be made a tolerable place to live in was by bringing everyone together.

Montville's groups became caught in a tangled web of perceptual and attributional forces. The deciphering of who thought what about whom when and why and whether it was reality or fiction that was being conveyed became the essence of a large portion of the groups' interchanges. Yet despite this, there were some dominant perceptual forms that each of the groups took on and that became the basis of the attributions they made.

In general, the *uppers* developed a *pessimistic outlook towards the other groups*. They saw the middles as being less than competent to fulfill their allocated social functions. They saw the lowers as being rebellious and uncooperative. The uppers' pessimism generalized to making them afraid that the middles would be too incompetent to act as social mediators or implementors

132

of the Elites' wishes and that in their weakness they would be seduced into a power coalition with the Outs. In their pessimism, the uppers also came to the conclusion that the only way to get anyone to do what they wanted was by the use of force or coercion. Accordingly, they developed a punitive, untrusting, and depriving orientation towards the other two groups.

Montville's *lowers,* caught in the encasements that go with the experience of powerlessness, developed a pessimism as intense as that of the Elites, though expressed in different forms. The lowers came to *view the actions of those above with both suspicion and disbelief.* This suspiciousness developed as a natural corollary to the group formation processes we discussed earlier, where it became evident that no matter what the Elites did, the Outs interpreted it as a threat in some way, even when Kenloch was not even thinking about Westville. One of the unintended consequences of the upper group's determination to keep the lowers deprived was that the powerless ended up interpreting all of the Elites' behavior as an expression of "their ongoing determination to oppress." When Westville was not feeling suspicious they tended to be apathetic and rebellious, a behavior that is very characteristic of powerless groups (Sayles, 1958).

As they came to adopt a "we don't care" attitude, the total system became balanced in the sense that the polarities (Elites and Outs) both looked at their world through pessimistic filters and both adopted a stance of "we care primarily about ourselves and aren't too interested in what's happening to anyone else."

The *middles,* locked perilously in the middle of the uppers' and lowers' pessimism had a strong propulsion to counter the pulls on them from opposite sides. Their typical *reaction to the others' pessimism was to be optimistic,* countering the uppers' and lowers' belligerence towards each other with often hollow-sounding rhetoric about being interested in doing things "for the good of the system." It often appeared that the more pessimistic the Elites and Outs were, the more optimistic the middles sounded.

Use of Information

The second major category for examining the characteristics of Montville's groups is how they used information. At a cursory glance, it's evident that each of the three groups used information in different ways. Both the Elites and Outs moved towards information-withholding postures—though each for radically different reasons—while the Ins couched themselves primarily as information sharers.

Since we've already discussed the topic of communication significantly, in the earlier sections of this chapter, most of this section will be cursory. You will recall that by "information" we mean not only basic facts but how reality has been given shapes and forms and how meanings have been attached to these forms.

The uppers *used information withholding as a major way to force middles and lowers to be dependent on them.* Throughout Montville, the Elites took the stance that the less others knew the more influence the powerful would have. When the uppers did communicate with others it was invariably in the form of directives, never a sharing of how the Elites struggled to put reality together for themselves.

Like the uppers, Montville's Outs *withheld information,* but in their case it was *primarily a way to protect themselves.* As we've discussed, the powerless group concluded that the most effective way to be powerful was by being united and the most effective way to be united was by being secretive. Hence the lowers' information withholding acted as a defense against their fears and vulnerabilities.

How middles use information is contextually related to the postures of uppers and lowers. With each of them engaging in information withholding, with each having pessimistic views of the other, with low trust and both holding the dynamically conservative posture of trying to change the others' behavior but resisting all pressures to change themselves, *middles gravitate towards an information-sharing stance.* They do this (1) to develop an independent power base, (2) as a way to suppress pessimism and generate a more optimistic tone in relations between groups, and (3) as a method of depolarizing tensions in the system. While Montville's Elites and Outs were engaged in behaviors that increased tensions, Hannover tried to lessen the resultant pressures by attempting to couch themselves as champions of information sharing.

Modalities for Dealing with Conflicts among Groups

The last two categories for examining the internal characteristics of Montville's three groups are the ways they dealt with conflict that occurred both among groups and within groups.

Before discussing specific instances of conflict at Montville, it is important to acknowledge that underlying all discussion of conflict is a basic ideological question of whether conflict is socially "good," "bad," or "neutral." In the last few decades, social theorists have spanned the spectrum on this ideological optic. At one extreme is the view that "society" is a fundamentally cooperative activity, and that conflict is a pathological force that comes with barbaric intent to undermine social stability (Drucker, 1950; Mayo, 1945; Parsons, 1954). In this perspective, conflict is a social scourge that must be eliminated or at least minimized if human progress is to roll in on the tides of inevitability. Another perspective proclaims that conflict is endemic to the very nature of social relations, that it serves some critical social functions and provides a cleansing and abreactive force to enable society to remain fundamentally stable (Coser, 1956; Dentler and Erikson, 1959; Simmel, 1955). A further notion, given modern rebirth in the work of Hegelian and Marxian dialectics but found permeating the ancient philosophies of the East (Lao Tsu, 600 B.C.), is that society predictably creates conditions of social antagonisms out of its structure. Hence, rather than it being an integrated cooperative system, society at best may be viewed as a relatively integrated system of conflicting structural forces. In this framework, society is not a set of social structures but a process whose "order lies solely in the lawfulness of its change" (Dahrendorf, 1957).

The importance of recognizing that the social meanings of conflict can vary is that it opens the possibility of asking under what conditions individuals or groups will focus on one ideological framework for viewing conflict as opposed to others. I've noted earlier that the ideologies I hold may well be primarily a by-product of the position I occupy in the social structure. If this is correct, perhaps if I am located in a position of power, I'll see conflict generated by others as a disruption to the status quo and therefore pathological. However, if I'm powerless, the existence of conflict that generates the possibility of change may provide me with my only moments of hope and optimism that my condition of oppression can be overcome; hence, I'll see conflict as socially "good." If I'm caught between the polarities, as happens when in the "middle," I may well be forced to recognize the dialectical components of conflict—that it can destroy "what is" and therefore be pathological or socially regenerative, depending on whether what gets destroyed is something I want to see preserved or changed.

The above comments are relevant to our discussion of all group conflicts, independent of whether they're expressed in external or internal processes. In many ways the mere distinction of conflicts as being internal or external is a grossly distorting delineation, for groups invariably attempt to deal with threatening within-group conflict as being a consequence of among-group tensions, and many legitimate clashes at the intergroup level get expressed as internal group turbulence. However, I'm going to make this artificial distinction for my discussion here with the hope that it will help to simplify sufficiently to enable some clearer pictures to emerge about how uppers, middles, and lowers deal with conflicts. First, I'll look at external conflicts.

In general, it has been found that groups engaged in conflicts that represent a major external threat respond with increased group cohesion and solidarity (Coser, 1956; Janis, 1972; Simmel, 1955). In addition, common experience and research have shown that whenever a social system is fragmented the emergence of a superordinate goal, such as occurs in a community following environmental disasters (earthquakes, floods, fires, etc.), can activate a level of social cohesion that is never evident during normal conditions (Alinsky, 1971; Sherif, 1956, 1958). It would be easy to deduce from these observations that significant conflict among groups will automatically produce internal group cohesion. Such a generalization is inaccurate. It is only really when that conflict creates a threat to a group's existence that cohesion automatically results. Hence, severe conflict between two equal groups will augment inner cohesion for both (Blake and Mouton, 1961), severe conflict

135

between unequal groups will increase cohesion for the less powerful group but not usually for the powerful group. It has been found that when groups of unequal power are forced to negotiate, they operate on very different internal processes (Haskel, 1974), even when it appears that the separate interests being battled over are equally critical, for underneath there's always another set of conflicts—those that go with the ongoing power to subjugate on the part of the powerful and the struggle to change the social conditions of subjugation on the part of the powerless (Dahrendorf, 1957).

The Montville experience suggests that conflict among groups of unequal power will trigger those *with power* to respond by becoming *increasingly assertive, punitive, and dictatorial, withdrawing "privileges" and withholding authority necessary to implement delegated responsibilities.*

Montville's Outs followed the predictable pattern of responding to conflicts with others by *increasing their cohesion and commitment to their unity as their primary goal.* This was most evident after the attempted meal cancellations. This type of provocation by the Ins and Elites repetitively served to coalesce the Outs, giving their unity purpose and enabling them to act with force as one body.

For Montville's middles, conflict with other groups had a different impact than it had on Elites or Outs. For them, it *created a greater sense of disorientation, triggered their indecisiveness, and made it increasingly difficult for them to act.* This flows understandably from their delicately postured location between two opposing groups whose relationships were always precarious to manage. Hence, among-group conflict tended to immobilize the middles.

Handling Internal Conflicts

Each of Montville's three groups experienced conflict and tension within their ranks, but they handled it in very different ways.

How Kenloch dealt with internal conflict could be seen in their early deliberation on the phantom plan. Soon after the Elite members started to brainstorm how to implement their scheme, they stumbled upon the problem of how they were going to make decisions. The quick agreement was consensus. But they did not address how they would deal with a member who refused to agree. Shortly thereafter, Lennox, feeling that he wanted to experience what it would be like to have his power visible, began to resist the phantom scheme. Kenloch faced its first expression of dissent from within. They dealt with it in a creative way, agreeing to develop a unique, visible role for Lennox so he would feel content. Faced with possible dissent, they consensually created legitimacy for the dissenter, agreeing to disagree.

Westville, within the first few hours of its life, had also agreed on consensus decision making for their group. But when confronted with the possibility that some members might wish to act on individual initiatives, they concluded that this would be a problem with which the group would have to deal. Dissent was not legitimized. They did not agree to disagree.

During Montville's history, internal tension for the *lower group* evolved into a major problem for them. As their disagreements about whether to be "proactive" or "reactive" intensified, their internal cohesion and the integrity of their group unity became threatened, causing them to "get under each other's skin". This generated a lot of volatility.

Hannover, during its first hours together, did not even take time out to contemplate how they would make decisions together. Individuals merely took initiatives, which others followed or resisted. If resistance was strong enough, the initiative was squashed and they dwelt in a state of inertia until someone else, no longer able to tolerate inactivity, took an initiative. If the initiative was supported, the group followed in that direction until they collectively ran into a blind alley or hit an immovable blockade.

In the three Montville groups we see three markedly different ways of dealing with internal conflicts. The *lowers* used what I call the "capitulation method." They called it consensus. But it wasn't. For theoretically, a consensus emerges when a potential solution is constantly changed until the dominant wishes of all concerned are adequately met or equally compromised. This isn't what the Outs did. While they made initial attempts to find a perfectly compromised outcome, this was impossible and what emerged instead was a decision that a large enough portion of the group could agree with. When this occurred, the others who may still have been in opposition were expected to suppress their disagreements. So rather than each member of the group overtly assenting to the resolution, as would occur in a true consensus setting, the lower group simply kept modifying a potential resolution until they reached a point where those who disagreed were willing to give up on their position and concur "for the sake of the unity of the group." This is why I call it the capitulation method.

As noted earlier, the *upper group*, although adopting an initial consensus approach, also agreed from the outset to tolerate dissent. In contrast to the lowers, they were not forced by the social structure into the position of needing to preserve a public display of unity. In fact the Elites, quite to the contrary, had its group members behaving in extraordinarily contradictory ways, e.g., when Richard charaded as Hannover's major negotiator. Generally, upper groups handled internal tension by what I refer to as a "critical mass method." This bore some similarity to the spirit of a "majority vote," but it was a majority with a difference. Usually, if we traced the resolution process from its beginning, the outcome was not a majority perspective at all. It was invariably that of the minority, but of a minority that held weight or "critical mass" in the overall set of internal group relationships to be able to dominate the majority. The vast literature on the social influences at force in groups highlights that there are many ways in which individuals and small minority subgroups can shape the opinions and behaviors of others in particular and desired ways. For example, it is possible for an acknowledged "leader" who singularly holds one particular opinion to sway enough of the group members to go along with that position (Janis, 1972).

In the upper group, a critical mass that began in the minority only had to compromise and build to the point where it became a majority. There was no need, as with the lowers, for the dissenters to capitulate for the sake of the group. A facade of unity is not necessary for the upper group. The dissenters' views can be made public, for Elites basically agree to disagree (e.g., minority reports from groups like the Supreme Court are to be expected but not from a union or tenant association).

Montville's *middle group* was never really able to separate out for itself what were internal as opposed to external issues. The existence of their on-going external conflict generated disorientation and indecisiveness within their ranks. This disorientation became a major source of their internal tension. In Hannover's mind, to deal with internal tension always required them to be able to gain mastery over external tension. However, this proved impossible for them to achieve. Every act on their part seemed to carry such far-reaching consequences that whenever they experienced a new pressure, the only way they could think of dealing with it was to "check out" all the possible implications of their actions. Hence they were forever focused on trying to gain an understanding of "where everybody is at," "where they're coming from," and "where they wished to go." It was always the middles' hope that by finding out as much information as possible, a path to resolution would be self-evident. But this was not to be. All the data they could gather merely confirmed that Elites and Outs wanted different things, and such discordance simply para-lyzed the middles and generated more internal tension.

As we've noted repeatedly, the middles' solutions to their problems al-ways seemed to make things worse for them. The more internally paralyzed they became, the more dependency they developed on data from the whole system as to how they should act. The more data they got, the less desirable any action became and the more they became trapped in stagnant paralysis. This response to internal tension, displayed by Montville's middles, I refer to as the "common understanding approach." Its replica can be found every-where in society. If you don't know what to do, conduct a study. This buys time in which to do nothing. As usually happens, the results of such studies are inconclusive, suggesting the need to study it further.

In *summary,* internal conflict is handled by the three Montville groups in very different ways: Elites by the "critical mass method", the Ins by the "common agreement method", and the Outs by the "capitulation method".

Conclusion

It is time to conclude these conceptual speculations on the intergroup relations operating at Montville. I must now explore whether these tentative learnings from the power laboratory simulation have relevance elsewhere. So, it's on to the Ashgrove school system. There I'll attempt to see if the rela-tionships among groups are caught in structural encasements such as I found

138

in Montville. Further, I'll want to observe whether the various groups displayed any of the characteristics that seemed so evident at Westville, Hannover, and Kenloch.

In conclusion, let me summarize the major ideas that I formulate in my reflections on the experiences of Montville.

Structural Encasements

The relationships among all of Montville's groups became an expression of three major structural encasements.

The *uppers'* relationships became shaped in such a way that they were never able to gain insight into the consequences of their behavior.

The *middles,* dependent for their existence on the preservation of the very conditions they were trying to change, engaged in relationships that became imprisoned by the need to delicately preserve functional relations with both uppers and lowers.

The relationships of the *lowers* became totally encased by the protection devices they designed to create and preserve group cohesion and unity.

All three groups developed characteristics that I'd like to suggest may be typical of groups in general that occupy the positions of upness, middleness, and lowness.

1. Perceptions and attributions. The first is the dominant perspective that each group developed of the Montville world and the attributions that accompanied that world view.

The *uppers* tended to see those below them as less competent and less reliable than themselves. Hence they developed a pessimistic outlook, which caused them to delegate responsibilities but not the authority necessary to implement those responsibilities adequately.

The *middles* viewed the system in more optimistic terms than either of the lowers and uppers, rejecting the extreme views of the lowers' incompetence and the uppers' untrustworthiness. They resorted to systemwide ways of thinking about issues, using moral and ethical frameworks of persuasion.

The *lowers* responded to those above with suspicion and disbelief. They viewed the action of others as manipulative and self-serving, being uninfluenced by the moral persuasions of the middle group.

2. Use of information. How the three groups used information differed significantly.

The *uppers* used information withholding as a major way to force the middles and lowers to be dependent on them.

The *middles* used information sharing as the centerpiece of their system identity and as a method of developing a group power base.

The *lowers* used information withholding as one of their major protection devices to preserve group unity.

3. Modalities for dealing with external conflict. Each group developed a different way of coping in situations of conflict with other groups.

The *uppers* dealt with external conflict by becoming increasingly assertive, extrapunitive, and more dictatorial, withdrawing "privileges" and withholding authority necessary to implement delegated responsibilities.

The *middles* responded to external conflict by becoming more disoriented, indecisive, and impotent.

The *lowers* reacted to external conflict as a threat and accordingly increased their cohesion and commitment to their group unity.

4. Modalities for dealing with internal conflict. Each group handled conflicts within their own group in significantly different ways.

The *uppers* dealt with internal conflict by "critical mass" methods.

The *middles* used "common understanding" methods when torn by internal tension.

The *lowers* handled conflict within their ranks by using the "capitulation" method.

Part 3

Ashgrove

Ashgrove

Introduction

Having formulated, out of the experiences of Montville, some tentative images about how hierarchical intergroup processes operate, my quest led me to the point where I wanted to see whether similar dynamics were occurring in an ongoing social system with the same type of consequences. With this goal in mind I decided to look for an organization that had a number of clearly defined groups whose functions were explicitly and sharply delineated and that were embedded in an obvious hierarchy of administrative accountability. I thought immediately of a public school as a good possibility.

My search for an appropriate school system led me to Ashgrove, a small New England town that had its origins in a deep-rooted farming community. Culturally and ideologically it had been identified with Yankee protestant republicanism. But since the 1940s, influenced by the ever-increasing national mobility, Ashgrove had grown threefold and gradually been transformed into a Catholic-dominated township of democratic, conservative ilk with a significant proportion of the workers commuting to nearby larger industrial cities.

The social and political turbulence of this period meant that the town's public school system had likewise been going through significant phases of growth. Accordingly, it provided a natural and rich, real-life laboratory of dynamic intergroup processes and offered an ideal base for comparison with my Montville observations.

To keep the study manageable I resolved from the outset to restrict my investigation to the town's one high school together with the groups that formed the authoritative structure that overarched the school. The critical groups of interest to me, arranged hierarchically, were:

the public,
the town politicians and town administration,
the board of education,
the office of the superintendent,
the school principals,
the teachers, and
the students.

In my early days in Ashgrove,[7] as I searched for a structure that might help me synthesize what I was observing, one thing kept striking me. This was how unpredictable the behavior of the various groups seemed to be from situation to situation. It was different from Montville where the Elites mostly acted like uppers and the Outs like lowers. But here at Ashgrove, the opposite was emerging. Sometimes the board of education appeared controlled and unflustered, like typical uppers. At other times they looked chaotic, turbulent, and suspicious, like lowers—in fact very much like students.

I agonized for ages in my search for parallels between Montville and Ashgrove, until one simple thought struck me. I had failed to recognize that my upper-middle-lower framework was relative and not fixed. In hindsight, this was understandable, given that I'd developed it in Montville where there were only three major groups that had preserved their Elite, In, and Out status throughout. I shifted to thinking of the upper, middle, lower structure as relative and then the parallels between Montville and Ashgrove became self-evident. With this perspective on the school system, when the board of education was unflustered and controlled I could see how these behaviors were aligned with their relative position of upness with respect to the superintendent's office and the school principals as groups below them. When the board's behavior was suspicious and chaotic, it was easy to identify how they were lowers relative to the town politicians and the public above them.

After I made this conceptual shift of treating the upper, middle, lower framework as relative, by the mere arbitrary act of drawing organizational boundaries around a subset of the critical groups, I could view these groups from the specific vantage point of upper, middle, or lower positions. For example the principals were in an upper position when relating to the teachers and students, in a middle position between the superintendent's office and the teachers, and they were in a lower position with respect to the board of education and the superintendent's office.

By delineating the whole social system in this way it became possible to explore the interaction patterns among three key groups, the board of education, the superintendent's office and the principals, for each of the relative positions of upness, middleness, and lowness.

Table 1

Definition of Clusters for the Three Primary Groups in Each of the
Hierarchical Levels of Upness, Middleness, and Lowness

Viewing the *Board of Education* as the Primary Group

Relative Position			
Upper	*Board*	Politicians	Public
Middle	Superintendents	*Board*	Politicians
Lower	Principals	Superintendents	*Board*

Viewing the *Superintendent's Office* as the Primary Group

Relative Position			
Upper	*Superintendents*	Board	Politicians
Middle	Principals	*Superintendents*	Board
Lower	Teachers	Principals	*Superintendents*

Viewing the *Principals* as the Primary Group

Relative Position			
Upper	*Principals*	Superintendents	Board
Middle	Teachers	*Principals*	Superintendents
Lower	Students	Teachers	*Principals*

Given the clusterings represented in the above table, it is evident that the behavior of three groups, the board of education, the superintendent's office, and the high school principals, can be examined for the interactive configurations of each of the relative upper, middle, and lower positions while other groups (for example the students or the politicians) must be restricted to only one (lower) or two (upper and middle) positions respectively.

With this framework it is possible to see once again, although it is much more complex, the operation of the structural encasements, social comparison processes, and dynamic conservatism forces that we were attempting to make sense of in the Montville experience.

Table 2
Main Characters at Ashgrove

Politicians

Paddy Maloney	Town Mayor
The Factory	Chief Power Broker

Board of Education

Ron Kingston	Democrats—Chairman
Craig Hewett	
Mike D'Onofrio	
Matthew Lodell	
Luise Taylor	
Rodney Saunders	
Gerald Bomford	Republicans
Julia Langdon	
Reuben Kaufman	

Superintendent's Office

Dr. Eddie Rhodes	Superintendent
Don O'Sullivan	Assistant Superintendent
James Levine	Business Manager

Principals

Lewis Brook	Principal
Brendan Collier	Assistant
Peter Maher	Assistant
Bob Walder	Assistant

Others

Patrick Sheehan	Football Coach
Carlo Esposito	Opposition's Football Coach

And so I turn to Ashgrove. My purpose in this part of the book is to simply tell the Ashgrove story as best I can, exploring the extent to which the Montville images and the intergroup material we discussed in part 2 help us understand an ongoing everyday social system.

It's a Sticky Wicket

My first task was to establish contact with the school system and to attempt to negotiate a mutually agreeable way to go about doing my study. Since the phenomenon I wished to explore was concerned with how groups, with differential power, related within the context of a total organization it was eminently clear that how I entered the system would influence profoundly both the nature and quality of the information that would be made available to me and what crevices of the total organization I'd be granted access to. The hierarchical structure of the social system made it likely that if I made a successful overture to the board of education they had sufficient power, if they so wished, to virtually force the superintendents and the high school to participate in my desired study. But if the lower groups agreed only as an expression of compliance with the dictates of their superiors, I knew this would make the data I uncovered to be of dubious value since it was likely they'd tell me only things they'd be willing to have their bosses know about.

In addition, gaining entry involves crossing organizational boundaries. It would be a dreadful error to assume that once I'd crossed the external boundaries of the organization I would be sufficiently inside to pursue my objectives. That would be naively ignoring the myriad of internal boundaries that are equally critical, especially since the very concept of structural encasements between groups of unequal power delineates that there are very different boundary relations operating at the various levels of the hierarchy. Montville had taught me that to understand the inner operations of any two groups or their relationships with each other I must enter radically different mindsets. I must make myself fully available to absorb how each group uniquely understands itself and the forces it's subjected to from outside.

I resolved to attempt a multiple entry approach by contacting each group at more or less the same time and asking each to decide for itself whether it wished to participate. I felt that if I did anything other than this, I almost certainly would get trapped into one set of the organization's inner structural encasements and my study would be rendered ineffective from the outset. I made two principles pivotal in my approach: (a) each group was to have total autonomy to grant or refuse me entry without any possibility of repercussions from other parts of the system; (b) no group was to encourage or discourage other groups from participating, either directly through pressure or indirectly through implied sanctions. I calculated that this would force me to deal with each group on its own terms.

The first people I spoke to were the superintendents, Dr. Eddie Rhodes and his assistant Don O'Sullivan. They were intrigued with my ideas and Rhodes quickly indicated he'd be willing to support my studying the high school. I responded, "No, I must be clear. It's you who I want to study—that's all I'm asking from you. I'll approach the board and school separately." Rhodes and O'Sullivan were a little taken back. They'd never been approached this way before, but they caught on quickly to what I wanted to do and why I was beginning this way. They thought my chances were slim but were interested enough to say okay for themselves and that they'd not stand in the way of or encourage any other groups to participate.

As I left, Eddie Rhodes wished me good luck, assuring me "it'll be a sticky wicket." In all the years I've been in the United States I've heard that cricket phrase used often, but I've only ever met two Americans who really knew what it meant, although most use it accurately in its metaphoric sense. Rhodes was one of these two people and he immediately endeared himself to me as a result.

For all the other groups, except the students, I used rather standard procedures for establishing an agreement to proceed. It was hard but eventually I gained at least some acceptance from all groups, with people's reservations made explicit—or so I thought. I was very careful to point out that there could be both positive and negative outcomes for the system as a whole, ensured them of confidentiality of individuals' responses, and offered them feedback on my findings about how the groups interacted, and so forth.

Needless to say, each group dealt with my attempt to cross their boundaries by methods congruent with what their boundaries were like. The board wanted to check my credentials, wanted to know who was behind me, what type of prestige such a study would bring to the school system, and whether I would help solve what they referred to as the problem of communication in the schools. They never mentioned how effectively the board communicated with the schools. I felt a lot like I did when I talked to Montville's Elites and I suspected this was because I was tapping the board's upper encasement. With the superintendents, principals, and teachers, I sensed myself activating middle encasements. Dealing with each of these groups involved spanning a wide range of concerns eventually leading to an agreement that everyone seemed willing to accept though it was never fully clear to me what that agreement was. It was just like Montville's Ins.

Gaining entry to the student group proved to be very difficult. That was understandable since they were the lowest group in the structure; I expected I'd hit their lower encasements. They were a sufficiently diversified group for me to feel that no form of entry I'd read about in books seemed logical. Every alternative seemed problematic. If I were to arrange with a teacher to allow me to go into a classroom to hold an informal discussion, they would probably think of me as a teacher and filter out things they wouldn't tell teachers. If I were to be introduced by one of the principals, suspicions would be raised as to whether I was spying on the principal's behalf. There was the students' representative council, but everyone knows those councils are not very representative. No already established student body seemed ideal. It was clear there were many pitfalls to be avoided, yet to find an adequate alternative was hard. Just to walk up to a student, with role *in vacuo,* was difficult, for most teenagers are caught up with the hustle and bustle of doing their own thing, even if it's only sitting around and living out the youth culture or talking about the fact there's nothing to do. My major concern at this stage was to establish a contact with the students that would help me to get through the irregular facade and get meaningfully into the life of the students' culture.

While I was still thinking about what to do, I noticed there were three areas the students tended to hang out—in the courtyard, in the cafeteria, and in the bathrooms. Teachers were forever chasing students out of the bathrooms because this was where the major drug passing took place, so they said. The special attention given to the bathrooms by the teachers had made this space critical for the students.

The courtyard was where ninety percent of the cigarette smoking was done by students in the school. The official rule said there would be no smoking in school buildings. Students translated this literally, arguing that since the courtyard was not a building, the teachers could not stop them from smoking there. Not that there was much of a fight. The principals and teachers had given in quickly and tacitly approved smoking by simply never going into the courtyard themselves. If they had, they'd have gotten high. The marijuana in the air was thick. It was easiest to just stay away.

The other area the students considered their own was the cafeteria. It was a zoo. Lunch sessions were held every thirty-three minutes from 10:36 A.M. to 1:21 P.M. At the end of each session three hundred students would try to escape through two small doors while three hundred hungry students with equal energy tried to push their way in. On my first excursion into the cafeteria I noticed four teachers who were marching gestapolike around the perimeter, generally twenty paces behind each other. When I asked them what they were doing, they glibly replied "keeping control." This seemed a strange response given the degree of chaos that constantly reigned in the lunch hall. When I asked why they walked around the outside they said "it's too rough in there," pointing to the mass of students pressing, shouting, fleshconsuming, and throwing handfuls of french fries. "Would you go in there?" I saw their point. I asked them how effective they thought they were being as control agents.

"Not very!"

"Why do it then?"

"You have to have someone here in case a fight breaks out!"

"What would you do if a fight broke out?"

"Call an ambulance."

I laughed. They were serious.

One thing that was most clear to me was that if I were to enter the cafeteria for more than a short period, students would view this as some form of transgression on my part. There were strong student norms that made them feel most protective about their own space. It occurred to me that one way of gaining entry to the student population would be to violate these norms of keeping their territory sacrosanct and then negotiate with them, on their terms. Negotiations were certain to be difficult, maybe even impossible. But if I managed to survive the entry traumas, it seemed the chances would be reasonably good for me to develop adequate access to the realities of the students.

So on one rainy day I nervously marched into the cafeteria and sat down at a vacant table. My intention was to spend a few minutes casing out the place and just seeing what would happen. Scores of eyes that previously one might have guessed would be indifferent to anything around them, found a new puzzling focus. ME. It was clear to all that I wasn't a student, I was too old for that. I wasn't a teacher, I was too casually dressed for that. It appeared that having disposed of those two potential categories someone decided that I must have been some form of "enemy." Within a moment, one of the students had picked up a sloshy kernel of corn, left over from his lunch plate, and using it as a missle, collected my left ear with a sharp sting. I quickly developed two hypotheses as to what this meant. Either it was a random object in flight, which my ear had intercepted accidently—an unlikely possibility— or else I'd just learned one of the sanctions applied to breakers of the norms of the students' culture. I paused to see whether I could gather more data to confirm or deny either of my hypotheses. One of the joys of this type of research is that the social scientist doesn't have to go hunting for large periods of time for appropriate data; it generally emerges from the system with such obviousness that no statistical test of significance is necessary. Within seconds I'd received one such deluge of significant data. This time it came, not with the impact of one singular data point but rather with the bombardment of no less than fifty corn kernels, which left their impact from the top of my head to the base of my spine. This confirmed, without the slightest doubt, the appropriate hypotheses and I determined quickly to acknowledge with both a smile and a frown the direction from which the projectiles had come. I also concluded that nothing short of a major interactive attempt on my part would bring success to this venture, and with the added motivation of wanting to avoid a premature burial in corn kernels, I slipped quietly across to the nearest table of students and started talking.

I introduced myself, telling in two sentences what I was doing and asked if anyone at the table would be willing to answer a few questions for me. "Sure, let me introduce you to my buddy." I'd tell my story again, only to be introduced to yet another buddy. After I'd been passed around the table I got angry. "If you kids don't want to talk to me, just say so. But don't give me the run around. Is there anyone at this table who'll answer any of my questions?" "Sure Mister, we'll answer your questions, so long as you answer one question

150

first," retorted a cheeky voice from one fellow who would show me only his back. I was impressed with the reciprocity of this request and the deal was made.

Those students took off. I don't think I've ever been through such a third degree. They thought I was lying. What was extremely puzzling to me, however, was why this was happening. Towards what goal? It was clear that the students were "checking me out." My story about being a researcher interested in organizational psychology was clearly not believed. I quickly deduced that they considered this to be a cover story but I couldn't work out what they thought I was. A half hour later, after getting myself very emotionally bruised, it became clear to me what had been going on. They had thought I was a narcotics agent. No sooner had it occurred to me what this was all about, when one of the students began to open up as a sign of my having passed their test. Drugs became an immediate discussion topic and as the moments passed I began to feel more accepted. A major display of their acceptance of me came when one of the girls got up to leave, took me by the hand and said, "Come on, I'll take you into the girls' bathroom and show you how it all happens." At that moment I knew I was "in" and that my battle with these students was over.

During these early discussions I was quickly made aware of the geographical divisions of the students in the school cafeteria. In one region sat a group who characterized themselves as the dropouts—that was the group I had happened upon initially. At the far end, in one corner, were the jocks, in the other corner the collegiates. Their shorter hair and less energetic behavior confirmed their difference. In between were the marginals—the people who hadn't decided yet what they wanted to be. I felt that while I was at it, I'd attempt to get on speaking terms with another type of student. So I took off for the college-bound students.

They too put me through a grilling. They had similar suspicions that I might be a narcotics agent. However, they conducted their interrogation with greater sophistication and more precision, taking less time and leaving me feeling less bruised. Again I felt accepted in my researcher role when they willingly entered into a lengthy discussion on their own use of drugs, punctuated by light chatter about sports and girls for the moments the football coach, all two-hundred-fifty pounds of him, who was on patrol at that time, was within earshot.

The most overwhelming aspect of my early contact with the student body was that it opened up a way of understanding the realities of these teenagers that no other adult in the town had access to. For example, at that time and to this day, no principal, teacher, or Ashgrove adult will concede that the school system has ever been infiltrated by narcotics agents. I must concede that it is possible those adults are right, but I don't believe it. It may be those students were merely fantasizing, but I was the one who got grilled and they displayed

151

interrogation skills I'd never seen before and which I swear could only be developed by extensive and vigorous experience. Further, by so injecting myself into their subcultural norms, the students gave me insight into things like the geography of relations among the various student groups within the cafeteria, which I probably would have never thought to ask about if I'd encountered them in a more formalized way.

I guess if I had never been to Montville and seen the paranoia of a powerless group I may have assumed these students were just romanticizing or simply giving me a hard time for the sake of it. However, in this setting I chose to interpret that I had banged into and eventually learned how to penetrate the walls that constituted the lower encasement of the student group.

My entry to Ashgrove taught me three things that I promised myself to pay attention to for the remainder of my stay there. First, I, as a researcher, would get caught up in their intergroup dynamics and would forever be jostled by whatever structural encasements were active at the time. Second, having gained acceptance with each group by negotiating my way through the boundaries of one of its structural encasements gave me no guarantee that my agreement would hold up when another of their structural encasements became active. Therefore I would have to be willing to renegotiate my way in and out of events, over and over again. In other words, entry would never be over. It would always be an issue in some way or another. Third, I promised to remember that whenever there was conflict, there would also be powerfully different versions of reality and that I must constantly adopt a multifaceted approach. To this end I decided that whenever one group convinced me they were right and another group was wrong, I would immediately take off and stay with the adversary group until their version of reality seemed equally plausible.

Eddie Rhodes was right. It was a sticky wicket.

Budgetary Intrigue

Perhaps one of the most personally threatening aspects of my observations of Montville and the theoretical material I've been presenting is how easily reality seems able to be changed. If it is accurate that reality is so unstable then it seems to me that any knowledge we have is also very temporary and quite able to be fractured. I defended myself against accepting this idea with rationales such as: "Well Montville was not the real world;" or "It just hadn't adequately stabilized but when it did, reality would also get more secure." Of course I hoped that since Ashgrove was a reasonably stable system I would find social reality to be less precarious.

I had been somewhat prepared to discover that different groups saw the same event differently as was evident in my first encounter with the students. However, I was unprepared to be bombarded with so many examples of how easily a person in any regular organization seemed able to shift reality sets with virtually no awareness of doing this. I am going to tell here just one Ashgrove story to illustrate this. However, I could easily tell many such stories on all individuals and all groups in the school system. This one is about the superintendent, Dr. Eddie Rhodes.

There's a season every year when the board of education and superintendent answer to the town fathers for the accomplishments and failures of the educational system. These occur in the context of budget hearings. Ashgrove, like most small New England towns, has a type of participatory democracy. The town holds public meetings that form the basis of advice to the mayor and the mayor's staff on how to administer community services. All financial matters get filtered through a board of finance, six crusty old townfolks appointed by the mayor to act as conservative custodians of the town's fiscal matters. Late each spring they hold public budget hearings to scrutinize proposed educational expenditures. The procedure goes as follows. The elected board of education and the superintendent prepare a budget, which is submitted to the board of finance, who hold appropriate hearings and then forward it to an educational committee and a communal town meeting for either further reductions or approval. When all departments' budgets have been approved an appropriate tax rate is set.

It is evident that the board of finance holds a lot of power, which must be dealt with delicately. Since the sole purpose of its existence is to reduce expenditures by detecting unnecessary monies that have been padded into proposed budgets, it makes no sense to submit an unpadded budget, for they'll find a padded component come what may. Hence the process goes as follows: work out what you need; add a little extra; hide it; but make it sufficiently visible so that's what the finance board locates and throws out. The name of the game is hide it so it can be located with a struggle but don't make it so hidden it can't be found. There are sophisticated, informal rules to guide these processes and it doesn't make sense to deviate from them. For example, to submit an unpadded budget is like playing with fire. It's tantamount to telling the board of finance they have no important part to play in the financial matters of the town. That's equivalent to telling them they're redundant, a sure provocation for a battle. From the board of finance's perspective, every budget has a "padded component." They will find it, or if necessary create it.

Eddie Rhodes, as superintendent of schools, knew this procedural game. On each of the previous two years his budgets had been severely butchered, well beyond the padded component. Into the bargain, he had been caught in very tense exchanges between the board of finance and the board of education, and Rhodes had been made the whipping boy. In fact, he'd been subjected to so much abuse that this particular year he resolved to try to change the rules. His approach? Present a straight budget. Great folly!

In this setting Superintendent Rhodes and the school board were middles located between the board of finance as uppers and the school system in general as lowers. Rhodes played out middleness to perfection.

The board of finance meeting started with Dr. Eddie Rhodes being asked to speak on behalf of the board of education and present the rationale for their budget. He was called to the podium. In front of him was the board of finance, six sleepy old men sitting behind a long table. Behind him was a row of board of education members. Behind them were several rows of people euphemistically referred to as the public. In the back of the room there were several teachers who were members of the teachers' contract negotiating team.

Rhodes started. With a flourish he announced that they had decided this year to present a "straight" budget. The board of education was asking for no money that was not absolutely essential. He admitted that in previous years they'd asked for more than was necessary, "But in these days of fiscal limitation, it would be immoral for us to seek support for anything that was not totally critical." Rhodes presented a stirring address, filled with all the right rhetoric, drawing an occasional "hear, hear!" I've listened to a lot of sermons in my time, but this was one of the best. By the time he'd finished, every one of my guilt buttons had been pressed and I was convinced no one in Ashgrove would ever pad a budget again. The public also seemed taken in by him. However, the members of the board of finance were clearly not believing a word Rhodes was saying. They made faces conveying mock humor at the superintendent's "routine." In the back seat the teachers weren't even listening. With a fine-toothed comb they were delicately tearing the budget figures apart, looking for the monies they suspected had been padded into the budget to cover their proposed salary increases.

While I was still wondering what all this meant, Rhodes was cut off by one of the finance board members who wanted to complain about the way the budget was presented. He was aggressive. "I want to be able to compare this year's proposed budget with last year's proposed budget. You've given me the comparisons not with the proposed previous budget but the one actually approved after we'd made our reductions." In actuality, there was a simple way to make the comparisons, but for some obstinate reason he didn't want to have to do it that way. He interrupted the meeting for five minutes with procedural trivia, however, his concerns really had nothing to do with the way the carefully documented budget had been presented. Rather it had to do with establishing clearly in everyone's mind who were superiors and who were subordinates in this setting. He wanted to get the board of education and the superintendent into a defensive posture as part of a maneuver to expose the "inevitable pad", which Rhodes was claiming didn't exist.

Dr. Rhodes, well accustomed to this ritual, fought back, gently indicating that the budget had been presented in the form that he believed would best enable the board of finance to do its work and in keeping with the formats that had been satisfactory in previous years. However, he contritely acknowledged he'd be willing to change it to some other format if that were now more preferable.

154

Once this disagreement over the budget structure had stirred some conflict, the aggressive finance member became highly conciliatory, indicating "perhaps I was being overzealous in my criticisms; it seems to me that the system is improving in that our two boards are understanding each other better this year." This whole exchange had a patronizing air and certainly forced Rhodes into the double bind of having to be contrite or aggressively reactive, either way boosting the finance board's sense of its power.

The next hour passed with Rhodes and education board chairman Kingston defending why so many increases were necessary. Everything they said was followed by probes calculated to embarrass or to discredit. Most of the attacks were trivial and diversionary, rarely with substantive thrust, but always with the psychological impact of diffusing the potency of any argument as to why extra education money was needed. The general orientation of the board of finance seemed fixated on "We don't believe what you're telling us and we'll use every trick in the book to try to find out where the budget pad is."

The finance board, as uppers, were clearly not believing what the middles were saying. They kept stirring up conflict and then blaming the superintendent and the board of education for not being more competent. Every time the middles found some leverage, the uppers turned it back on them trying to drive them into an impossible corner.

Soon after the substantive material of the budget had been dealt with, one board of finance member opened up what promised to be a chaotic debate. He asked what the board of education proposed to do about the salary increases that would flow from the contract negotiations that were going on with the teachers. He noted that no additional money had been added into the budget to cover these anticipated additional expenses. Education chairman Ron Kingston replied that they had deliberately left them out since the negotiations stood at a very delicate point. He argued that "any public declaration of what we, as a board, expect to have to pay would be tantamount to making an explicit offer. For strategic reasons we determined we would not do this at this time."

The difficulty for the town financial processes was one of timing. For months the board of education and teachers had been negotiating a new salary agreement. It would probably take several more months before a settlement would be reached. For weeks, everything had been deadlocked with teachers demanding twelve percent increases while the board of education were offering two percent. Privately, the board had resolved to go up to five percent but no higher. However, strategy determined that they had to get the teachers down to about eight or nine percent before the board made a firm five percent offer. Then an arbitrated settlement would probably come in, splitting the difference at around six to seven percent. The town could tolerate that. However, it would be months before it could be finalized as to what additional monies would be needed. The problem was the town property tax rate for the next year which by law had to be set the next week. It was a perfect Catch 22. The board of finance clearly would have to make a guess as to what a final settlement might be in order to set an appropriate tax rate. However, this would have to be kept secret otherwise the board of education's strategic position would be totally undermined in their contract negotiations. Yet this secrecy had to be kept super secret, for the town of Ashgrove ran its government on the basis of public and open hearings and meetings.

For the moment, the finance and education boards were in a fix. Here they were in a public hearing and they couldn't talk about the fact they had to keep certain secrets because the public was present. As with most things there was a ritual to deal with this. Very subtly, the issue was sidestepped by Rhodes and the education board agreeing to wait around till after the hearing had ended to meet with the board of finance in its executive session, when the public would not be present.

The secret executive session was started off by an assault by one of the finance board. "We're going to have to work together to sort this problem out. I hope you can see what a difficult position we're in as a result of not having your predictions for salary increases that will flow from the new teachers' contracts. I want to know why you didn't have the sense to estimate them and include them in the budget."

"We've told you why we didn't do that," replied Kingston. "Because it would clue in the teachers about the increases we're going to give them."

"I didn't mean that you should have an item in there called 'increases in salaries' but you sure could have helped us out if you'd padded your budget to cover those expenses."

Eddie Rhodes smiled. "How could this man, the great detector of the 'budget pad', be suggesting we should have attempted to hide some money there?" He was determined to score some points. "We decided it would be most inappropriate to try to hide money in there—first, because it would be unethical" (faint smile) "and we've been most determined to play these financial issues with you straight; second, if we'd hidden money in there you'd have been sure to find it anyway in the probings we've just gone through and then the information would be public. What's more, we attempted that two years ago and got accused of trying to get the same money twice."

"Yeah, I know, I know! Okay, well, we're going to have to work this out together. We're going to have to help each other over this hurdle if we're to get it straightened out."

At this point the upper-middle distinction between the two groups began to disappear. Everyone relaxed. The powerful public preorchestration of both boards disappeared. They stopped behaving aggressively. Cans of beer were opened. They no longer were Dr. Rhodesing and Mr. Chairmaning each other. Now it was Bill, Eddie, Ron, etc.

For the next hour the boards of finance and education, together with Eddie Rhodes, acted like classic Elites. They plotted and schemed. They came up with several potential solutions all of which involved "budget padding." In the final analysis the town would have to hide the increases somewhere and only a portion could be slipped into the education budget. From their point of view the major problem was how to keep everything under the table. Eventually, they produced a solution that read like a crossword puzzle: $25,000 was to be padded into the sewerage budget; $10,000 into the police budget; $15,000 into public works, etc. Politically it promised to be a fine solution. The problem was it was highly illegal. If they had been caught they'd have probably gone to jail. However, not a soul, Eddie Rhodes included, raised a single word of objection. This was not only unethical, by Rhode's standards of four hours before, it was also illegal; but in this setting no one was concerned with questions about "not playing the game straight," or "the immorality of padding the budget." The two boards cordially parted company for the evening, with the education group pleased by their efforts and reasonably confident they would get most of the money they asked for.

The budgetary events created no further ripples in Ashgrove that year. The teachers' salary money was eventually effectively padded into other departments' budgets, no one got caught for illegal actions, and the teachers, months later, settled for five percent increases.

Probably the only person who got really disturbed through all of this was me. I became captivated by the question of whether Superintendent Rhodes had any insight as to how easily he'd switched from his highly moralistic posture about the budget padding when he was a middle to being a willing accessory to illegalities when he was an upper, all in the space of a few brief hours. He seemed to have no consciousness that his behavior had been inconsistent. Several months later I talked with him about my observation. He replied and I believed him, "My God, Ken, I can see what you're talking about when you put it like that. I want you to know, however, that this is the first time it's ever occurred to me that my behavior that night was remotely inconsistent."

In this little event in Ashgrove I was intrigued by how much relevance the theoretical images developed from Montville seemed to have. First, it was clear that people and groups could, quite unknowingly, shift reality sets just as easily as happened in Montville. Secondly, the groups spent a lot of effort posturing in order to develop solid power bases, with the middles resorting to overarching concepts like morality while the uppers were making it clear they intended to call the shots. Third, while the middles got carried away with their appeal to transcendent concepts such as social ethics, neither uppers nor lowers believed them. Each polar group saw the presentational format of the middles as merely a ritual to be ignored. Fourth, secrecy played a big part. The board of education and superintendent were claiming to be open and honest while talking out of their middle mouths. However, they were quite blatant

157

about being closed and secretive when in an upper perspective, both in keeping from the teachers their intent to offer a salary settlement of five percent and when they moved into "padding money into the budget" with the board of finance.

Armed now with the conviction that my theoretical image about relationships among groups of differential power had as much relevance for Ashgrove as for Montville, I proceeded to look systematically into the town's school system.

Early Struggle

I felt that in order to have an appreciation for the Ashgrove of today I needed some historical perspective. After asking a few simple questions it was clear to me that one central problem dominated how people understood the previous decade of this New England school system. The focus had been made where the ninth grade should be located. For many years, Ashgrove had ached and groaned its way through a number of decisions, then reversals, followed by reversals of the reversals, in an attempt to impregnate the school structure with the most ideal format. The turbulence of Ashgrove's transition from a stabilized farming community to a growing satellite middle class residential area had excessively stressed the community's educational structures. In the early 1960s it had been obvious that more schools would be needed. Originally, the situation was simple. The town required a new junior high school immediately and a second senior high school about a decade later. The difficulty was that the picture had become clouded by educational innovations that suggested that open-spaced classrooms would be the prototype of the future and that the junior high concept of a school for grades seven and eight should be replaced by a middle school that spanned levels five to eight.

The fiscally conservative town fathers, wanting to postpone spending their money until the very last moment, had procrastinated as long as possible by fanning disagreements over what type of school structures and what grade alignments should be adopted and using these disagreements as an effective stalling device. By the end of the 1960s the overcrowding situation had become desperate. Action had to be taken. Accordingly, the town elected Paddy Maloney, who had been chairman of the board of education for twenty years, to Ashgrove's mayoral seat, with the explicit charge to pump some much-needed adrenalin into the atrophying school system.

The town entered into a period of feverish planning, resulting in a resolve to develop the ideal school system, escalating the originally projected costs from three million to nine million dollars. New industry was attracted to the area to provide an additional source of taxes that would compensate for this increase in expenditure, thereby saving the townsfolk from additional economic pressures. The possibility of a new middle school was moved from fantasy to potential reality.

During this time of initial high activity, someone had the foresight to pause long enough and ask the board of education an awkward question. "What grades and how many students will we try to house in this new facility?" "What's the matter?" retorted somebody, impatient with the prospect of procrastination. "Let's build a school and make it flexible so that we can house any cut from fifth to ninth grades." The word flexible had a musical appeal. "For nine million dollars we should be able to buy flexibility as well as classroom space." This logic seemed irrefutable at the time. However by the fall of 1969 a decision on grade alignments had to be taken. A lengthy and vigorous debate and a lot of corridor politicking had produced a resolution—the middle school would house grades five through eight, the high school grades nine through twelve. That left one problem, overcrowding in the senior high school. As a temporary solution the board of education decided to renovate the old junior high school, making it an annex to the high school until they could build a second complex that everyone agreed would be needed by the mid 1970s.

In reviewing the history of the grade alignment battle I came to see theoretically perhaps the most potent aspect of how hierarchical relationships among groups of differential power shaped the structure of each group's realities and in turn their actions in the system. What I saw was how each group could simultaneously be a middle, upper, and lower. In particular I came to recognize how a group experiencing itself as caught in the middle could, without any realization that this was happening, be experienced by other groups as acting from either an upper or lower perspective.

Once I came to appreciate how subtly but significantly the upper, middle, lower framework could shift from situation to situation, and even from one phase to another phase within the same situation, then I was both overwhelmed and excited by how similar Ashgrove seemed to Montville.

On the history of the grade alignment battle it was easy to understand the board of education's behavior when I looked at them as middles sandwiched between the schools as lowers and the town politicians and tax-paying public as uppers. In classical middle fashion they seemed to have given birth to some creative ideas and then found themselves unable to make the major decisions necessary to transform their blueprints into reality. Their original problem had been school overcrowding and an obsolete junior high school building. To cope with this, they had designed a nine-million-dollar middle school but done it in such a way that they still had to renovate a decrepit school building and make it into a cumbersome annex to the overcrowded high school simply in order to get by. The board of education, like the middles at Montville, seemed to have dealt with their central problem of overcrowding by a series of patchwork solutions destined in the long run to create as many problems as they eliminated.

In looking at the board as middles it made sense that they would change their minds over and over as they were buffeted by the political storms around them. Hence it was not surprising to find these years filled with vacillations.

The fall of 1970 had brought with it the hope that the new nine-million-dollar intermediate school would be functioning within the year, but construction had fallen behind schedule and each passing day added a little extra tension to an already anxious board of education. The town fathers had begun to feel the political squeeze at the massive outlay of educational money and in response had started to ask aloud as to whether a second high school was absolutely necessary. It occurred to them that if only the board of education had designed the new intermediate school for grades five through nine instead of five through eight, the pressure of overcrowding on the senior high would have been lifted and the town might in the long run avoid having to build a second high school and thereby save ten million dollars.

The town politicians, angry that the expenditure of all this money would not solve all the educational problems, decided to act. They resolved to force the board of education and the superintendent's office to shift the ninth grade out of the high school into the new intermediate school. They calculated that this would alleviate the overcrowding and spread the benefits of the innovative middle school across a larger number of students, bringing with it the corollary political dividends. For the politicians, who could be seen as uppers in this situation, this solution seemed perfect. However, they lacked critical information. Hence, not surprisingly, this realignment solution contained the seeds of its own destruction. The politicians had failed to recognize that the elementary sector also needed radical overhauling. For years, the population pressure on the lower schools had demanded the use of obsolete buildings and church halls, many of which had proved to be educationally unsatisfactory. This was one reason the new middle school had been required. However with the promise of relief, the elementary schools had stopped complaining so the politicians had forgotten the desperateness of their need. The major complaints had been coming from the high school, so the politicians figured that this was the group in greatest need. The reality was that the whole school system was hurting.

The new middle school could alleviate either the elementary chaos or the senior high crowding. It could not do both. However the politicians, failing to recognize this reality, blindly plotted to scheme for a grade realignment.

The moment the politicians' (upper) plans became clear, there was a loud public outcry that was strong enough to jar the politicians into a middle position. With the public suddenly provoked into action thereby activating a more powerful force above them, the politicians gravitated towards a typically middle reaction of placation, offering a token gesture as a solution. They decided to rapidly construct a classroom extension at the high school to accommodate an additional two hundred students. This seemed to work, at least from the politicians' perspective, for their opposition became temporarily muted. Fooled by the meaning of this silence, the town fathers slipped back into an upper position and unilaterally decided, after a respectable period, to once again set in motion their realignment scheme. Little did they realize that the whole school system was sitting on a volcano that was waiting for a final catalyst before erupting. The realignment plan was destined to become that catalyst.

Ashgrove's politicians chose a board of education meeting in October 1970 to refloat their realignment scheme. For their mouthpiece they picked two Democratic board members who had ears closest to the voices of the town fathers to formally move to have grades six through nine housed in the new middle school, not the originally planned grades five through eight. This was a simple act, designed to test the prevailing reaction among other board members and in the community at large. However it detonated an explosion, fueled by years of repressed anger, that was to become a fight that would last several years, claim numerous battle casualties, and leave scar tissue to haunt Ashgrove's educational system for the next decade.

That evening the board room became the scene of suppressed tempers as intellectual muscles were sharpened for the exchanges that lay ahead. Some of the Democrats had got a clear message from the "Factory," the headquarters of the town political king, as to how they should vote. But they were cautious about blindly obeying the dictates of the town's master manipulator, for even if one's opinion were similar to that of the "Factory," it was important to avoid all possibility of being labelled his puppet. Superintendent Rhodes and Assistant Superintendent Don O'Sullivan, in coalition, were taking a firm position. They were adamant that the middle school should house grades five through eight.

The scene looked fearsome. Within minutes of the removal proposal being floated, the room erupted. The public and board members became so angry they started to shout at each other. Rather than risk civil war, the board quickly backed off by deciding to table the proposal and debate it at a later date. This was a standard technique in Ashgrove. Whenever anything got too hot, the strategy was to postpone it and then work out a preorchestrated decision that could pass through the public political machinery smoothly. Hence, the spirit behind the postponing of the realignment motion was to allow time to orchestrate the planned change with minimal "bloodshed." A hollow dream!

The interval between that October evening and the first November board meeting was characterized by a frenzy of emotional attacks. Coalitions began to form. Irrationality raged rampantly and the political corridors became ablaze with traditional trade-offs and bargaining exchanges. It was not until the first battle casualty was claimed that anyone was shocked into asking, "What are we doing to ourselves?" And what a price the town had to pay! In the midst of a vigorous and public debate with a group of four hundred parents over a school issue, with emotions intensified by the grade alignment fever, the high school principal, John Meadow, found himself stressed to the limits of physical and psychological tolerance. In the middle of this public argument he suffered a massive and premature heart attack and died.

At the dawn of a new day, dragging hearts heavy with guilt, burdened with fear and disoriented with uncertainty, the town paused to bury its leading educator and to confront another crisis, the finding of a new principal.

The shock of Meadow's death dulled Ashgrove's creative reserves. For the immediate they resolved to merely elevate one of their two assistant principals to the vacant role on a temporary basis. Then the only decision they had to make immediately was which assistant to appoint. In one way the obvious choice was Brendan Collier, the more senior of the two. On the other hand, Lewis Brook, a younger man, promised more energy and stability for he conceivably could serve as principal for many years ahead. Brendan saved the board of education the agony of needing to make a decision by indicating he was not willing to step into the principal's role under any conditions. So on a hollow Monday evening, the board of education drafted Lewis Brook for the job, gave it to him on an acting basis, and preserved for a clearer day a long-term decision.

I anticipated that after Meadow's death finding a new permanent principal would have been the board of education's top priority. It so happened I was wrong. I was expecting that the board and the superintendent would have felt a sense of upper responsibility to act quickly in consolidating their middle group (in this case the high school principals) in order to keep the activities of the lowers (teachers and students) flowing smoothly. I also expected that the board would have been shocked to their senses over their collusion as middles with their uppers (the town politicians) and recognize how unproductive their participation in the grade realignment schemes was proving to be. This didn't happen either.

The board seemed blind. For a whole month they simply ignored the principal's situation. To my mind this upper facet of their function was so critical it should have been their top priority. Instead they returned to the preoccupation of their own middleness, namely the grade realignment where they were caught between the town politicians and the school system as a whole. As middles they continued to behave indecisively. For two board meetings held every other week, grade realignment was debated and retabled with no resolution.

Each time a potential vote was to be taken, it became clear that four votes would be cast for the grade five through eight structure and four votes for a six through nine format. Such a deadlocked situation would demand a tie-breaking vote from the Democratic chairman, Ron Kingston, who was always reticent to use his tie-breaking power for his own personal reasons. He knew that when the board was so precariously divided this represented accurately a reflection of the deeply felt divisions that existed in the Ashgrove community at large. There Kingston was professionally vulnerable. He was a prominent local lawyer and depended on not alienating his clients. He feared that if he took sides on an explosive and polarized educational issue, his law practice could easily be placed in jeopardy with half his clientele. He knew the balance of forces on grade realignment was overwhelmingly precarious. Hence from his point of view it made most sense to postpone the decision and try to orchestrate a resolution that enabled him to never have to take a public stand on the subject. For ages Kingston had refused to be publicly drawn into the realignment controversy. The tie vote was being created by one Democrat repetitively voting with the Republicans, and it made most sense to Chairman Kingston to try to force that Democratic member to vote with the rest of the party than for him to have to pay a high professional price for breaking the deadlock. Each time a deadlock vote emerged, Ron Kingston pushed his fellow board members to postpone the decision to buy time for a further preorchestration attempt.

In Ashgrove the standard ploy for effecting such a delay was to request the superintendent undertake another study such as calculate population trends by an alternative technique or conduct another financial analysis that differed trivially from previous investigations. The content of the request was usually unimportant. The process was what was critical. It was set up to provide an escape, albeit temporary, from the board's inner tensions. In other words, when the board, as a group of middles, was torn by its own inner tension, it attempted to get rid of these tensions by moving into a constellation of relations where the board members were uppers and then transforming their within-group conflict into between-group conflict. Mostly they carried out this operation by engaging the superintendent's office in a particular manner. They would present their group's inner tension as an academic problem, which needed more information to resolve (a typically middle orientation). However they delegated the task of obtaining this information to the superintendent (a typically upper act). In the process the board members made their request for a further study sufficiently ambiguous that no matter what Superintendent Rhodes or his staff came up with it would be unsatisfactory. From the board's point of view it would be inadequate *because* it didn't provide a way for members as uppers to solve their inner conflicts, conflicts that in essence were really middle conflicts that the board was struggling with because it was caught between the polarities of the town politicians and the school system in general.

When once the board was able collectively to define the report of Superintendent Rhodes and his staff as inadequate, then the board was able to experience itself in agreement (i.e., its inner tensions for the moment were gone) about its being in conflict with the superintendent's office. Instead of having to focus on its own within-group tension the board could turn its attention to the between-group conflict that it had helped create. In addition because the board was in an upper position and caught in the propensity to see problems as the fault of others, it also would dismiss the problem it was then encountering with the superintendent as being due to his incompetence.

163

By this sequence of procedures the board would have transformed its inner conflict into between-group conflict and in turn transformed the between-group conflict into a dual attribution. First, the conflict instead of being within the board was with the superintendent's office. Second, the conflict was Rhodes' fault.

I should add in passing that the way I've been talking about this dynamic implies that the board of education was knowingly carrying out its operations with the intent of making the superintendent appear incompetent in order to hide from its own problems. I don't think it worked that way. The board, like all groups, was simply paying attention to some things and ignoring others, and this side of its actions was a blind spot. It fell into the shadows of the upper-middle relationship of the board and superintendent's office.

Despite numerous attempts to stall and preorchestrate a negotiated solution on the grade alignment deadlock, it eventually became obvious to everyone that the board of education was becoming paralyzed and the school system was being torn apart. Hence as the battle reescalated, the town political chiefs again decided to seize the upper position and act. They conceded that their timing had been inappropriate when they made their original realignment proposal; however they were quick to point out that their timing was off because others had kept from them critical information. They were arrogant enough to claim that their interventions to date had been fine in spirit, thereby preserving the self-proclaimed right to meddle when it suited them. These politicians knew they had the power to win the realignment issue but they feared it would be at too high a price. Nevertheless they were not willing to back down entirely. They made a compromising move.

At the next board of education meeting, two of the board members— lackeys of the political puppeteers—floated a thinly disguised and poorly reasoned proposal. In essence it was to place only grades six through eight in the new intermediate school and leave the high school unaltered. The irrationality of this move was obvious. It meant that not only would the elementary and high schools remain overcrowded but the new, intermediate facility would be grossly underutilized, an intolerability given the previous arguments of the town politicians. The political folly of this attempt was its transparency. Everyone could see clearly that at the opportune moment of surprise, when the opponents' backs were turned, the town Democrats would plan to slip the ninth grade out of the high school and into the middle school, thus achieving their original objective.

Outraged at the manipulativeness of this ploy of the Democratic town fathers, the three Republican members of the nine-person board of education indicated their determination to fight this issue to the bitter end. These three Republicans had always sided with what they labelled as the progressive educational forces in the town and had been outspokenly in favor of the five through eight grade alignment. In this they had been supported by both Superintendents Rhodes and O'Sullivan and they felt convinced they could get

164

one Democrat to "defect" and vote against the town bosses' dictates. These Republicans used great procedural skill. They amended and tabled and reamended and untabled and retabled the original motion so many times that only they could finally sort out what was happening. They also pulled off guilt induction routines of extraordinary finesse, seducing one Democrat and eventually Chairman Ron Kingston to vote on their side, sealing a five to four voting victory in favor of the middle school retaining grades five through eight. Against all odds, the town political bosses were defeated in this the second round of the grade alignment battle. However in the process a series of forces were activated that were to reverberate constantly through the political and educational system in the months ahead.

In reflecting on the history of the grade alignment debate to date it was clear how the middles—in this case mostly the board of education and the superintendent's office—had been torn by internal tension, vacillating between the polarized political tensions of those above and below. Likewise the town politicians and the board when in the upper location had displayed the characteristic structural encasement of being blind to the consequences of their behavior and aggressively blaming others when conflict with middles and lowers had produced outcomes contrary to their own liking. The lowers—in this situation, the schools and occasionally the superintendent's office—had remained steadfastly resistant during this period, each being very clear that their unanimous and unifaceted concern was that the politicians come up with the money to upgrade the rapidly deteriorating educational facilities. The board of education's middle encasement was expressed in numerous ways, not least of which was a very visible internal paralysis. They'd have characterized their vigorous and feverish activity as "*decision making.*" From an observer's perspective, however, their behavior looked more like "*decision avoiding.*" Their repetitive postponements, their constant request for more studies to be conducted so that the best possible decision could be made, their political negotiations in corridor conversations designed to preorhestrate decisions, looked mostly like system paralysis. A lot was happening, but at the same time, nothing was happening.

It was also fascinating to me that soon after the town politicians had been defeated on the grade alignment issue, for a while, like classic uppers, they became very vindictive. They seemed to need a scapegoat and made the superintendent, Eddie Rhodes, the target of their attack.

For several weeks, from dark crevices of Ashgrove's complex political networks, attack after attack was launched on Rhodes, culminating in the following bitter sentiments in the *Ashgrove Courier.*

> If this is what we can expect from our school administrators, Dr. Rhodes and his top level advisors can all take their leave immediately. They don't even have to say goodbye, just fold their tents and steal quietly into the night.

Looking at it all from another point of view, it was also possible to picture the town politicians as middles caught between two opposite sides of the public, the side that wanted to keep taxation low and the side that also wanted to have a good school system. In Ashgrove at this point of its history these two sides tended to be two large coalitions of people each of which took just one perspective as its own and attacked those who took the other. This external battle was in many ways a public playing through of tensions that resided within each member of Ashgrove. Almost everyone, in reality, had a fiscally conservative side and an educationally progressive side. However with the battle raging publicly, individuals tended to pay attention to only one side of their inner tensions by participating in the external fight, denying that they shared as much inner investment in the position their opponents were battling to win. Such tensions of equal force are destined to move towards a deadlocked position. It's the very fact that we all feel so deadlocked about such forces internally that feeds our investment in having a resolution generated externally. However we transport our inner investment in the deadlock into an outer domain, so it's not surprising that the resolution is just as hard there also. If we concede this point, then it is possible to look at Ashgrove's politicians and see them as middles caught between the countervailing forces of both these facets of the community upon whom they were dependent for their legislative mandate; they were encased in the precarious task of trying to keep contradictory forces simultaneously happy. From this vantage point it is understandable why the political bosses appeared indecisive, manipulative, and inconsistent, all images typical of middleness.

Positions Vacant

For years I've been interested in two theoretical issues that had seemed quite separate to me until I went to Ashgrove. The first of these is the Freudian concept of repetition, which intrapsychically can be thought of simply as a propensity to behave in any situation similarly to the way one has behaved in that situation previously. Interpersonally the notion of repetition can best be understood in concert with the concept of transference. This is our tendency to relate to another person in a similar manner to a prior relationship, most commonly a parental figure, either transferring to that person attributes of the parental figure (or whoever is being identified with) or transferring to the current relationship the unresolved tensions of the previous relationship. The second issue is contained in the popular idea of history tending to repeat itself. Each of these issues is important but at a surface level neither is really complex nor hard to understand for any social theoretician.

After exploring Ashgrove's grade alignment battles I found myself thinking about these two issues side by side. In particular I wondered whether the unresolved conflicts of the grade alignment struggles would merely get transferred into and played out in another historical event or whether the various groups who'd been party to the battles would learn of and from these struggles and formulate alternative ways of dealing with the conflicts, maybe even transforming them into something constructive.

The answer to this question was easy to find in the story of how the school system dealt with the selection of new principals for the high school.

It was more than six weeks since principal John Meadow had died. There was a pressing need to attend to the problem of the high school principal. Lewis Brook had been waiting anxiously either for confirmation as principal on a permanent basis or the freedom to return to his assistant role. As it so happened the board of education had no stomach for undertaking a national search at this time. So with little thought and no public debate, but with the decision carefully preorchestrated behind the scenes, they moved to appoint Lewis as permanent principal. The town bosses gave Brook the appointment with a solid vote of confidence, but the job had a price. He was told he would have to be more tough minded than his predecessor John Meadow, although they were not explicit about what being tough meant in this role of principal in a school they also wanted to consider as progressive. For some, it meant that students should be whipped, at least psychologically, for failure to live by this township's standards, which teenagers universally considered to be outmoded. For others it meant that they should pursue a vigorous educational program encouraging that the social environment of the school complex both mold and be molded by the evolutionary developments in which the youthful generation were caught. For yet others it meant that the principal should provide an efficient babysitting institution that would insure that the young folk were off the street, out of sight, and away from trouble.

Members of the community had strong and diverse ideas about what they wanted in a school and clearly hoped they could all be achieved simultaneously. Hence, it was built in that no matter what the principal and his assistants did, they were certain to be praised by some and criticized by others. To be tough from one perspective by definition made him weak by another. Hence, Lewis had little alternative but to learn to live with the inherent conflicts of middleness in which he usually found himself caught.

This was an anxious time for him. The deceased principal's papers took weary hours to peruse, file, or dispose of and the public's agitation was still so high that vultures were sitting ready to pounce on any folly.

His initial tasks as principal were difficult. In the immediate, it was necessary to make a quick-acting appointment to the vacant position of assistant principal. He looked cursorily around his staff to find someone with a reasonable level of seniority and experience who at the time had a light teaching load and who could be drafted with minimum disruption to the school.

The one person who met these criteria best was Bob Walder, senior English teacher, baseball coach, and coordinator of English for the junior high and senior high programs. Bob had been a most successful teacher, was well known for his published high school text material, and had a great rapport with students and teachers alike. Brook made a quick and automatic appointment, hardly even thinking about whether he wished to endorse Walder as a candidate for the position on a permanent basis. Had Brook thought about his actions in endorsement terms, Walder may not have been given the position. However this was the last thing in his mind at that time, for all he wanted to do was return the school to a quick equilibrium.

In order to select a new assistant principal, a committee of Superintendents Rhodes and O'Sullivan and Lewis Brook was appointed. They were to make a recommendation to the board of education who would, by state statute, either ratify the nomination or reject it. They could only appoint someone recommended by the selection committee. Thus if we looked at these groups from my hierarchial framework, the board was upper, the committee middle, and the assistant principal candidates were lowers. In the events that unfolded all three types of structural encasements were evident, the uppers being blind to what they were doing, the lowers attempting to resist what was being done unto them, with the middles perpetually torn.

As the selection process started an unexpected debate occurred. For some time there had been rumblings in the Republican and liberal quarters of the town that suggested a third assistant principalship at the high school should be created. This idea had never been taken seriously but in the guilt-stirred atmosphere after Meadow's death it surfaced as a formal proposal at the meeting of the board of education after Brook's appointment had been confirmed. The Republicans wanted a third assistant principalship established because, they argued, the administrative load of running Ashgrove high school had become very onerous and the town could not afford to run the risk of overstretching Lewis Brook as they had John Meadow. In addition, the Republicans claimed that there was need for new blood in the system and in particular they were eager to hire a woman assistant principal.

The Democrats responded to this proposal with outrage. They took the position that it was fiscally irresponsible and bureaucratically expansionist. They also rejected the idea that new blood was needed in the system, resolving to select a new assistant principal from the current teachers in the system. Their stance was summarized by one of the Democrats, who argued "We have some really good quality *men* in the school now, and I see no reason why we should bring in someone from outside to supercede these people. That would be bad for morale."

Recruitment procedures were initiated. The selection committee was instructed to choose one candidate from amongst the current Ashgrove teachers and recommend *him* to the board of education for appointment as the new assistant principal.

Within the high school itself there was much speculation as to who would be likely candidates and who would receive the much coveted support of the principal. Peter Maher, director of vocational education in the high school, was one potential candidate. He was a large-framed, jolly, and extremely out-going man who was involved in almost every club and community project in Ashgrove and loved and was loved for his activities. He enjoyed his contact with students and genuinely had their interests at heart, particularly those who found little meaning or motivation in the highly competitive, academic courses. Peter wanted to be an assistant principal, however he was eager to avoid the embarrassment of being rejected. He decided to talk to Brook. He was not fool enough to seek his endorsement but if the principal viewed him as totally unsuitable for the position, he wanted to know it. Brook liked Maher, had enjoyed contact with him, and although he'd had limited administrative experience, Lewis Brook encouraged him to apply.

Bob Walder, presently acting assistant principal, was a clear applicant as were a number of other senior teachers in the school.

Rhodes, O'Sullivan, and Brook set to the task of interviewing the candidates, finding four of them to be acceptable. Maher was everyone's number one choice. So he became the natural nominee of the committee. However, while they'd been going through the selection process, it was brought to the attention of Superintendent Rhodes that there was a reasonable amount of support in the town for Bob Walder, and it had been suggested that maybe some consideration should be given to this factor. The problem was that Walder had interviewed very poorly and had ended up in fourth position. So even if political considerations were to be contemplated, as might have been consid-ered justifiable if the selectors could not discriminate between the first two candidates, they clearly were rejected as irrelevant in this case.

At the first January board meeting in 1971, Superintendent Rhodes re-ported that the selection committee had completed its task and that it was recommending Peter Maher to the vacant position.

However, the backdrop to this particular board meeting had become highly confused. Over recent days, news had been leaked that Maher was to be given the nomination and while there was no one specifically opposed to him, there was a strong community lobby for Walder. Both candidates had kept distant from this lobbying, though naturally they were intensely anxious about the outcome. Walder had a national reputation for his contribution to education; as a baseball coach with a good record he'd developed great rapport with students and he carried the image of being a strong disciplinarian. Those who spoke *for* him focused on these issues as his strengths. Those who spoke *for* Maher leaned heavily on his capacities in vocational education and his good relations with industry and townsfolk. Phones rang hot for days. Super-intendent Rhodes, who'd developed an image of being less than malleable in such political situations, received only a dribble of calls, but Assistant Su-perintendent O'Sullivan, more identified with the town's covert activities, was plagued to death, as were several board members. Their dilemma however, was that even if they were willing to be influenced by the town folks, the pres-sure was approximately equal for both Maher and Walder.

Democratic board member Craig Hewett was the leader of those supporting Walder. He was still smarting over having lost in the recent grade realignment battle, having thrown his weight behind the wishes of the town fathers. In these times of political confrontation, he was not about to lose again. What's more, he had the political skill to win.

Craig was a friend to everyone. He had the capacity to converse with all the extremes of the community. He could hold his own with both the little old lady on the street and the eloquent professional. He was effervescent. He found it easy to generate a lighthearted atmosphere and to imbue any situation with a resonance of its own. A few minutes with Craig Hewett usually was therapeutic, even when he was vehemently disagreeing with you. Hewett was willing and able to defend his position on virtually all issues. And he did it with color. When it came to the topic of school discipline, he was particularly vigorous. "I'm very concerned about the way the high school schedules classes and the lack of control of the staff," he would say. "Worst of all I think we're unfortunately drifting along with the country as a whole in an ultra-liberal approach. One problem with the current operation of the school is that the kids have too many choices and too much free time. That can become tantamount to inadequate direction. Most children in the high school age group need direction. They particularly need something specific to do. Never put a child in a position where he has nothing to do! That's where we make our worst mistakes as adults!"

It was Bob Walder's ability to keep students engaged and to be a disciplinarian in a nonalienating way that made him an appealing candidate for the likes of Hewett. Walder certainly had style. He was the kind of person who if he hit you, you'd be inclined to say, "Gee, thanks. That was really kind of you." The students loved him.

Strongly supporting Hewett in the lobby for Walder was fellow Democrat Matthew Lodell, the current grandfather of the board with twenty years of tenure. Ideologically Lodell and Hewett usually ended up on the same side of most issues, though for very different reasons, and hence they behaved similarly but experienced very little affinity for each other.

Matthew Lodell had a very firm view of his role on the board. He had a little descriptive routine that he'd recited so many times that anyone could have mimicked him word for word. With the warmest sincerity and a touch of naiveté, he espoused the straightest version of democratic participation that could be found anywhere. "I think the board of education should always work hand in hand with the town officials; we should listen to what they think is best and decide how to handle the educational needs in the light of the dollars that can be afforded." Matthew's ear, though often not hearing correctly, was ever tuned to the voice of the fathers. He lived out his democratic philosophy as fully as he could and spoke to the townspeople of his ilk with great regularity, sharing his perceptions of the "inside story" and gathering responses that he could use to shape his votes. It is doubtful whether he ever asked himself the question of whether the people he spoke with represented an adequately wide spectrum of opinion!

In support of Hewett and Lodell was Democrat Mike D'Onofrio who had been siding with the Republican trio in the grade alignment deadlocks. As a result he had fallen out of favor with his fellow Democrats. This made Mike anxious because, as a politically ambitious young lawyer, having failed to toe the line of his party's bosses, he felt particularly vulnerable. However, he always claimed he voted his own mind, and on this issue he considered Walder was the best candidate.

This group of three Democrats for Walder (D'Onofrio, Hewett, and Lodell) were hotly opposed by the three Republicans and Democrat Luise Taylor who bristled at the idea of making this type of decision on political grounds. They formed an automatic group in support of Peter Maher, not so much because they thought he'd be the best assistant but because he'd been the candidate chosen by the selection panel and should be appointed as a matter of principle.

Apart from Chairman Kingston, that left Rodney Saunders, a quiet, unassuming, serious-minded, and affable Democrat, holding the balance of power. With extreme pressure from the group of "Democrats for Walder," Saunders was swayed in their direction, thereby locking up a tie vote on the assistant principalship in a very familiar four-all stalemate. In these circumstances once again, Chairman Kingston held the power to break the tie but once again he had good reasons to refrain from voting because of the personal and professional costs to his legal practice. He'd just been through the grade alignment battle eventually deciding to pay the cost by voting against the town fathers. He was in no mood to be in this situation again. It became obvious to him that in order to avoid this problem he'd have to get the Democratic board members to agree to a procrastination so that a preorchestrated, covert solution could be developed.

At the next board of education meeting when Peter Maher was nominated to fill the vacant assistant principal's position, before there was any discussion there was a successful motion to table the issue until the next meeting. This avoided, at least for the moment, any public blood bath between the pro-Walder and pro-Maher forces.

Peter Maher was somewhat dismayed by the outcome of that board meeting. For days before he'd been most anxious about the prospect of losing the position. He knew he was to be the nominee of the selection committee, but having become attuned to the political gossip of the town, he suspected that his ratification might be rejected.

When the board made no decision that night, Maher began to wonder about the implications of remaining a candidate. He hated the prospect of losing on political grounds, and concluded that, rather than run this risk, he'd withdraw. When he went to tell Principal Brook of his decision to withdraw, Lewis talked him out of it, assuring him that the selection committee still intended to have him appointed.

Maher agreed to continue but felt he had to insure some calm between him and his colleague, Walder. Bob and he had been basically friendly and the prospect of allowing events such as this to fragment a working relationship was distasteful to them both. Maher assured Walder that if Bob were given the position, he'd abide by the board's decision and not attempt any political reprisals. Bob Walder appreciated this overture and realizing in many ways that he was the underdog, admired Peter Maher for his efforts to keep the calm.

Whatever form of synthetic tranquility could be charaded in the high school was clearly lacking in the town those next two weeks. Eventually, it became clear to Democratic board members that no adequate political solution could be produced with the appointment of either Maher or Walder, for all the community had become stirred up and anyone who'd originally been occupying an open-minded middle ground had become polarized into either the Maher or Walder camp. The last thing the town needed within its education system was another bloody battle to anger a large portion of the public.

After a while it dawned on some of the Democrats that had they not vetoed the Republicans' original attempts to create a third assistant principal's position a few weeks earlier, they'd now be sitting on the perfect political solution. Both men could have been appointed. The danger of such a bold fantasy was that to try to reverse their earlier rejection of the extra assistant's position would have some overwhelming political costs, to say nothing of its personal costs in terms of mere embarrassment. Despite all the obvious hazards, this idea of creating an extra position so both Walder and Maher could be appointed emerged with irresistible force. Political pragmatism began to father a new courageousness among the Democrats and moved them to make plans. Previously the Democrats had rejected the suggestion of a third administrative position on the grounds of fiscal irresponsibility. This would be trickery. They decided they'd have to present their advocacy for the third position at this time as an expression of their liberal progressivism. They knew it could backfire, but felt it was worth a try.

The boldness of this political maneuver on the part of the board Democrats angered the Republican trio who, though originally in favor of the extra administrative position, now rejected it vehemently simply as a reaction to the Democrats' manipulativeness. The three Republicans tried desperately to recruit one of the Democrats to their side so they could block this political compromise. One Democrat began to sway towards the Republican camp, making Chairman Ron Kingston fearful that once again he'd be confronted with a deadlocked board with four votes in favor and four against the creation of the third assistant principalship. Kingston dreading this prospect decided to diffuse the possibility by telling the Democrats that if one of them voted with the Republicans, he would cast his tie breaker in favor of the third assistant-ship. With this declaration, the board chairman averted the potential deadlock and broke the movement the Republicans were trying to mobilize.

As the board Democrats moved to preorchestrate the dual appointments of Walder and Maher, one further obstacle surfaced. Nobody had thought to check out whether Superintendent Dr. Eddie Rhodes would be willing to go along with the appointments of both Maher and Walder. It so happened he wasn't. Rhodes had become very angry over the gamesmanship of the previous months and what he considered to be the blatant disregard for the educational well-being of his school system. He understood the political constraints every-one operated under, but he felt these had inappropriately dominated educa-tional concerns. The board knew that they could only ratify whomever Superintendent Rhodes nominated for the assistant principal's position. When he was asked, Eddie Rhodes indicated that if two assistant principals were to be appointed he would nominate the selection panel's number one and number two choices. Maher had been number one so that was no problem. Walder had been ranked number four. That was a problem.

The board Democrats were furious when they heard Rhodes' reaction. They had not counted on what they described as the superintendent's obstin-acy, which they could see was about to produce another double bind. With their patience running out, the board Democrats decided to force Rhodes to comply with their wishes. The strategy was simple. They would reject the su-perintendent's number two nomination and invite him to nominate the third person on the panel's list. They would then reject the third nominee and invite the submission of the fourth candidate, Bob Walder. They would accept this nomination and pull off their delicately preorchestrated scheme.

Democrat Mike D'Onofrio was dispatched to recruit Eddie Rhodes' compliance with the scheme. Mike was an obvious person to carry out this task because he was a good friend of Rhodes and had been one of the super-intendent's strongest supporters. Rhodes was disgusted by the proposed method of forcing him to do what the politicians wanted. He felt things closing in on him. By this time he'd become convinced Walder should not be appointed under any circumstances. When he told D'Onofrio this, the schism between these two men became greatly deepened. Mike let loose with a series of ac-cusations about how obstinate Rhodes had become; "You're so inflexible, you'd be willing to subject the whole school system to a devastating political battle over Walder—simply so that your elitist principles could be upheld!!" The blow was crushing. Mike pulled rank. The conversation became clarifyingly simple.

"You will nominate Walder."

"I won't."

"You *will*."

"I *won't*."

"Then your contract's up in six months."

"I will."

Apart from wanting to keep his job, Eddie Rhodes knew he was trapped. He knew that if he fought the Walder issue further, the town would erupt and he'd be held responsible for creating the problem. It became starkly evident to the superintendent that continued postponement of appointments and increased politicization would insure worse damage to the school than conceding to the political wishes. Seeing no way out, Rhodes reluctantly agreed to participate in the plan to create a new position and make easy the appointment of both Walder and Maher.

At the next board meeting the tabled motion to appoint Maher was lifted and subsequently retabled. It had been hoped to push through the creation of a new assistant's position that evening but one of the antagonists astutely pointed out that this could not be done without it being first placed on the agenda, which had not yet happened. So the whole topic was retabled until the next meeting when, if the board wished, they could validly create a new position.

Walder and Maher were forced to sit out yet another two weeks of ambiguous tension while the politicians continued with their games of procrastination. At the next board meeting, the preorchestration unfolded like clockwork. A quick motion and vote, and then there were two positions that needed to be filled. The superintendent was called upon to make two nominations for the vacant positions. Reluctantly he recommended Maher and Walder. An appropriate motion was formulated and the appointments made—all affirmative votes except for Republican Julia Langdon, who was so disgusted with the whole event she abstained in protest.

So it was that Walder and Maher took up their new positions, relieved that the battle was over but very strained by the way the appointments had been made and the many weeks of painful delays.

In this story, we can find all of the social theory issues we've been focussing on in our exploration of Ashgrove thus far. In addition we can see the ongoing playing out of the deeply entrenched conflicts of the town's school system with the same behavior patterns being repeated. It was as if the board as uppers had learned nothing from their earlier experiences. By the time I'd unravelled the principal's story, I felt convinced that the board of education in their upper mentality had no comprehension of the consequences that flowed from their behavior. They seemed totally imprisoned by the structural encasement of uppers. The question of whether history would repeat itself seemed relatively trivial by this point. It seemed to me that the natural forces would lead in this direction.

This realization drew two strong feelings from me. One was depression. I felt overwhelmed by the question of what would it take to jog a group like the board out of its prevailing behavior patterns to stir the exploring of possible alternatives. I had little sense of any answer. The second feeling I had was intense curiosity. I was fascinated by the idea of trying to understand how the relationship among the high school principals may have been shaped by the way they came into being as a group. It's to this topic I'll now turn.

The Walder-Maher Phenomenon

It was two years after the appointments of Walder and Maher that I first met the group of Ashgrove principals. Encountering them was a strange experience. It felt a lot like talking to a schizophrenic. Events that they discussed seemed to hold significantly different meanings for each of them. Maher and Brook appeared to have somewhat common pictures of reality. Walder and Collier talked about seeing the world in similar ways although in their agreeing they appeared to differ. There was very little similarity among the Brook-Maher-Walder-Collier perspectives on anything. In addition others' opinions of this principal group varied widely. For example teachers and students unanimously praised Walder. They considered him to be by far the most popular and effective principal of the four of them. They also felt Maher was not very effective, that Lewis Brook was a "mixed bag", and felt that Brendan Collier, while being a little rigid, was mostly helpful. However, the superintendents and board of education members, all of whom were above the principals, had the exact opposite picture of Maher and Walder. They thought that Bob Walder was totally incompetent while Peter Maher was by far the best of the group. Their views of Brook and Collier were somewhat similar to the students and teachers. In my early conversations most people when looking at the principal group commented that "they seemed to have a problem with communication" but none offered any meaningful explanation as to why that might be.

In my earliest thoughts about this group I gravitated towards the idea that it would be best to look at them first from a middle perspective and see what images emerged. I started with the assumption that probably what happened was that they as a group played out internally certain of the tensions that they had to juggle as a group responding simultaneously to the educational pulls of teachers and students and administrative/political pulls of the superintendents and board members. What initially intrigued me, however, was what forces might have shaped the particular configuration of tensions that were being displayed by these four principals as a group. I decided to go right back to their beginning days together and see if I could untangle the flow of events to help shed some light on what I was now seeing two years later.

The difficulties seem to start right at the beginning, the moment Lewis Brook decided that Maher would be more appropriate than Walder for the vacant assistant principalship. Brook's problem was that he had unintentionally given Bob Walder an advantage in the competition for the position by appointing him in an acting capacity immediately after John Meadow's death. It proved to be an advantage only because both Walder and Maher lacked experience and given the repetitive delays in making an appointment, the board was giving Walder a good base of experience that the pro-Walder forces in Ashgrove were attempting to use as part of their promotion of his application. In addition, the more experience Walder got on the job and the more he was coming to be seen as competent by teachers and students, the harder it was for Principal Brook to defend his strong preference for Peter Maher. To compensate for this unintentional advantage, Lewis Brook took pains to find fault with anything Walder did. Whenever he spoke of Walder to the superintendent or anyone of his superiors, Brook deliberately worked on conveying the message that Walder was unsuitable for the job, criticizing him outright or damning him with faint praise.

Brook also took on the task of pushing Maher, praising him for everything he did so much so that board members started to view Peter as Brook's "fair-haired boy."

In the early days, Brook's responses to Maher and Walder were reasonably simple. Whatever happened he focussed on Peter Maher's strengths and Bob Walder's weaknesses. If Lewis felt ambivalent about anything he almost mechanistically split his negative feelings off and projected them onto Walder and took his positive feelings and mapped them onto Maher. He would take the simplest of differences between Bob and Peter and escalate them into a major schism, damning Walder's position and praising Maher's. This split in Brook's reaction to Walder and Maher commenced about the time the assistant principal selection committee met and chose Peter Maher. Initially there was nothing malicious in Lewis Brook's reaction. He merely figured it was the only strategy he could use to counter the politicians' meddling in his school. However, by the time the dual appointment of both men was made, Brook's attitude seemed somewhat entrenched.

The process of the joint Walder-Maher appointments made Principal Lewis Brook very angry. While understanding the political realities that had dictated the dual appointment, he resented the situation so bitterly that after the appointments had been made he continued to criticize Walder and praise Maher. I suspect at this point he wanted to prove that he'd been right and one way to do this was by making sure Walder was seen as incompetent even though this could be self-defeating for Lewis in the long run. Whenever Principal Brook approached Walder to do something administratively, it was always asked with a reluctance and a grudge. Walder didn't like this. It made him nervous and in his nervousness he appeared indecisive and underconfident; it's this characteristic Brook could use against him. These were the things being told to his superiors.

A basic problem, however, was that while Walder's superiors were coming to accept him as less than competent, those below him, the teachers and students alike, were forming a radically different picture. Bob had always enjoyed an excellent rapport with his students. His skills as a first class teacher and a popular baseball coach had enabled him to develop close and significant relationships with students. He was always firm but empathetic and found it reasonably easy to discipline without producing alienation, an extraordinary skill in an era when most authority figures were automatically suspect. Part of his strength was his ability to be lighthearted—often taking neither the students nor himself too seriously. He had the gift to differentiate between the mere exuberance of adolescence and the deepset, destructive rebelliousness of the minutest minority of students. He understood how demoralizing it was to be treated as the latter when reality was the former, and he took great care to avoid confusing the two. To some people it appeared that Bob was weak with his students and that a part of his relationships with the teenagers was "a joke." Those who made that error missed the very essence of his strength.

In comparison, Lewis Brook had always tended to have an aloof approach with students, especially when it came to discipline. He felt the need to be perceived as "tough" and "detached" and couldn't understand how Bob could be effective in discipline while allowing himself to be close. This reflected a difference in styles that Brook was quick to diagnose as Walder's problem of overempathy. Lewis believed this made Bob popular but ineffectual.

It was correct that Walder lacked interest in administration. He treated these duties as essential but ungratifying so he set his own priorities as students first and administration second.

While Peter Maher lacked experience in administration, he had a clear and keen mind for the detailed thoroughness that was required for this part of the assistant principal's job. This side of Maher excited Brook because it promised to lessen some of the excessive administrative burdens he himself felt in his role. On the other hand Walder offered no such prospect. Hence, Brook felt he'd get more help from Maher than Walder.

In the early days after the dual appointments had been made, there were clashes among the principals over how discipline should be carried out. Brook and Maher both believed that to discipline effectively it was necessary to be aloof. Walder considered closeness to be a prerequisite. Their clashes would lead Walder to express disdain about the paperwork that took them all away from the critical tasks of being an educator, while Maher and Brook countered with claims that good education could only occur if there were efficient administrative machinery.

These differences between Maher and Walder activated an early differentiation between the roles of the two new assistant principals. Maher became seen as being more attuned to the issues of administration while Walder focussed more on the concerns of teachers and students. This may have been an effective way to work provided everyone agreed. However they didn't and their minor differences became so blown out of proportion that Walder began to feel that Maher didn't pay enough attention to the students and teachers on a day-to-day basis while Maher concluded that Walder didn't pay enough attention to administrative issues. To compensate Maher would do more administration to make up for Walder, while Walder took on more disciplining and developing stronger contact with students to make up for Maher's "overemphasis" on administration. Walder didn't mind this informally evolving arrangement. Maher resented it deeply for as time passed, Peter felt increasingly imprisoned by the administrative burdens of his role while he saw Bob becoming freer of it everyday. This split heightened Brook's affection for Maher and disdain for Walder. They never talked about what was happening but it was clear to both of the new assistants that they each resented the rewards the other was obtaining—Maher the support and praise of Lewis Brook and Walder the warm rapport with teachers and students.

The two men eventually became imprisoned by the roles they had gravitated towards. Walder, with his administrative muscles underexercised, became less competent in administration than he was capable of, while Maher found himself without the time to respond adequately to teachers' and students' concerns. Nowhere was this more evident than in discussions over the "detention" system Ashgrove used. To discipline a student, teachers had to gain a principal's prior approval. Maher was often many days and sometimes weeks behind in authorizing and disposing of "discipline slips." This frustrated the teachers because they always felt punishment was meaningless if it wasn't reasonably immediate. Walder, on the other hand, with significant free time (as Maher would point out), was able to process "discipline slips" that came to him within the day. As a result, he received high praise from teachers who came to symbolize him as "their man." While Brook and Maher became more close, Walder felt more alienated and he turned to teachers for nurturance and support. Since teachers liked Bob it also meant that they were very ready to accept his interpretation of Maher and Brook as the "bad guys." This reinforced the schism for it guaranteed that those above and below the principal group would look at them from very different vantage points.

Brendan Collier, the third assistant principal (who'd originally stepped aside after John Meadow's death, thereby making it possible for Brook to become principal), felt very excluded by the complex web of emotions generated by the other trio. Brendan and Lewis had never been close but they had learned how to work together comfortably. There had been many reasons why Collier had not wanted to be principal when John Meadow died, not the least of which was that as a sixty-year-old he'd grown tired of trying to keep up with the pace of changes in the school. He'd concluded that there were very few rewards to be achieved by being ambitious or subjecting his life to extraordinary strains.

Under the reign of Principal John Meadow, Brendan Collier had attempted to straddle the two sets of tensions that constantly pulled a principal—the imperative to be attuned to the needs of those below and the demands of those above. Collier had carried the role of managing school finances and in this task he'd lived out perfectly his "middle function" by never losing sight of the fiscally conservative interests of his superiors and the concerns of subordinate teachers who always had superb reasons why they wanted extra money for some irresistable educational innovation. His attempts to mediate these tensions caused some people to like him, others to despair over him. Some saw Brendan as a "fuddy-duddy" or "no-hoper" while others characterized him as "the most underrated person in the school system." Both of these perspectives on him were correct, for he showed different facets of himself to the various people with whom he interacted. As a result he had a number of people "for" him and a number "against" him. In addition, his allies and adversaries were well distributed amongst his subordinates and his superiors. This stood in sharp contrast to Walder and Maher where everyone recognized that in the event Walder and Maher were to be the two candidates to replace a sudden departure by Principal Brook, superiors would want Maher while subordinates would chose Walder.

The three assistant principals at Ashgrove High School showed different ways of handling the tensions of middleness with which they had to struggle, individually and collectively as a group. As they attempted to mediate in the extreme pulls from those above and below, they experienced a great deal of tension. One mode of dealing with this might be characterized as the Collier method, constantly taking the external tensions inside him, letting them percolate around as the separate pulls intersected within his person, and then arbitrating on them as he felt best. An alternative was the Walder-Maher method where the balance of the tensions became maintained by each of them being responsive to different sets of tensions. In this mode, the pulls that were felt intrapsychically in the Collier case were experienced interpersonally in the Walder-Maher framework.

By the time I'd got to this point of unravelling the principal group's history I found no need to explore much further. It was self-evident why they were such a hard group to be with. Each of them had such a different way of dealing with the tensions they experienced as principals and in turn each of these different ways of confronting tension generated a special configuration of forces that left a bizarre paralysis in their relationship together. What happened was that every event they experienced together had different meanings for them because they looked at events from divergent vantage points or they focussed on different aspects of each event, then extracted their own meanings from the things they experienced together. In listening to them talking together it was evident they weren't communicating but this was because they listened with ears that were calibrated by meanings different from those being used by the speaker. Walder listened to everything through the filter of how it would affect his good relationships with subordinates and his poor relationships with superiors. Maher listened through ears calibrated to augment his good relations with Brook and other superiors while simultaneously hoping to diffuse his anxiety over how he related with teachers and students. Collier listened with the hope of quelling the turmoil he had to struggle with inside. Brook listened with the overriding concern of keeping the politicians and public "off his back" so he could work on building his educational program without outside interference and without having to constantly put up with subordinates he considered to be incompetent.

Every communication amongst them sounded like all of them were pulling in opposite directions. In a way they were, for their inner realities were pointing in different directions. Each of them was sensitive to different pressures and to the same pressures in different ways; hence words that passed among them carried different messages. They would often walk away after an exchange believing they'd understood each other and having reached an agreement about how they'd act and then go off and all do things in such diverse ways that it looked like no discussion had ever taken place. For our future reference, I'm choosing to refer to this as the Walder-Maher phenomenon.

There was one additional complexity in this group. Brook's tendency to side with Maher forced Walder and Collier to often coalesce, even when they were not in agreement, merely to resist the force of the Brook-Maher pairing. This meant that very often as many as three or maybe four different vantage points would be collapsed into two, which would then be played out as a clash between a Brook-Maher coalition and a Walder-Collier coalition. This meant that very often issues the principals had to resolve were addressed, not on the basis of their merits but according to the particular alignments that were prevailing within the principal group at that time.

It is conceivable to me that the split in the Walder-Maher relationship could have been made quite functional so long as a mechanism could have been developed to coordinate their respective contributions. However without that integrating device, which Principal Brook almost certainly would have had to create and manage rather deliberately, the split roles all four of them played only entrenched the inner schism of their group to an impossible level.

The theory that I was understanding for the first time in observing the interaction of this group of principals was how as middles they dealt with their inner tensions. Previously I'd appreciated, as we've discussed earlier, that many of the internal conflicted dynamics of a middle group could be meaningfully thought of as a playing through of what were basically external system conflicts that they were caught in the midst of and that they introjected and acted out on behalf of the system as a whole. What was new for me here was seeing that within the principal group there were different ways of handling those conflicts and that these differences, which might have been made complementary instead of contradictory, were a source of covert conflict in and of themselves. In addition, as each principal attempted to deal with the conflicts he experienced as best he could, hoping to lessen the problem overall, it usually made things worse. It was almost as though the harder the group worked to avoid having its conflicts be a problem the more they became paralyzed by those conflicts.

One concluding comment I want to make about this story of the high school principals is that in my opinion the way the board of education made the decisions about the Walder-Maher appointments ended up having profound implications for how the principals (as lowers) developed as a group.

However at no point did any board member even suspect that the "problems of communication the principals seemed to have in working together" (as Hewett explained it) were in any way linked to their own behavior as a board during the complex and procrastinated turmoil of the Walder-Maher appointments. Again I saw the upper structural encasement operating in the relationship of the board with the principals.

The Superintendency

During my first days at Ashgrove I started to question whether my upper, middle, lower framework was too simplistic when applied to a social structure as complex as a school system. The realization that I could think about these hierarchical relationships in a relative way had been a first major breakthrough for me. Soon there was to become a new puzzling issue however. This was whether a group embedded in a hierarchical exchange with other groups would be able to shift its own inner reality sets so that it could see itself in upper terms *and* middle terms *and* lower terms as I, an external observer, was finding it easy to do. Or would a group always see itself in upper *or* middle *or* lower ways?

Slowly I came to realize that each group seemed to stay mostly with one framework for viewing itself. This was particularly clear when I looked at the superintendent's office. While the principals, viewing themselves as middles caught between the superintendents above and the teachers below, looked at an act of Eddie Rhodes as though it was from an upper, the superintendent did not see the upper facet of his actions. He would see that same behavior not through the eyes of the principals in lower(teachers)–middle (principals)–upper(superintendents) spectrum but through a lower(principals)–middle(superintendents)–upper(board) configuration. In other words Rhodes saw himself as a middle, even when it may have been more appropriate to view himself as an upper or a lower. Middleness seemed to be his prevailing mentality.

I would like to explore this theme by discussing Superintendent Eddie Rhodes, examining how he gravitated towards experiencing himself as middle even when an upper or lower orientation might have made more sense. I've chosen stories about Eddie Rhodes to highlight this point although I think there were many indications that most Ashgrove groups tended to do the same thing. Before starting I should point out that often I'll sound like I'm discussing the person Eddie Rhodes and not Ashgrove's superintendent group. However when I do talk about him as an individual I'd like it to be understood that I'm discussing him as a representative and figurehead of this group as a whole and that because his figurehead role is so large many external group issues get actually put into him specifically whereas they more appropriately belong in the function of the Superintendency in general.

Eddie Rhodes had come to Ashgrove under strange circumstances. The previous superintendent had been eased out over a ludicrous salary issue. He'd been trying to negotiate an increase to $20,000, which the board refused on the grounds that a town the size of Ashgrove could not afford anything more than $19,950. This $50 difference was trivial but had been given special symbolic significance. Nevertheless when Ashgrove began to look for a new superintendent they had been unable to recruit a satisfactory replacement at less than $23,000.

For months the superintendency had been left in the hands of Don O'Sullivan, a man in his early thirties who had been assistant superintendent for the previous two years. In that short time he had won the hearts of the townsfolk. Don had been holding the school system together, brilliantly orchestrating the feverish development of the new middle school and sensitively walking the tightrope between vigorous political tensions. He spoke the political vernacular fluently. Unlike his predecessor and his eventual successor, Don had a natural empathy with the town. Since he marched to the drumbeat of the locals, many wanted him to be superintendent. However he didn't want the job. He was ambitious and hoped some day to be a school superintendent, but he was still young, underqualified, and somewhat afraid of the wonder-boy image people were packaging him in. He knew the tinsel could easily tarnish. He'd been feeling overburdened by the acting superintendent role and was convinced he needed a few more years experience as an assistant.

Eventually the position was given to Dr. Eddie Rhodes, a man in his late forties who had been assistant superintendent at nearby Winslow County. Rhodes had the stature of the English gentry. Though dressed with an extroverted flamboyance for the times, his nature was quiet and reserved with a touch of reassuring confidence. He was not easily ruffled, at least not outwardly. He carried the stamp of strong, deliberate, and liberal views on education. Generally the Ashgrove school board liked him and had voted unanimously on his appointment.

When Superintendent Rhodes arrived in January 1969, he felt no need to march immediately into the limelight. The system had operated smoothly under O'Sullivan's guidance previously and both men were keen to preserve tranquility in the transitions. The major public activity of the day was the hyperactive planning for the middle school. O'Sullivan was totally immersed in this project. He belonged to all critical committees and found himself propelled to the center of the town's arterial system. The superintendent felt no compulsion to wrest this position from his assistant. In fact he viewed his managerial role to be that of encouraging his subordinates to work to the fullness of their capacities. Rhodes and O'Sullivan discussed this explicitly and both agreed that Don should continue to carry the major load of coordinating the middle school's plans.

Rhodes, instead, turned himself to the more mundane, but much overdue, task of overhauling the budgetary system, which he undertook in league with James Levine, his highly meticulous and thorough business manager.

The days and weeks sped by. The school system functioned smoothly with the low visibility of the new superintendent and generally people who'd had contact with Eddie Rhodes felt warmly towards him.

Given Eddie's reserve, townsfolk became curious about his private life. He'd arrived in Ashgrove without his wife and family. Initially he'd dismissed this simply on the grounds of family expediency. Winslow, his old home, was not far away; he could always, and regularly did, get back there for the weekends. Some of his children had married and settled in the region and as a family man he enjoyed spending time with them all. Hence, he'd decided it was best to separate out his private life from his work life, giving his weekdays to his job and his weekends to his family. This period was, however, a time of considerable marital stress for Eddie, eventually leading to divorce, a topic discussed often at Ashgrove cocktail parties.

It was reasonably easy to delineate the superintendent's role into each of the upper, middle, and lower positions. Formally he had two prime functions in the school system. As senior educator, he was charged with the professional responsibility of developing and nurturing the educational life of the town. From this perspective the superintendent's office was in an upper location overseeing the principals and teachers (middles) who in turn were responsible for the classroom activities of the students (lowers). At the same time the superintendent's office acted as the executive branch of the board of education. In this function, the superintendent and his staff acting as administrative executioners of the political will of their elected superiors were middles sandwiched between the political interests of the board (uppers) and the educational pressures of the schools (lowers). Both groups above and below, the politicians and the educationalists, expected the superintendent to be the custodian of their interests. Hence, Rhodes was constantly required to manage and negotiate the delicate boundaries between these two sets of often conflicting interests. In this middle position the superintendent always had to walk the tight, unclear, difficult-to-identify, thin line between precariously balanced polar opposite tensions, displaying not only educational and administrative expertise, but also a keen capacity to manage conflict.

In addition to the above, Eddie Rhodes and his office were lowers with respect to the board of education (middles) and the town politicians, in particular the Factory (uppers). Although Ashgrove was officially controlled by the mayor and elected officers in City Hall, there was another key actor whose influence must be included. Ashgrove had a very powerful behind-the-scenes puppeteer. Operating out of "the Factory", he'd for years wheeled and dealed his way into an invincible position, finally building and then spreading his multimillion-dollar operation into every crevice of the political and town machinery. He personally kept a low profile, accepting no visible political posts.

However, he called the shots and like his good friend, the late Mayor Richard Daley of Chicago, could usually achieve what he wanted to with minimal effort. He summoned people at will to his Factory. When he called, people responded. He "owned" several mouthpieces who compliantly spoke the words he shaped, thereby protecting him from having to ever defend any of his own stances. Many people feared him. No one ignored him.

Eddie Rhodes thought it wise to keep himself free from the Factory's influence and scrupulously avoided direct formal contact with him. They would meet in the cocktail circuit and cordially exchange pleasantries but they never directly confronted each other on school-related issues or made their feelings, pleasant or otherwise, known to each other. In this regard, Superintendent Rhodes felt obliged to answer only to the board of education who in reality provided a middle buffer between the superintendent's office and the real Ashgrove uppers, namely the Factory and his cronies.

The tensions surrounding the superintendent were played out in strange ways. On virtually any issue, if Rhodes took a stance supportive of the educationalists' view, the politicians described him as "rigid, obstinate, inflexible, and unable to accommodate to the obvious realities around him." If he sided with the pragmatic demands of his politically focussed superiors, defining decisions in terms sufficiently vague and veiled to cover all contingencies, his principals and teachers would describe him as "wishy-washy, malleable, and easily co-opted."

The place where these binds became most intense was during the struggle over where the ninth grade should be located. Here Rhodes had taken a firm stand arguing that educational and not fiscal considerations should be made primary. He won, but was then made the whipping boy of the Factory and Ashgrove's economic brokers who accused him of being too radical and unresponsive to political pragmatics. Soon after this he'd been pressured to breaking point to give in to political considerations over the Walder-Maher appointments, leading to the accusation that he was easy to buy off.

As Rhodes became more aware of those criticisms he found it hard to please anyone. For months he was passive. Then, realizing how ineffective he was being, he attempted to respond to his critics by becoming more forthright with those who saw him as rigid. However, the net result was that instead of each group consistently applying one label to him, everyone came to attach both sets of labels to him, describing him sometimes as wishy-washy and other times as rigid. This eventually degenerated to the point where no matter what Rhodes did, people described it as inappropriate, leading finally to the accusation that he lacked the necessary characteristics to run a school system.

There were some powerful system forces that converged on the board–superintendency–principals relationship that colored profoundly the confusing view Ashgrove had of Dr. Rhodes. Eddie was always required to sit at the conflict point between the board and the schools. He could manage that conflict in any number of ways.

On the board's side if something surfaced that demanded the superintendent's action, if it had occurred previously and if precedent or explicit board policy had been established the superintendent would take action in the spirit of historical or stipulated guidelines; or if there were no real political issues involved, Rhodes may have merely taken the appropriate actions, as would any chief executive, saving the board from having to deliberate trivia. On the other hand there were other situations that the superintendent felt the board should debate and arbitrate on which he routinely added to the agenda of each board meeting. When the board came to deliberate these issues the superintendent referred to them, one of two things tended to happen. Either they would come quickly to a decision about what should be done or else the board would become highly split and agonize at great length about how to proceed. In the former case, the board responded to the superintendent with the tone of "Why do you pass such trivia on to us? It's your job to handle these things without taking our precious time!" In the latter case, the board strained by lack of agreement would look to the superintendent to provide definitive data to convince them of appropriate actions or else provide "strong leadership" to free them from their own fragmentation. If he could not provide the data or felt that the available data left ambiguity about an appropriate course of action, then the board relieved themselves of their own feelings of fragmentation or helplessness by criticizing the superintendent for his indecisiveness and lack of leadership.

In reality the only time the board ever really took a look at their superintendent was when he was raising an educational issue that was pitted in some conflictual way with either fiscal concerns or the hybrid values of the Ashgrove community in general.

The board developed a very unbalanced picture of their superintendent. Since he took a lot of actions independently, they only ever focussed on what he felt dependent on them for, and in this realm their images of him were very distorted. If the board resolved the issues efficiently the superintendent was boring and wallowing in trivia. If the board was fragmented, the superintendent was wishy-washy. If the superintendent managed the board-schools conflicts effectively, so virtually nothing was passed to the board for deliberation, the superintendent was lazy and doing nothing of value. He simply couldn't win.

In the superintendent's relationship with the principals a different set of images emerged. They felt "cut-off" from him, especially Principal Lewis Brook, who didn't live in Ashgrove and who was not well connected to the informal grapevine. Often events occurred at board meetings and got reported in the press without any formal or official word being passed to the school. Hence Lewis was forever being embarrassed and irritated by a parent or informed citizen who would confront him on school issues raised at board meetings that had never been discussed with him. Brook would get outraged over this and demand to be informed by Rhodes about anything that might be of relevance to his school. The superintendent would agree to keep him informed. The problem was that Brook and Rhodes had two totally different images of what was relevant to the high school. Eventually Lewis became demoralized by the situation and came to believe he would never be consulted or advised of decisions the board was deliberating. He saw Rhodes as being aloof and noncaring and learned to reciprocate by indifferently excluding the superintendent's office from things important to their functioning. It became a vicious cycle. After a long series of administrative actions such as the Walder-Maher appointments and the ninth grade location debates that appeared blind to the stresses of his position, Lewis Brook became very apprehensive about what might be done to him next. He genuinely believed his voice counted for very little in the final analysis when it came to the board's deliberations relevant to his school, and he reluctantly accommodated to the prospect that "the worst could always possibly happen." For Brook, hearing nothing came to mean not that nothing was happening, but that "all hell was about to break loose."

In the absence of clear information from above, Brook grew to look for other cues to develop a basis from which to synthesize and create his own reality of what was occurring. He learned to read between the lines, sometimes accurately but mostly inaccurately. He became so dependent on his private synthesis of reality that whenever the Superintendents Rhodes or O'Sullivan did speak with him, much of Brook's energy seemed focussed on confirming his construction of reality, rather than listening to what his superiors were saying. For the superintendents, this was most disconcerting because, whatever they said, they felt Brook was not hearing correctly or was interpreting in a radically different manner from what they intended. Regularly, the superintendent or his assistant would put down the phone after talking to the high school principal and exclaim with confusion, "Why did the principal respond that way to what I said?" To make things worse Eddie Rhodes was unable to perceive how totally disorienting it was for Lewis Brook to have such limited information on what the board was planning or how their processes operated, and instead he concluded that the principal was simply threatened by contact with the superintendent's office. Genuinely wanting to minimize the stress they generated for the high school, the superintendents wrongly decided that it would be best if they tried to be less threatening by leaving the principal and his assistants to their own resources as much as possible. Rhodes' solution meant that Lewis came to feel even more "cut off", which augmented Brook's fear that things could fall apart at any time and, in cyclical fashion, led him to depend even more heavily on his own constructions of reality. In this way Rhodes' actions towards Brooks ended up augmenting the very problem he was trying to solve.

One example of how this self-defeating cycle occurred was what happened to the superintendents' bimonthly administrative meetings with all the principals from all of Ashgrove's schools. These initially were conceived as problemsolving sessions, but the diversity and complexity of the difficulties raised and the range of interests represented was too great to ever get closure on anything. The principals became so frustrated with these meetings that they were abandoned with no appreciation of how critical a function they fulfilled in providing a forum for exchange of information between the school principals and the superintendent's office. It was not until they were ended did the principals realize how deprived of information they could get. Yet no one wanted to suggest reintroduction of these meetings. They were too horrible. Being in a bind, everyone did nothing until it was too late and Rhodes' relationship with Brook had become ossified in communication paralysis.

Ashgrove's convoluted opinion of their superintendent was augmented by the overall anxiety in the town at large. Even though Rhodes was in no way responsible, the construction of the new intermediate school had been stalled by disputes and technical problems, causing its opening to be postponed a year. Overcrowding had escalated to crisis proportions and the Factory had been suggesting that the town would never be able to afford a second high school. This was very irritating to Lewis Brook and the others who had to live daily in the turbulence of too many adolescents in too small a space; they took out their anger on Rhodes.

It was the spring of 1971. That December Rhodes' first-year contract would end and he was afraid he would be made the sacrificial lamb for the unresolved turmoil of the system. In particular, he was frightened that the board of education would simply ignore the need for contract review, let it run out without debate, and then leave him at the last minute with insufficient time to search for any alternative position.

Unknown to Eddie Rhodes, the Democrats over the preceding months at their clandestine caucuses had spent a lot of time debating what they referred to as the "Rhodes situation." Two board members, Lodell and Hewett, wanted to have him summarily dismissed, as did Mayor Maloney, who felt he was paid too much and that he had not developed a good rapport with the town politicians over financial matters.

There were, however, some moderate voices who supported Rhodes. Chairman Ron Kingston, while conceding that the superintendent's first term had not been a resounding success when examined from the perspective of how the board or town officials related to him, overall considered that the past two and a half years had been satisfactory from the perspective of the school system as a whole. Kingston felt the superintendent "droned on at times, but then so do most of us." D'Onofrio had a private friendship with Eddie Rhodes and since he considered loyalty among friends to be primary he spoke up in Eddie's support. Of the other Democrats, Luise Taylor was inclined to go with the opinions of those who thought he should be fired, while Rodney Saunders found himself torn between the two opposing camps.

The three Republican members of the board were firmly behind Rhodes. They felt he had been very effective in standing up to the manipulations of the town Democratic bosses. They thought he'd been a good, successful, and sincere superintendent, and that he was being given intolerable grief by a town too immature to entertain his stature, too rigid to respond to his initiatives.

Many townsfolk criticized Eddie Rhodes for very trivial issues such as how he dressed or the fact that he had a moustache. Deep down the feeling was simple. Rhodes just wasn't of the Ashgrove ilk. He was not Catholic, he was not extroverted nor easily provoked into a hot political fight; rather, he was calm and poised and fiercely dedicated to preserving his autonomy from behind-the-scenes political pressures. Thus, in contrast with his assistant Don O'Sullivan, Eddie Rhodes was not privy to all the town's gossip, or used as a sounding board, dragged away into a dark corner of a cocktail lounge to be informed of the latest piece of political drama. And in essence, that's what people wanted. Someone who could be baited into a fight. Someone who would flirt with the trade-offs that gave the town its very vibrance. Not someone who could retain his aloofness and objectivity. Whoever heard of an administrator who wanted to be objective? Why, not even a small town judge would be expected to be so superhuman!

When Rhodes' future in Ashgrove was eventually debated by the board of education, a lot of chaos was generated. The board met in secret, kept no notes, and recorded no minutes. Hence, it is not possible to be certain of the processes that lead to the board's decision that night. The outcome was clear. Rhodes was to be given a $1,000 per annum salary increase and his contract would be extended for only one year, not the customary three years. It seemed in retrospect that this extension was a compromise reached by those who wanted the superintendent dismissed outright and those who considered this to be totally unacceptable. What motions were voted on, in what order, or how the votes were cast were never made explicit. But the division of those for and against was clearly delineated that evening. Three Republicans plus Mike D'Onofrio were for Eddie Rhodes. The other four Democrats were against, thereby generating the regular situation of a four-four deadlock, which Chairman Kingston had to settle. He orchestrated the one-year extension proposed and cast his vote in favor of this solution. It is of interest to note that this voting was identical to the way the board members had voted on the ninth grade issue six months earlier.

Rhodes was furious. He'd grown tired of the way he'd been treated and with an uncharacteristic outburst of assertiveness challenged the board to tell him directly if he should interpret their action as a dismissal. He called for a full board meeting in secret session with none of the public or press present and asked that all the facts be put on the table. In particular, he wanted to know whether his pending divorce had influenced anyone's votes. He went around the board room and asked each person present, one by one, whether his marital situation made any difference to his or her vote. All assured him that it didn't. Then he asked for a statement of their evaluation of him. In summary form, the main things declared were: "(a) you're not forceful enough in your encounters with the town fathers and the public at large; (b) you do not handle public relations at all well; (c) you haven't achieved anything since you've been here."

Rhodes felt the blistering sting of these criticisms but he took them in his stride. He asked for an elaboration, then lawyerlike he delivered his defense. He talked at length about the educational innovations he'd introduced, the change in leadership style he'd brought to Ashgrove, and the streamlining of administrative and budgetary systems. He concluded with a flourish. "One thing I'd like to know is what type of leadership do you want from your superintendent? Do you want a shallow extrovert, a public relations type? If so, I'm the wrong man for the job and I wish you'd fire me. If you want someone who can take things calmly and use his administrative skill to keep the system functional without loud fanfare or public demonstration, then I feel I have something significant to offer. I'd like to know which of these two types you want, for if you want the type of person I'm not, I know deep down it would be best for me to leave."

That evening nothing decisive emerged. Rhodes was given a good hearing and the board for one of the first times saw their superintendent exercise the full force of his intellect and personality. They adjourned to debate another day what they should do with Rhodes.

After several weeks of silence Hewett arranged to see Rhodes and reported that the six Democrats had met privately and come to a decision as to how they wished to proceed. "We decided that you defended yourself well the other evening and from our current perspective feel we do not have reason not to renew your contract for another three years. However, we do have a proposal. We'd like for you not to push us for a decision for the moment about your future. Let the political heat fall off and the public interest subside and then later on we'll renew your contract for another three-year term." It had impressed Eddie all the time Hewett was talking how ironic it was that it happened to be Craig who was carrying this message, for he had been the strongest voice in the campaign to force Rhodes out of Ashgrove. However, the diplomacy became increasingly clear as he realized that since this message was being conveyed by the person who supported him least it sounded believable. They cut a deal and a few months later, good to their word, the board of education without fanfare voted unanimously to extend his contract another three years.

After seeing how the superintendent group functioned in Ashgrove I became reasonably convinced of one additional prison that they seemed to have been caught in. In some regards they were trapped in the binds of uppers. In other ways it was middles and lowers. However even when they were in the upper or lower encasement they looked at their experience only in terms of

189

the underlying dynamics of middleness. Rhodes in particular, seemed blind to anything other than the forces that went with his middle experience. I began to wonder to myself as to what type of forces the superintendent could unleash if he allowed himself the freedom to dwell fully with the upper or lower location and to experience these facets in other than a middle way. We'll return to this theme later.

In concluding this section I want to briefly note that the superintendent group pushed and pulled as middles did not fragment like the Hannover Ins did at Montville. In fact relations within the superintendent's office were intensely colleaguial. Each of the three professionals, Rhodes, O'Sullivan, and the business manager, James Levine, understood each other well. They saw their differences, both in capacities and styles, as strengths and they used them complementarily. They were able to talk about this relatively freely, even down to acknowledging that O'Sullivan was seen as the popular, dynamic force in the school system, while Rhodes was perceived as indecisive, aloof, and aristocratic. I think one of the main reasons why this group didn't get torn apart was because Eddie Rhodes took most of these middleness tensions and dealt with them within himself. He seemed to get intrapsychically torn apart in ways similar to how Hannover was ripped up as a group. Don O'Sullivan did likewise. Hence the forces that could have destroyed this middle group of superintendents were not played out in their group, but rather within each of them individually. The group was able to survive in fact as a result, but with a large personal and individual price.

Brook's High School

Despite the fact that Principal Brook and Superintendent Rhodes had very little appreciation for each other, in reality their situations were extraordinarily similar. Brook spent much of his time trapped in binds of middleness that were, in the final analysis, almost identical to those Rhodes experienced. However, when the principal was in *his* middleness, the only facet of the superintendent he paid attention to was his upper side; whereas conversely, when Rhodes in his middleness looked at Brook, the dimension of his subordinate he made focal was the principal's lower side. Since the upper and lower pulls were the tensions that made middleness so difficult Rhodes saw Brook to be part of his problem and Brook saw Rhodes in turn to be part of his problem. Hence they never came to comprehend how much their respective middleness gave them in common. I always felt, when listening to them talk, if only they could have altered the spectacles through which they looked at each other, their experiences were at a basic level so similar that they were in a position to understand each other almost perfectly. Instead they didn't understand each other at all.

190

There were three broad domains in which Lewis Brooks' middleness was most evident: on the topic of changes, in how he dealt with communication, and in the struggle with the overcrowding of his school.

Perhaps the most critical problem for Lewis Brooks was the community hysteria over drug taking. Ashgrove high school students, like their peers right across the country, had become the children of the drug age. Trying marijuana was like learning to walk; it was simply part of growing up.

Lewis Brook felt keenly the pressures from the town over student drug taking. People seemed to hold him responsible for not having stamped it out. Brook knew that some drug activity occurred in the school; but he also knew and understood his students well enough to be confident that they were not ruining their lives by the occasional hit. Experiments with drugs, along with unkempt, long scraggy hair, or the occasional outburst of a student profanity, were not an indication to Lewis Brook that the teenagers of the day were all rotten as some of the community constantly implied. Rather, he saw this behavior as a sign of teenage struggle for individual identity in a confused world and in a somewhat uncertain school environment.

As principal of the school, however, he felt obliged to manage the complex tensions that the drug topic produced. On the one hand he was committed to scaling down the overconcern that came from the community; on the other hand he was determined not to overact with his students.

Ashgrove's board of education in general represented the dominant parental attitude (uppers). On the drug topic, the high school students represented the dominant youth culture (lowers). The teachers, principals and administrators vacillated somewhere in the middle, sometimes able to identify with student attitudes, other times with that of the adult Ashgrovite. Hence, every time someone started getting upset about drug taking it unleashed in Lewis a lot of tensions.

For Brook, the only way he could reduce the external pressure was if the community were convinced that there was very little drug taking occurring. To save himself from overacting within his school it was easiest to simply avoid noticing it as much as possible. If he saw, he had to take action. Then it would get in the press and feed the hysteria. Lewis tried not to see, so hard in fact, that many people came to believe that he was too stupid to notice the realities that were before his very eyes. To uppers and lowers, it appeared either that Lewis was blind or out of touch. To Lewis, as a middle, turning a blind eye made strategic sense.

How Lewis chose to deal with his middleness tensions infuriated his teachers, not so much on drug-taking issues but on administrative themes such as finances or discipline, where he adopted a similar approach. Lewis often felt that the middleness binds paralyzed him. However the teachers, as lowers, did not interpret Brook's inaction as stuckness. They saw it as obstinance, incompetence, or indifference. Further, the harder they pushed the principal to act in their interests, the less flexible he seemed to become. Of course from an upper-middle-lower perspective this is understandable for the lowers' pressure merely heightened middle paralysis. After a while the teachers gave up on Brook. Rather than pressure him to act as the agent of their interests with the superintendent's office and the board they started to bypass him. Teachers began to seek out influential parents and board members and tried to get changes by pressuring the superintendent and the principal from above. This led to some very messy scenes.

The scenario degenerated to the following: the superintendent would receive a complaint and be asked to investigate it; he'd call Brook and ask for all the relevant information that should be considered given the concern; Brook would feel defensive because he had been kept in the dark by his teachers (because they no longer believed he would act in their interests); he'd want to know who reported the incident and would be very embarrassed about not knowing what was going on in his school; he'd then want to find out which teacher had been "talking out of school"; the teachers in turn, like classic lowers, would protect each other and then Brook would look stupid as he launched on his witch hunt.

I used to feel sorry for Brook. Here he'd been attempting to lessen his own frustration and the double binds of his office by pressuring the superintendent less than he as principal was being pressured. However in his attempts to make things easier for himself he was in fact making them worse because the teachers were learning how to exert force on him from above. This infuriated Brook.

To make things worse he was being cut out of the communication system and losing his power to delicately manage and control the forces he was having to keep in balance. Eventually he resorted to something that seemed incomprehensible. He sent out a directive to his teachers saying that no one could speak with the superintendent, a parent, or a board member without first discussing it with him. He did not stipulate the consequences of violating his edict but he made it clear that this would be viewed as personal disloyalty and as a direct disruption to the educational interests of the school. To me this was amazing, for here was Brook, the veritable complainer about the problems of inadequate communication in the system, explicitly and deliberately trying to block certain communications. I understand that what Lewis wanted was to reinject himself back into the center of communication in and out of his school. It was obviously his hope that this would provide a way to lessen the polarities pulling on him. But it was far too late.

The teachers were not to be defeated by Brook's ploy. They found a way to circumvent their principal. In the next few months a large number of them applied for sabbatical leave, which automatically gave them an interview with either Don O'Sullivan or Eddie Rhodes. These interviews usually began with a request to destroy the sabbatical application and an explicit acknowledgment that this was just a ploy to be able to talk to the superintendents about things teachers felt Brook was trying to hide.

As a result, Rhodes and O'Sullivan continued to be fed information about what was going on within the high school, while Brook blindly believed that his system for stopping the "leaking" of information should be working. He continued to be amazed, however, by how much the superintendents seemed to know about his school. He never worked out how it happened but he did begin to suspect that there might have been "spies" in his midst.

To me this seemed so reminiscent of Montville and the middles dual preoccupation with the spy theme and their getting caught in the impossible binds of the guerilla-entrepreneurial scheme.

Apart from the drug and communication issues, Lewis in his middleness got totally overwhelmed by the problems of overcrowding in his school, caught between the uppers who wanted to spend as few dollars as possible and the students who were collectively creating great chaos simply by their mere numbers. The school had been forced to operate what they euphemistically called the extended school day. It was packaged as an educational innovation but it operated like an administrative nightmare. It worked as follows. Each school day was divided into fifteen segments called modules. Course content was parcelled into essential and elective components, and students could design individualized programs that best represented their educational and personal interests. Each student was expected to spend approximately two-thirds of the day in class or highly structured activities. The remainder of the time could be directed to more personal interests such as craft, library, private project or relaxation activities. The spirit of this design matched perfectly the dominant youth culture of the day of highly individualized education and maximal flexibility. This scheme might have worked except that when students were not in class there was nowhere to go and little to do. The cafeteria was always overcrowded. The library was too small and the gymnasium was always occupied with sports classes. Hence, despite the fact that the program was designed to enrich the educational experience of the students, the lack of available space for extra activities meant that there were always a lot of students with virtually no place to go and nothing to do. Since nobody liked the teenagers to be milling around in the corridors and bathrooms, students who had not found a crevice of the school structure to hibernate in during the free modules were rounded up and herded into the auditorium where they were expected to sit quietly until they could return to some formal activity. Teachers who were not teaching were rostered to act as conformity officers, which meant keep all otherwise unoccupied students in the auditorium and make sure they remained quiet. Teachers and students both resented this immensely.

Brook realized he had to take action. But what could he do? For years he'd lobbied for a second high school, believing that by 1980 there could be as many as two thousand students. As the school system vacillated back and forwards over where the ninth grade should be located and with the slowness of the opening of the new middle school, he became afraid that he'd be asked to carry as many as seventeen hundred students in space ideal for several hundred less to the end of the 1970s.

Exasperated by the school system's refusal to address the problems of overcrowding at his school, Lewis Brook decided to do his own study of population estimates. He was frightened by the results. It appeared that the High School population would increase from fifteen hundred in 1972–73 to 1746 in 1977–78, just enough to make his school completely unmanageable but not enough to truly justify the gigantic expense that a totally new high school would demand. He decided to bite the bullet and ask for more space at his school, knowing this would mean that the second high school would be dropped. He argued that a new fifteen-hundred-pupil high school would cost ten to twelve million dollars whereas additions to his high school of a new fieldhouse-type gymnasium with supplemental locker, storage, and team room facilities, a new classroom wing, a vocational-educational area and a second cafeteria, converting the present gym into a library and dividing the present library into a sound-proofed instrumental music area could be done for as little as $1.5 million, half of which would be underwritten by the state. He felt this was not an unreasonable cost for a facility that could carry the school system into the 1980s.

The immediate response to Brook's new population figures and the proposed building extensions was confusion. There were some who felt that the impetus for the second high school was being diffused by these student population estimates. Others considered that this building extension would be an ideal solution. Yet others used this as a rationale to support their original contention that the ninth grade should have been moved to the intermediate school. This latter group was still extremely annoyed by their earlier defeat and saw the information emerging through Lewis Brook's study as providing a new leverage to their position. Originally, they'd reacted by saying, "If you won't move the ninth grade, you won't get a second high school." With Brook's proposal in hand they started to say, "If you won't move the ninth grade, don't expect us to help in resolving the high school overcrowding problem by any method."

For several months, the board of education, the superintendent and the high school administration found themselves paralyzed by the intensity of the community's contradictory reactions to Brook's proposal. Eddie Rhodes, sensing another fight in the air, decided he should do his own study of population trends, just to be ready for the detonation of the inevitable explosion.

Rhodes came up with a surprise. Contrary to everyone's belief his figures indicated that the high school population was peaking at about fifteen hundred students and that within two years they would begin to decline, so that by 1980 instead of there being the anticipated two thousand or more high school students, there would be as few as 1,350.

The superintendent felt his findings were so important he should release them straight away. Paying little attention to the political implications he made them public. Lewis was outraged. For years he'd depended on everyone's belief that the population would increase for leverage in his campaign to obtain relief for his overcrowding difficulties. And here was his boss taking away his major ammunition. Principal Brook felt abandoned. Immediately, he suspected that the superintendent had been bought off by the politicians and had fudged his figures as part of some political maneuver. He feared that the superintendent had given up on his repeated support for Brook's concerns of overcrowding. This was not true however. Rhodes had done his studies completely alone and without political pressure and he had not changed his position that even with the current high school population more space was needed.

Lewis concluded that with the superintendent becoming a turncoat there was no alternative but to fight him publically. He decided to create a forum in which the superintendent's findings could be discredited. Wanting to stack things in his own favor, he invited Eddie Rhodes to present his findings openly to the high school teachers. Reluctantly and foolishly, Rhodes agreed.

The faculty assembled at 1:00 P.M. one afternoon. Rhodes was nowhere to be seen. At 1:10 both embarrassed and annoyed, Lewis Brook stepped to the microphone and blandly declared, "The superintendent was expected to be here by 1:00 P.M. It's now ten after and I've decided to give up on him; but let me tell you what he was going to say." He quickly summarized Rhodes' findings of a peak population in 1973–74 and then a decline. He concluded, "But I don't believe this; in fact, I'd like to write a book on it. I'm very unsure of the validity of his study and am convinced that there are so many other unexplained variables such as the current drift to the East Coast, that have not been taken into account, that I don't think this study can be considered at all definitive."

With this, Brook suggested that the teachers make use of the allotted time by breaking into departmental groups to discuss other issues and then conclude at their usual 2:10. At about 1:30 Dr. Rhodes called Brook to apologize for his lateness and to announce that he could be there by 2:00 P.M.

Superintendent Rhodes was very flustered over this delay. He'd been detained in a meeting in the state's capital that morning. When it was clear that he could not make the appointed hour, he vacillated about what to do. On the one hand, he realized that the teachers would be aggravated at his delay; on the other hand he felt if he didn't turn up at all it would look as though he was afraid of criticism of his population study and was taking refuge in his being unavailable for public debate. When all these factors were put into the decision, he concluded that he had to go.

When Brook announced to the faculty who were by then dispersed in rooms around the school that Rhodes would be there at 2:00 P.M. and that everyone should reassemble for his presentation, everywhere in the building an audible groan of complaint could be heard. That meant that the teachers would be kept in school an extra hour, and they experienced in this act the feelings their students regularly had on detention occasions. Thus it was a reasonably hostile and nonempathetic audience that confronted the superintendent when he arrived. Their opinions had already been molded, partially by Brook's earlier comments, and now it was evident they had to compliantly sit out an hour of boring statistics as a gesture to the political football game at which they were mandatory observers.

Rhodes' presentation was an academically fascinating dissection of the available population figures and extrapolation from possible trends. He certainly had been most thorough in his research and he presented his study in the most detached, academic form he could. But within five minutes no one was listening. People courteously turned to pages of statistics at his direction, but these responses were automatic and no indication that the material was being absorbed. By the end of the hour everyone was bored, and teachers obviously so annoyed at having been detained, that no one had any energy to challenge or even query his findings.

When it came to question time, no one said a word. Everyone just wanted to leave.

All in all, everybody lost something as a result of that occasion. Principal Brook did not succeed in getting his faculty to discredit the superintendent's findings. Rhodes convinced nobody, bored everybody, and left bad feelings, first over his being late, second over detaining everybody, and third over being "such an unstimulating man", as one angry teacher expressed it. The teachers all lost an hour of their personal time, lost some faith in the system's sensitivity to what really mattered to them in their educational task, namely overcrowded conditions, and they lost a little respect for their principal over his unnecessary backhanded slap at the superintendent in his absence.

By this stage of my understanding of Ashgrove I began to wonder seriously, and somewhat dispairingly, whether Rhodes and Brook would ever be able to understand each other. To my mind they were both so alike. The forces contributing to their experiences of middleness and the binds of their prison were so similar. Yet their experiences of each other's realities were so radically different. I kept saying to myself, over and over, if only they could step back and look at themselves from a distance, if only they could trace the impact of the three types of structural encasement on their experience of themselves and each other! Then I would stop. "Remind yourself, Ken, that you seem unable to do this in your own life. Why do you imagine Eddie and Lewis could do it!"

A Clandestine Caucus

Since my first day in Ashgrove I'd heard of the board Democrats' policy of "postponing and preorchestrating" whenever they were unable to resolve their differences in public. I knew their orchestrations took place in secret caucus meetings but it was hard to obtain reliable information on what actually occurred during those private sessions. I'd been fascinated to watch the boards of finance and education operate in coalition during the budgeting sessions and I'd grown curious about what might transpire in the Democratic meetings, especially since after one of their late night clandestine encounters there were as many versions of what took place as there were people present. One day I unexpectedly stumbled into an event that gave me an intriguing inside glimpse at these forces operative in their Democratic caucuses.

I tell this story primarily to highlight one aspect of how the board made its decisions. However, many other important themes may be found in this incident. Some of those I've already drawn attention to, which are illustrated again in this event, are: (1) the ongoing blindness of the board as uppers to the consequences of their behavior; (2) the extent to which the lowers, in this case the principals, experience themselves as pawns in others' power games; (3) the ongoing pulls and tugs on those who feel trapped in the middle; (4) the meddling of uppers, here the board, in affairs not remotely related to their function; (5) the repetition of old patterns of interactions between groups where the situation cries out for different actions; and (6) the overwhelmingness of the pressures that can converge on one individual when the system starts to behave in frenetic and strange ways.

Everybody in New England knows that the quality of the educational system of small towns can be gauged by how good their football team is. Over the previous few years, Ashgrove had fared badly, especially in the game on Thanksgiving morning against their archrival. They had lost eight out of the past ten Thanksgiving Day games and the town had grown tired of having indigestion while eating roast turkey. The old school simply had to do better.

Both Hewett and Kingston, keen sportsmen and active alumni of Ashgrove High School, felt obliged to remedy this situation during their tour of duty on the board of education. But how do you cure such a problem? After years of trying more acceptable methods, they'd decided the most effective system would be to buy off their main opposition's football coach. For years they'd been preparing the ground with well-timed rhetoric such as: "The problem is Ashgrove has no strong full-time athletics director who could oversee the program in all the schools and assure that essential sporting skills are inculcated and nurtured in the early years;" "We need a constant flow of good sporting blood through the middle school and eventually into our high school teams;" "We need an ideal man as athletic director who can therapeutically channel the destructive and self-damaging frustration of our teenagers into aggressive and ego-building sports;" "Some schools that have a good sports coach can boast a history of students whose lives seemed initially vacuous but were transformed by the injection of temporary meaning by strong physical involvement in sports while the emotional shakiness of their adolescence passed." Hewett and Kingston made good political mileage out of these slogans, which the town loved. However to date they'd not had an opportunity to effect their plan.

Hewett and Kingston believed their own rhetoric and wanted someone like Carlo Esposito, coach of their major opposition, to come to Ashgrove. The problem was Carlo had been so popular and successful where he was that it always seemed impossible that he could ever be interested in Ashgrove. Hewett had discussed with him the possibility of moving on numerous occasions over recent years. Though Carlo had been flattered by the thought, he had simply laughed his rejection. Even if Esposito were interested, he knew enough about politics to realize that engineering the creation of the job and lining up the forces so that Carlo could get the position would be very difficult.

Every time Craig Hewett and Ron Kingston thought about their scheme they got stuck on one problem. What to do with Patrick Sheehan. He had been football coach for years and if an athletics directorship were created he would be a strong inside candidate. However Craig and Ron were convinced he would not do well in this special role. He was a great teacher, a popular man, and a very promising future administrator, but they felt, and Patrick in the privacy of his own mind may well have agreed, that he did not have the peculiar mix of characteristics that made one of those truly outstanding sports coaches. However, Sheehan's political support in the town was so strong that if he sought such a prestigious sports directorship it would be virtually impossible to deny Patrick the position. Hewett and Kingston would have to mount a massive political campaign to undermine Sheehan's candidacy. Both Ron and Craig knew they had to avoid precipitating such a showdown and had decided to bide their time.

One day they were suddenly presented with an unexpected opportunity. Brendan Collier had reached his limit with the tensions of his job and the strains within the group of principals at the high school. He decided to retire that summer, two years before everyone assumed. One afternoon Brendan took Lewis Brook aside and told him of his intentions to resign and asked that Brook keep it a secret, telling no one for at least ten days. Brook gave Collier his word but accidently let it slip during a conversation with Board Chairman Kingston that very afternoon. Ron picked up on it straight away. Embarrassed, Lewis told Kingston it was strictly confidential and asked that Ron tell no one because of Brook's prior promise to Collier. Kingston, agreeing to keep it quiet, went straight to the phone.

"Craig, we've got our chance to do our Esposito plan!"

"How come?"

"Collier's quitting!"

"When?"

"This year!"

"When shall we move?"

"Tonight. I'm going to call a secret caucus of the board's Democrats after our regular board meeting tonight."

"Where?"

"Let's see if we can meet at D'Onofrio's. No one could see us in Mike's basement and his home is off the beaten track. Craig, would you call him and ask if it's okay for tonight at midnight?"

"Okay. By the way, Luise Taylor will be back for the first time tonight after her operation. Let's keep the board meeting going until she's too tired."

"That's a good idea. It'll be easier to pull off without her."

The scheme was to preorchestrate Patrick Sheehan's promotion to the vacant assistant principalship, pass a rule that no principal could be a senior sports coach, create the special athletics directorship, undertake a national search, reject all applicants as being unsuitable, and then when their grand scheme looked like it might die before being given birth, draft Carlo Esposito from his school district, packaging him as the only man in the country who could do the job. They'd have to move quickly and with careful synchronization.

That night the whole board of education met at their regular 8:00 P.M. time. The agenda was short. The meeting could have been completed within one hour. I assumed that the Democrats were eager to end early so that they could get to D'Onofrio's for their caucus. However the board meeting dragged on and on, with endless, highly conflicting debate over trivia. I was confused as to what was happening. Suddenly it became clear. At about 11:30 Luise Taylor very apologetically excused herself, claiming that she was exhausted, that she still needed a lot of rest as part of her postoperative recuperation. Within minutes of Luise's departure the board meeting ended. All the things that had seemed important to debate in detail all night were now brushed aside. Later I came to understand that this stringing out of the meeting had been part of Hewett's and Kingston's plan so as to postpone commencing the caucus until after Luise had gone home. Since they feared she'd oppose their plan, having her absent was quite strategic.

As the five male Democrats arrived in the dark at Mike's home in the early hours of the morning, there was a spirit of mystery. Ron and Craig sat side by side on a couch; Mike was wandering around pouring beer and scotch; Matthew Lodell was sprawled in a comfortable chair; Rodney Saunders was on the floor.

"What do we have to discuss tonight?" opened Lodell impatiently. Kingston started with the news that one of the assistant principalships at the high school would soon fall vacant.

"Who's leaving?" shot in Matthew.

"Can't tell you. It's still secret, and I know only in strictest confidence."

"I bet it's Collier," cut in D'Onofrio.

"I'd prefer not to say. Don't you understand this is confidential?"

Mike insisted. "If you don't tell us, there's no point in even having this meeting. And since when did you decide you could keep privileged information from us. We're as trustworthy as you are."

"Okay, it's Collier."

Despite the fact Collier had told Brook of his intentions in the strictest confidence only a few hours earlier, it was inevitable the whole town would know by the next day. This group of Democrats were notorious for their inability to keep a secret.

"I don't believe it," retorted Lodell. "He's been my best friend for twenty-three years. I haven't heard it. He'd never tell you before he told me." Matthew was indignant.

"It's true," replied Kingston.

The atmosphere was tense. Despite their attempts to remain cohesive in public, there was very little unity in private settings. They could get really volatile with each other.

Hewett and Kingston laid out their plan.

Stony silence.

Eventually Mike spoke. "I don't like it."

"It won't happen," fumed Lodell. "I'll bet you're wrong about Brendan. He'd tell me before . . . ! Anyway, I just don't like it," angry at the idea of what it would cost to "buy off" Esposito.

"Why not?"

"I don't like the idea of deciding like this that Sheehan should be given the assistant principal's position!"

"Have you got something against Sheehan?"

"No!"

"Then what's up?"

"It's not that I have anything against him; it's just that I don't know whether he's the best man for the job. He might be, but this just seems to be the wrong way to go about selecting an assistant principal. We don't know he'll even apply; and if he does we don't know whether Rhodes or Brook would support Sheehan."

"Well, I've spoken to Brook," replied Kingston, keen to diffuse Lodell's discontent. "He's for Sheehan—thinks he'd be good."

"What about Rhodes? How do you know he'll go along with it?" asked Matthew still very perturbed.

"He'll be no problem," replied Ron.

"What do you mean, 'he'll be no problem'?"

"Well, one thing I've learned about Eddie Rhodes is that if you lean on him hard enough, he'll break."

"It sounds to me like we're setting ourselves up for another Walder-Maher appointment; and you remember how messy that was," added Mike D'Onofrio with equal concern.

"Well, we have the power here in this room," contributed Rodney Saunders speaking for the first time. "If we want to do it, we can do it, just so long as we vote together and no one decides to go off on his own," an obvious slap at Mike for his annoying habit of voting his mind rather than obeying the party line.

Hewett and Kingston sighed their relief the moment Saunders began to speak. They had hoped he could be swayed into their camp. It was obvious to everyone that D'Onofrio and Lodell would be against the plan. This meant Hewett and Kingston had to work on Saunders. If they could get him on their side then the caucus would pass it three to two. With Luise absent it would be easy. From there the scheme was to force the Democrats to vote as a block. That would pass on a three to two vote. Luise Taylor would then be given her instructions to vote with the Democrat's coalition and the scheme would pass in the board of education with five Democratic "yes" votes to three Republican "no" votes with Chairman Kingston abstaining. This was how the Ashgrove Democrats practiced democracy. A minority of two could pull off a five to three victory. So long as there was enough critical mass, others would be seduced into line to make it look like a majority decision. Saunders was the key. Hewett and Kingston would engage him in some standard "horse trading" with "you do this for me and we'll do that for you" type exchanges. If he could be swayed it would be easy.

I sat in amazement watching this all happen. The atmosphere was extraordinarily intense. Lodell sat for an hour simply pouting. He was so angry. However, he'd been brushed aside and was feeling very left out. Mike was silent, preoccupied with something else. Hewett and Kingston worked on Saunders. They negotiated vigorously. They promised support for some of his pet projects only if he'd capitulate to their interests in this plan. I felt the pressure was so strong that it was inevitable that he'd eventually concede. The thing that surprised me, however, was how easily two people, in this case Hewett and Kingston, could maneuver into a position where they were able to win when at least six of the nine board members were basically against them. The key had been making sure Luise was absent for this caucus. Everyone knew she was such a staunch Democrat as was Lodell that no matter what their opinions were, in the final analysis, they would always vote the party position. However had she been present, then with Lodell and D'Onofrio they could have formed an opposition block of three votes and the plan would almost certainly have been defeated.

Eventually, Saunders capitulated and the decision was made as planned. Two things promised to be complicated. Carlo Esposito would be available only if he were made a direct offer and it had to be a lot of dollars. "No haggling. Just make it big bucks!" Esposito had made his position clear. The second problem was Patrick Sheehan. The scheme demanded that Carlo be given a direct invitation and that meant Sheehan had to be removed from consideration. That's what made this opportunity perfect. All they needed to do now was to time everything delicately, line the votes up to assure success, and then sit back and watch the plan unfold.

At this point I began to smile inside. This group of Democrats was overlooking one critical issue and that was whether Sheehan would be interested in promotion to an assistant principalship. The board Democrats just assumed he would be, but no one had ever asked. I sat there thinking how ironic it would be, although by now in my mind somewhat typical of upper groups, if this whole scheme backfired simply because the schemers made one inappropriate assumption that they never bothered to check. It so happened that a few days earlier I had rather innocently asked Sheehan whether he wanted to be an assistant principal. He'd replied "Maybe someday but definitely not within the next few years and probably not ever here at Ashgrove."

Patrick Sheehan had been aware that within a year or two Collier would retire and then an assistant principal position would be vacant. For quite some time he'd been preparing himself for the possibility someday of being a principal and he certainly would be a strong candidate. He had spent the last few years shaping and running successfully a first class humanities department. He was immensely popular with students and fellow teachers alike. He stood tall at Ashgrove. A man just into his early thirties, he had a slightly retiring manner but he embodied sincerity. He enjoyed lighthearted encounters but still found it easy to be strict when needed. He was a man of integrity.

Sheehan, however, didn't want the assistant principal's job. He'd sensed for some time now the dysfunctional relations among the four principals. Patrick had been a strong supporter of Walder and he felt that Brook had undermined Walder destructively. While Patrick hoped to attain some administrative post, maybe in Ashgrove, someday, he didn't feel, for a wide variety of reasons, that this was the time. Although understanding local political processes well and knowing that it would be necessary to project an air of ambitiousness, he had privately determined that whenever Brendan Collier retired he would not be an applicant for his job. However, not a soul in Ashgrove knew this, least of all Principal Brook or this group of Democratic board members plotting and scheming in D'Onofrio's dimly lit basement. Hence my excitement and curiosity was at a peak as I left Mike's home at 2:20 A.M. that cold New England morning. I was looking forward to seeing how this story would unfold.

Hewett and Kingston waited impatiently for Brendan Collier to publically announce his retirement. The moment he did they swung their plan into action. Step one was promote Sheehan into the assistant principalship. To eliminate suspicion, they decided to conduct a national search for the position. However the day before applications closed they learned of their first set back. There were thirty-two applicants but Patrick Sheehan was not one of them. Rather unthinkingly they dispatched one of their political hacks to inform him that if he wished ever for a principalship he'd have to at least publically declare his ambitiousness and the appropriate way to do that was to present himself as a candidate for the Collier replacement. "We will interpret your failure to apply as indifference and lack of aspiration. It will go against you later." This message was made clear to Sheehan. In addition, Brook was letting everyone know his disappointment by spreading around the word that he'd been personally grooming Sheehan for this position for the past three years.

202

Patrick was subjected to a lot of pressure. He was flattered but confused. Something didn't seem right. Not knowing how to interpret what was going on, at the last minute he agreed to apply but with the clear private intention of performing poorly as a candidate to assure he would not be offered the job.

The selection panel of Rhodes, O'Sullivan, and Brook was constituted and they chose seven applicants to interview, including Sheehan. At the time when interviews were about to commence, Kingston and Hewett called on Rhodes and O'Sullivan to tell them of their grand scheme and to indicate that they wanted Patrick Sheehan's name to be the nomination for the position. This made Rhodes and O'Sullivan angry, but they were diplomatic enough not to say anything. They had been heavily bruised by their resistances during the Walder-Maher appointments and had come to realize that these situations were very complex and had to be handled with caution and skill. Privately they just hoped Patrick Sheehan came out looking like the best candidate. If he didn't, Rhodes and O'Sullivan didn't quite know what they'd do. For the moment they decided to worry about this later.

The superintendent, upset by the Democrats meddling in his turf, at one board meeting asked the board to read the top twelve files. Some members took the task seriously, Lodell in particular, who was coming to resent the scheming habits of Hewett and Kingston. He'd privately hoped that their efforts would be thwarted, though he was unsure he was willing to carry the responsibility for undermining their plan. "This Morgan guy looks pretty good to me," Lodell had commented. Hewett had countered with a sarcastic quip, pulling Sheehan's file out of the pile, throwing the rest of the documents across the table to Superintendent Rhodes with the injunction, "You can reject them all. Sheehan is the only candidate worth having."

The board requested the interview panel to present two nominations ranked first and second. After the interviews were completed, two candidates were considered outstanding, Patrick Sheehan and Irv Morgan. The selection panel agonized over who should be given the number one rank. They felt these two candidates were equally good, however they were so upset by the Democrats' scheming that they wanted to rebel and nominate Morgan. Eventually they gave in and ranked Sheehan number one.

The weeks had been racing by. It was now early July and the board was scheduled to make their formal decision on the assistant principal at their regular Tuesday night meeting. Sheehan was to be presented as number one candidate. The hot informal network quickly got this news to Patrick. He was dismayed. He had applied making a grudging concession to the pressures around him but he desperately hoped he wouldn't be offered the job. Now it looked as if he was going to be landed in something he didn't want. Regretably there seemed no alternative. He would pull out.

On the day before that Tuesday meeting, Superintendent Rhodes received a letter from Patrick Sheehan withdrawing his application, stating no reasons but concluding with the statement that "Someday I hope to serve as a principal in a forwardlooking high school."

This letter threw the system into chaos. Rhodes called Lewis Brook to tell him the news. Brook was incredulous. Reality seemed to be mocking him. He immediately sought out Sheehan and arranged for a quick meeting in the superintendent's office to discuss the matter further.

Sheehan felt driven into an inescapable corner. He had several reasons why he didn't want the assistant's position, but none of these were easily explainable to either his principal or his superintendent without hurting a lot of feelings. Patrick searched longingly for a rationale for his withdrawal that was both innocuous and would be acceptable to his two superiors. He stumbled upon an excuse, his desire to remain involved in sports. The board had announced a new policy that principals in the future could not coach sports. He explained that he wished to continue coaching football for another two years and since he could not coach as an assistant principal he would prefer to remain as a regular teacher for the interim. In this setting his excuse seemed reasonable enough.

For Brook and Rhodes, Sheehan's response produced an impossible bind. They believed they could probably get Sheehan to accept the assistant principalship if they let him remain football coach at least for a few more years. The problem was this would thwart the Hewett-Kingston scheme. Sheehan had been attractive to them primarily because his promotion would facilitate the appointment of Esposito. Nevertheless, Lewis Brook and Eddie Rhodes felt there was little alternative than to continue promoting Sheehan and try to get the board to reverse their new regulation about principals not coaching sports.

They asked Patrick if he'd accept the position if he were allowed to coach for another year. This threw the bind back on Sheehan. Feeling that his integrity would be at stake if he now refused, because his excuse for not accepting promotion would now look pathetic, he reluctantly said yes, but asked for more time to think it over.

Rhodes went immediately to Kingston because he knew that this would upset the athletic directorship plans. Ron was irate, but eventually conceded that if this were the only way to get Sheehan to accept the position then there was really little alternative. It offered the only hope of an eventual Esposito appointment. If they could get Sheehan promoted, Kingston figured they could always reneg on the football coaching issue in a year or two. By this time it was Monday evening, the day before the intended appointment was to be made. Rhodes reasoned with Kingston that it would be best to postpone further consideration of the athletics directorship for at least twelve months and then rethink the issue. Kingston thought about this suggestion for a long time and then angrily ordered the superintendent to do nothing until he had spoken with Craig Hewett.

For several hours the two master planners, Hewett and Kingston, sat with their heads together, but could see no ready solution. They were furious. Early Tuesday morning, after a long night of deliberation Hewett heard on the grapevine that Sheehan had resolved not to accept the appointment under any conditions. Rhodes was still expecting Sheehan to accept if the football coach issue could be resolved, when Craig called angrily to tell him the news. While Hewett and Rhodes were still talking, Sheehan left a message requesting a meeting alone with the superintendent immediately.

Patrick had decided there was no alternative now but to be direct. He apologized for the immense confusion he'd created, admitting that he'd been searching for a way to reject the job without hurting anyone's feelings. He confessed that the sports coaching issue had merely been a way to rationalize his rejecting the offer, acknowledging in retrospect that this excuse had been poorly thought out and had only fueled the chaos. He did not add that he'd heard informally about how he was being used in the whole Esposito plan but Rhodes suspected he had found out. Sheehan did say he didn't want to be a principal at Ashgrove in the current climate, hinting that the principals appeared to have difficulty relating but not saying how obvious and painful the whole Walder-Maher phenomenon was for most of the teachers in the school.

Superintendent Rhodes could see that Sheehan had now firmly decided and felt some empathy with the binds he had found himself in. Rhodes wished Patrick well, assured him that in everyone's eyes he would have made a good principal. They thanked each other and parted cordially.

Kingston was furious when he learned about this final withdrawal and asked Rhodes vindictively, "What would Sheehan do if we told him he couldn't coach anyway?" Rhodes responded "I'm afraid the Ashgrove school system would simply lose one of the finest men it's ever had!" Kingston decided to do nothing further.

The board meeting came and went. There was very little discussion about Sheehan's withdrawal other than the fact that he was a really good man and the board lost him. Irv Morgan was voted for the position and received unanimous support.

The Hewett-Kingston grand plan had become disembodied.

To this day Ashgrove has no athletics directorship, Patrick Sheehan continues as head of the humanities department, and the football team still loses to Carlo Esposito's team on Thanksgiving morning.

When I next spoke to Patrick Sheehan I found myself constantly thinking about Anthony from Montville, how the system was using him as a player in a script he could not unravel. Patrick knew the lines that were right for him to say, however he kept discovering they were not the lines others demanded of him. So many forces had been converging on him and meanings were being attached to his actions that certainly had no relevance for him. But they had relevance for others. And this is what could prove to be crazy making. I felt convinced that Patrick had made a lucky escape. The school system was in the process of putting so much significance into him, his thoughts, his wishes, that had he played along, he may well have lost any control over his own destiny. He would have become the focus of conflicted reality systems. Some would have seen him one way and others contradictorily. In fact he individually could have ended up having to bear within him the same kind of tension Walder and Maher carried in their relationship. Every bone in my body was now telling me that this is the stuff of which village lunacy is made. Had Sheehan gone along, unknowingly, he would have become yet another repository for the unresolved conflicts that oozed out of the underbelly of the school system.

Sheehan escaped. Only just. And I now began to wonder who would be the next potential victim.

The Unpredictable Italian

There's a proposition in social theory that claims every system needs a deviant. If there's not one around, the system will create one. It was hard for me to look at Anthony in Montville and not have all the everyday images of craziness come rushing to my mind. Yet when I got close to his reality and felt how the forces of the Elite, In, and Out groups seemed to converge on him, his behavior was reasonably easy to understand without having to evoke psychopathological explanations. In addition it was also possible to see what a critical function he played in that minisociety because his actions and how people related to him seemed to drain off much of the unresolved tension from the system at large. When there was tension that refused to go anywhere else there was always old Anthony, a ready receptacle into which bad feelings could be easily dumped.

One of Ashgrove's deviants was clearly Mike D'Onofrio. But his deviance was very powerful, so powerful at times that it could even be seen as leadership, given the precarious balance of the potential forces on the board. He was the one Democrat most likely to deviate from the party line. With a nine-person board and with the Republicans always holding at least three seats (a requirement of the law) Mike's willingness not to be a Democratic player meant that it was easy for the board to deadlock with four to four ties as it so often did. We've already discussed the import of this, given Chairman Kingston's reticence to vote as the tie-breaker.

In a way, since board members held some formal power, Mike's deviance proved to be a very potent force, often quite catalytic. A political analyst could, in fact, look at D'Onofrio's inclinations on issues and make a reasonably firm prediction on how things would unfold. For this reason when Mike spoke almost everyone paid attention, even if he was speaking nonsense. The paradox was that the mere fact that he was willing to deviate gave him his major power, and this power was augmented even further by the fact that people listened to him so intensely in order to see whether his conforming or deviating side were in gear. If he was in a conforming posture people didn't pay much attention. But when he was in his deviating stance, he got the limelight.

In a strange way, he was a barometer of the town. Average Ashgrovites, if they understood this phenomenon, might well have been able to see their own inconsistencies and ambivalences mirrored in Mike's vacillations and eventual behaviors.

This type of deviance held catalytic potential. And Mike didn't hesitate to use it.

What concerns me as a social theorist however is how this kind of catalytic action from a deviant with significant power generates so much unresolved tension among groups and people that it ends up being relocated in places where it doesn't seem to rightfully belong. The consequences of the actions of a deviant with power rarely appear to come back to roost on the deviant's doorstep. They seem to go somewhere else. Someone else goes crazy or gets killed off instead of the deviant whose actions originated the chaos.

D'Onofrio had been a member of the board of education for the past five years. He was a young, effusive, well-qualified, very successful, and much-esteemed lawyer in nearby New Bedford. He'd been elected to the board soon after he'd arrived in Ashgrove and had become popular quickly. He had many early political successes. He'd grown up in New Bedford and knew the physical, psychological, historical, and social layout of the urban region very well. His boyhood days had been spent in an Italian neighborhood, and with the determination of highly motivated, socially mobile parents he had been raised with all the opportunities any American boy could hope for. His path had been typical—off to college and then to law school and then back to his home city after a short apprenticeship period in New York to start practicing his new profession in the city he knew and loved so well and among the people towards whom he felt much fondness.

Mike would mention his Italian etiology within the first two or three sentences of any conversation with a new acquaintance. However he would distort his history, implying that he had grown up very poor and that he individually had lifted his family from poverty. Not true. By the time he was born, Mike's family was already middle class. He was proud of his ancestry, although he loathed the automatic association people made between an Italian and organized crime. D'Onofrio himself had been very strongly socialized into the Catholic religion and had adopted a rigid definition of right and wrong. Mike was so invested in seeing himself as a good, honorable man that he often failed to see many of the implications of his behavior other than that they conformed to his versions of morality.

In his law school days of indoctrination he had again been a victim of overzealous socialization. His loyalty to the law was so strong that he'd firmly convinced himself that there were no justifiable circumstances under which he'd consider breaking the law.

Mike was a character of strong contradictions. He could make a grudging concession to the ironies of his ideology, simultaneously by chairing Ashgrove's committee to elect George McGovern as president while supporting the mass arrests of the antiwar demonstrations during the law-and-order era of Attorney General John Mitchell.

He'd been so successful in his legal work that in a brief few years he'd climbed into a position of economic affluence. In contrast to Ron Kingston, his law practice was independent of Ashgrove. Hence he didn't need to rely in any way on the politicians of Main Street. This meant that he was envied by many, particularly those whose major sympathies were shaped by the Factory and who recognized Mike was free from those demands that the town's political bosses placed on so many of them.

D'Onofrio also had a strong relationship with Eddie Rhodes. He'd supported him both politically and personally. During the earlier grade alignment battle it had been Mike D'Onofrio who had regularly bolted from the Democratic ranks and voted with the more liberal Republicans in supporting the superintendents. This angered both the Democratic chiefs and his fellow board Democrats. At the time Mike had been glib. "If it costs me my political career, it costs me my political career. I'll live with that okay. However, I know I couldn't live with myself if I were to act against my conscience." He took comfort in this reassurance.

However, in the spring of 1973 Mike D'Onofrio was just months away from the end of his first six-year term. He had before him a critical decision concerning his future political interests. A couple of years earlier he'd been approached and asked if he'd take a position as an assistant attorney for the state. He'd refused, because deep down he wanted to be a judge, and although he hesitated to talk about it at this young age, he wanted to preserve that option if at all possible. To obtain a judgeship, however, he needed the Factory's support. He was a little afraid that the town bosses might swing against him but he was hoping his independent actions would not burn his political bridges. They perhaps might not, had it not been for the strange scenes of the federal election. The Factory had been one of the all-powerful Democratic gods for decades and it was hard for him to imagine that he could ever lose any of that power. The Democratic convention of 1972, however, brought a change. Although he'd not been thrown out physically by the McGovern caravan as had his friend and political ally, Mayor Richard Daley of Chicago, he'd been definitely pushed aside. He was still smarting with the indignity of this fact, vowing vigorously, "I'll never vote for McGovern," when D'Onofrio started his position as chairman of Ashgrove's McGovern committee. The Factory was furious and chose Mike's political future as one target to release some of his aggression. He passed the message along that D'Onofrio could count on being dropped from the Democratic ticket for the board of education election that coming November.

A therapist could have become exhausted trying to circumnavigate the huge fields of Mike's resulting despondency. After several months of playing victim, D'Onofrio resolved to go and talk about his future with the town's bosses. What transpired during these discussions is not really known. However, what is known is that Mike's behavior changed radically after those exchanges. He began to talk about how wrong he'd been originally in voting to keep the ninth grade in the high school, how he'd been deceived by the superintendent and Principal Brook and how if he had the chance to vote again he'd side with his party in favor of the removalist stance, not against it as he'd done previously.

Everyone was shocked. To a person, his fellow board members, foe and ally alike, concluded that the Factory had told him he'd have to get the ninth grade out of the high school in order to survive politically. Mike denied this accusation hotly. However, he did start to pour his energies aggressively into reactivating the old removalist debate.

Mike began to look a little crazy. Nobody seemed to have any interest in going through this battle again. In another showdown, at best he might have two votes in favor of removal, his and Lodell's. The original voting had been the four Democrats—Lodell, Hewett, Taylor, and Saunders—for removal. Against had been the three Republicans and two defecting Democrats, Mike D'Onofrio and Chairman Ron Kingston. At this time, both Hewett and Saunders had changed their positions. They continued to feel that the original fifth to eighth grade decision had been wrong. However, since the decision had been made that way, and the intermediate school as currently structured was proving to be successful, they felt to try removal at this point would be prismsighted and probably very disruptive. From their perspective, it would cause unnecessary chaos in the new school. They considered the only logic that could possibly be used to relocate the ninth grade at this time would be the saving of money, and Craig Hewett felt that a removal now would represent a dreadful waste. He even calculated that the costs of the removal alone would take many years before being compensated for. Hence, when summoned to the Factory to recruit him to the ranks of the new removalist forces, Hewett fumed his rejections. "I'll not be party to that. If someone will show me figures to prove the economic saving, I'll consider it. But otherwise count me out." Rodney Saunders took the same position. Luise Taylor's vote was of little immediate consequence because she was still convalescing after serious surgery. The votes for removal just weren't there. It seemed as though the issue would quickly pass.

It might have, had it not been for Mike who steadfastly refused to let it die. Despite the fact that for weeks Mayor Maloney had been trying to spark the politics of removal by publicly claiming the town could not afford to provide any additional buildings for high school students over the next few years, no significant fires for change had been lit. D'Onofrio, realizing that with every passing day his chances of pulling off any removalist action for the coming year and his political future with it were slipping away, chose the closing minutes of the last board meeting in April to make a sudden move.

He had not discussed his plan with his fellow board Democrats. Maybe it had not been a perfect idea, but it arrived with such an irresistible force that seemed to confirm its rightness. Mike drew himself to the edge of his chair and thumped his elbow on the boardroom desk. The bowed heads, lulled by an evening of indifferent debate, suddenly bounced to attention to hear the deliberate words of D'Onofrio's instructions to the superintendent. "By next meeting, which is May first, I want a report from the superintendent's office of the feasibility of removing the ninth grade to the intermediate school; and I want that topic to be placed on the agenda for that next meeting."

"What are you requesting in this study?" asked Rhodes, somewhat startled.

"I'd like a study that examines the feasibility, economics, and practicality of removing the ninth grade out of the high school. In any case, even if a report is not possible I want this item on next meeting's agenda. Oh, and let me be perfectly clear. My request is for 1973–74 academic year."

"That's next year!" boomed back Rodney Saunders, annoyed by the prospect that his own political image might be damaged just because of Mike's knee jerk reactions. "Why should I be made to look like a political hack just so he can get renominated," Rodney fumed beneath his breath.

Eager to avoid a bloodbath, Kingston closed the meeting.

D'Onofrio's action stirred a storm in Ashgrove. For two weeks all the formal committees relevant to the location of the ninth grade met and all the informal pressure groups returned to their dimly lit basements to paw over the dusty strategies that had been used or not used in the previous battles. The old anger resurfaced.

The Democrats became frightened by the intensity of the public reaction. Realizing they were going to get caught in the battle, they assembled in Mayor Maloney's office for a last-minute caucus. Everyone was present except Luise Taylor. D'Onofrio had a lot resting on the outcome of this caucus, maybe his political future, and he was extraordinarily tense. His vigorous desire for the transferral of the ninth grade for the 1973–74 year was being resisted most strongly by Saunders, Hewett, and Kingston, who believed firmly that everything had gone too far for any change now. They felt it would produce such a public outcry that it would take years for their party to recover. They had the superintendent's report that D'Onofrio had requested. Rhodes had looked at the issue from two perspectives—a mix of grades six through nine and of five through nine in the middle school. His conclusion was that "no matter which way you look at it, the problem is just like a balloon. Put pressure at one point and it reappears somewhere else. If we want to solve the problem at some stage our system will need more buildings. Removal of students will just transfer the problem from one building to another."

210

Everyone argued against removal except Maloney, the Factory, and Mike. They pushed hard but the trio of Saunders, Hewett, and Kingston would not move. Tempers were hot, but no matter what anyone tried, the resisting trio remained unflinching. Within half an hour the removal plan for 1973–74 died. But out of its ashes quickly rose the phoenixlike solution to produce the switch in 1974–75. This provided a compromise that situations like this demand. The gravitation towards this position was swift and unthought through. The resisting trio felt they'd won this immediate struggle and they now seemed very conciliatory. No one seemed very interested in whether it would be a wise decision for 1974–75. Having resolved the present, the future could take care of itself.

A major concern for the caucusing Democrats was how they should handle the logistics of this decision. They knew the public was in an uproar and that to declare their intention of removal in 1974–75 would be just as explosive as shifting the ninth grade immediately. They decided to table the motion completely and slip the 1974–75 scheme through in the early part of the summer while most people were away on vacation.

The next board meeting was scheduled for Tuesday, May first. Somehow, New England May Days in the 1970s had become almost synonymous with fear of chaos. This day was to prove no exception. The agenda for the meeting looked long and threatening. Such sensitive topics as the delicate situation with teachers' contracts, questions around busing of minority students, a brewing confrontation with a teacher over sick leave rights for maternity purposes, and debate concerning the superintendent's salary had all crept onto the agenda to help flame the realignment fires. The explosive power of any two of those items juxtaposed in one meeting defied speculation. No wonder each board member arrived with the determination to keep his emotions cool.

A vigorous collection of interested public filled "the gallery"—a dreadful misnomer for the messy ring of hard-seated chairs that spanned the drab room. The public had come primed for a fight. All board members felt themselves to be on display and the artificial cordiality between bitter political opponents was transparent. Kingston droned the meeting to a dull start. He and the superintendent "Dr. Rhodesed and Mr. Chairmaned" each other with the most aristocratic political airs. Not all board members were present. Luise Taylor was still convalescing, Reuben Kaufman had chosen to be late, and Julia Langdon was absent attending another engagement. Thus in the room at the time were just the five Democrats and Gerald Bomford, alone holding the Republican flag.

Gerald was the only black politician in Ashgrove. In a town all but lily white, he'd carved out for himself an amazing identity. He was clearly the leader of the three-hundred-person black community and he had the capacity and stature, if he so desired, to become simultaneously leader of the white community as well. During his high school days he had excelled in most that he attempted, sports and academics particularly. He had chosen a career of teaching for himself, with athletics and physical education as his prime cynosure. Over recent years he had held an appointment in a school district some twenty miles away.

There had been a number of occasions when attempts had been made to involve Bomford in Ashgrove's educational politics. He'd been actively sought out by both parties over the years but he'd refused. Gerald had never belonged to a political party. He'd retained an independent stance. However, he'd eventually relented and decided to run for the board of education on the Republican ticket. In this town Bomford felt the Republicans were more in the forefront of educational innovation and progressiveness. He was the first black person to hold elected office in Ashgrove.

It was hard to gauge the impact of Gerald's blackness in an era when racial issues were in such turbulence. Signs of prejudice towards Bomford as a man, if they existed, were extremely difficult to detect. His old school friend Craig Hewett was able to admit to feeling some prejudices towards blacks in general, "But Gerald, never! What can you say about that man! Gerald is Gerald! True, he's black, but somehow that never seems to be relevant for him. When I'm with him, I'm never consciously thinking of his blackness. I think I would feel the same way towards him whether he were white or red. Somehow he seems to reach beyond any stereotypes." Although this assertion could contain a tonnage of denial and camouflaged emotions, in reality Hewett's behavior was congruent with his verbal sentiments. The two men behaved like friends.

Craig and Gerald as a result of their positions on the board of education had found themselves regularly on opposite sides of political events. They had many an intense fight, each operating out of radically different concepts of education. However, their relationship seemed not to suffer as a result. Bomford had been slow to become highly active on the board. He took a calm first year to familiarize himself with issues and procedures but now in the brewing events of this spring, he had become more energized. This evening's board meeting was to be testimony to that.

Eventually the moment of potential crisis was reached. It was Matthew Lodell, with twenty years of board experience, who had been selected as the man to diffuse the explosion. "There are three board members not present this evening. I think it would be most inappropriate to discuss such a complex issue as this ninth grade move in their absence. I therefore move that the superintendent's report be tabled and referred to the Long Range Planning Committee." "Seconded," Gerald's voice flashed his approval. No discussion. Carried unanimously! The formal procrastinating act was completed.

"I'd like, however," continued Lodell, "to give the opportunity to the public to speak on this issue."

Craig Hewett quickly intervened and seized the initiative. He delivered an eloquent exposition on some of the historical background of the ninth grade problem. When he'd finished, a woman asked why there was a need to refer this issue to the Long Range Planning Committee. "If you had to deliberate this at a committee level, why didn't you do it before tonight?" A "nothing" answer caused her to rephrase her question. "Does this mean that you've decided that no change will be made for the coming year and that anything that is planned would be for later years?" Lodell replied "That would be a correct interpretation."

The public was incensed. They'd come ready for a fight and just as the battle was about to begin, one of the contestants refused to enter the arena. However, such predetermined emotions cannot be easily diffused with a simple political stroke. So fight they did. To attempt a rational exposition of what followed defies the cerebration of the human mind. One woman dominated the scene with her irrational outbursts for many minutes, cutting off with a high-pitched voice anyone who tried to speak. When she'd finished, another aggressor took over. The public went on and on. Through my eyes, the normally divided board looked amazingly cohesive in the face of this onslaught. They looked like classic lowers, with the public behaving like aggressive uppers. The politicians seemed like absent middles. At one point, Reuben Kaufman, who'd arrived a few minutes after the beginning of the attack, found himself defending a point with the logic of Hewett, and Hewett could be heard giving "wholehearted support to the position of my colleague Mr. Kaufman on that issue." What! Kaufman and Hewett, bedfellows? They normally found it impossible to agree with each other about what day of the week it was. I began to wonder if this was the same board I'd been watching all these months. No one seemed to be behaving consistently with his previous behavior.

Mike D'Onofrio played a low key role initially. For a while he looked like he would get out of this unscathed. But they got him. Although he really did tie the noose around his own neck. Hewett had suggested that this grade alignment had been hard to decide because the pro's and con's weighed about fifty-fifty either way. To this, an antiremovalist woman commented, "Well, that was the situation back in 1970 when the fifth-eighth combination was decided. What has changed?" Mike foolishly jumped in.

"We were unaware of the overcrowding problem at the high school back in 1970!"

"What do you mean, you didn't know where the kids were! Don't you know how many students there are and how much space is available?" D'Onofrio was cornered.

"Of course we know where the students are but. . . ."

"Well, Mr. D'Onofrio, I want to know where you were. What were you doing when it was overcrowded back in 1970?"

To get out of the situation Mike lied. He tried to be moralistic. He said he genuinely felt that with the evidence now available to him he'd voted wrongly back on that chilly November night in 1970. But his problem now was how to get out of the situation without implying he'd previously been incompetent. He tried to duck, but it backfired. Then he delivered a low blow, by making it look like the superintendent had misled him in the past.

"Who cares what the superintendent told you. It was your responsibility then, as it is now, to make sure you have the right information to decide."

Mike began to sound pathetic. Two or three more times when pinned to the wall, he came out fighting with his "I made my decision without the benefit of the knowledge of the high school situation at that time," but the more he spoke, the less believable he sounded, and eventually everyone started to ignore him.

While this was going on I sat struggling with how curiously the human mind operates. I'm convinced Mike had come to believe the rationalizations he was presenting so firmly that they had become his reality, despite the fact that I had found in the files the following letter written by him on the very day of that November 1970 decision he was referring to.

November 17, 1970

Dr. Eddie Rhodes
Superintendent of Schools
Ashgrove

Dear Dr. Rhodes and Fellow Board Members:

Yesterday I had the pleasure of a three-hour visit to our high school.

Contrary to preconceived notions and general heresay, I found conditions to be scholarly and orderly. At no time did I see roving bands of students nor did I see a generally chaotic condition.

The classroom situations were exemplary. Class size ranged from twenty to twenty-five in the general study classrooms and eight to twelve in the specialized study classrooms. I was able to draw a sharp impression of perserverance and eagerness on the part of students and a genuine professionality on the part of the faculty. The resemblance between our system and a university system is not only remarkable but encouraging.

The faculty appeared young and energetic and was representative of a broad geographical and academic base.

In short, I reaffirm my position that the instructional experience in our high school is praiseworthy.

Further, let me express my valid commitment to Mr. Brook who is playing a vital role in our overall operation.

Very truly yours,
Mike P. D'Onofrio

MPD:1jd

D'Onofrio had been one of *the* major actors previously in deciding that the high school was not overcrowded and therefore the ninth grade didn't need to be moved, but now he was trying to claim that he'd been in the dark and that the superintendent had been responsible for this earlier claim.

For a full hour, the grade alignment topic was bounced around with many irrational outbursts and very angry exchanges.

After taking as much of a beating as he felt the board should endure, Chairman Kingston decided to terminate the public debate. "We must end this discussion now because we have a very full agenda for tonight's meeting." The public rose *en masse* and stormed out of the building, clattering their way noisily down the ancient staircase of the old school building. The silence they left behind in the board room produced a ghostlike feeling. It was as if the soul of the system had just taken flight.

Outside on the lawn, the angry public paused to share their common disgust. Little groups huddled around in threes and fours, each addressing themselves to what they referred to as the "incompetence of Ashgrove's board of education." Only Republican Reuben Kaufman received any praise. They liked what he had said and in the aftermath, the alienated public elevated him alone to hero proportions.

Pregnant Politics

After the public left the board meeting that New England May Day the atmosphere became rather subdued. With the mob gone and the immediate assault ended the board emerged from the self-protecting stance they'd adopted while in that lower position. Now it was just themselves again, together with the superintendent, his assistant, and the business manager. No longer did they have to look at themselves mirrored in the anger of the hostile public, their superiors. No longer did they have to charade a unanimity. Once again their inner conflicts could surface and they could feel safe without having to suppress their differences or pretend to be something they were not.

I wondered what the transition from this highly defensive lower position back to their regular upper location would be like for the board. In particular I wondered how those deeply repressed emotions would work their way out into the open. As I watched them I found myself to be very anxious. There was an eerie feeling in the room, a sense of foreboding. By this time I had seen many Ashgrove groups operate, and I felt I had a good sense of how the relative hierarchial position influenced interaction in different relative locations. However I'd never watched a group go through an actual transition before, transposing themselves from one structural encasement to another. I sat back wondering what I'd see. What I saw was incredible. I've observed a lot of groups in my time, many of which have looked chaotic, stuck, frustrated, angry, and so forth, but never before had I seen one that looked more brain damaged. My sense was that all the energy that had gone into keeping things coherent during the exchange with the public suddenly imploded and the group experienced, within its ranks and with great intensity, the chaos and incoherence it had been experiencing just an hour before with another group. That is, the unresolved external chaos became expressed as internal chaos. What was striking about this was that the board seemed reasonably unable to recognize how irrationally it was behaving. This irrationality was obvious to the superintendent's group who were present in this setting as middles. However their attempts to interject or turn things around were glossed over completely.

Routine reports, a coffee break, and a low key discussion about teachers' salary negotiations had made the hour 11:00 P.M. Then the irrationality burst forth.

The theme. Sick leave for pregnant teachers.

Diane Grazio was a teacher in good standing, who after five years of marriage had become impregnated, as one male board member expressed it. For eight months she'd been healthy and had continued to work. However, the doctors had convinced her to rest for the final month in preparation for the birth. Over her years of service to Ashgrove, she'd accrued sixty-three sick days. She decided to apply for twenty of these before taking standard maternity leave.

The essential question embedded in Mrs. Grazio's application was a challenge to current policies of maternity leave. Pregnant teachers were granted maternity leave without pay; sick leave on the other hand was with pay. The principle she was fighting for was that since a woman may become ill during pregnancy she was entitled to sick pay for that period.

Her case triggered intense debate.

"We need to first decide what it means to fall pregnant!" offered Mike.

"Why?" asked Kaufman.

"Because if it's like catching the plague then it's reasonable to argue she's entitled to sick pay. But if it's like deliberately swallowing a tennis ball for the purpose of inducing a condition inappropriate for the tasks of classroom teaching, it's different!"

"Why would that make a difference?" replied Kaufman taunting his Democratic rival.

Mike, who had been reasonably silent since the public closed him down earlier in the evening, seemed determined to grasp the initiative on this topic. With a generous outpouring of his legalese he took off. "We should start by defining what is meant by the term of sickness." Like all good lawyers he paused for appropriate effect. "Sickness is an unforseen malady." Another pause. And then with a great burst of confidence as if with one swift blow of his legal mind, the matter would be laid to rest. "I don't think anyone in their right mind would view pregnancy as either unforseeable or a malady."

A hearty "hear, hear!" from some of his fellow Democrats.

"What do you mean, it's not a malady! It's certainly a malady if you're sick, and we all know pregnancy can produce some sickness." added Republican Reuben Kaufman, angered with the flipness of the Democratic stance.

"Well, if it's sickness, it's self-induced sickness," retorted Mike with a strange sense of confidence that this comment would prove the final blow.

"Oh, I see, you only intend to pay for sickness that is not self-induced. Well, tell me then, if one of our male teachers is out drinking one night and then reports the following morning that he's too ill to come to work, do you intend to refuse him sick pay?" Gerald Bomford joined the battle.

"That's a different case!" replied D'Onofrio dismissingly.

"I know it's a different case, but why don't you answer it all the same!"

Mike took the bait. "Well, we'd probably never know about it, so I guess we would pay him for his sickness."

"Oh, I get it. You'll pay for self-induced, foreseeable maladies so long as you don't know about it, and for self-induced, unforeseeable maladies and non-self-induced, unforeseeable maladies that you do know about, but not unforeseeable, other induced maladies you do know about!" Reuben Kaufman was also a lawyer.

"What!" Mike looked stunned.

"Why should I repeat it, you weren't listening!"

"I was!"

"Then if you were listening, it just goes to show you don't understand what you're talking about!"

"How's that?"

Kaufman was now gleeful. He had Mike in a corner. "Well, I want to know how a woman can self-induce pregnancy. Most pregnancies I've ever known about have required a male to do the inducing; so I would argue that pregnancy comes under the heading of 'other-induced malady' if you insist on that dreadful term!"

"What?" Mike was confused.

Assistant Superintendent O'Sullivan could keep his silence and his cool no longer. He exploded. "Listen, if I took a rifle and shot a hole in my foot I'd be entitled to sick benefits. It's a short-term disability. And I see pregnancy to be no different. This whole situation seems totally incongruous to me. If we had a teacher absent because he or she had recently had cosmetic surgery, we'd pay sick leave. But if a woman is ill because she's pregnant we'd refuse!"

"Then how's that different from a woman being sick due to pregnancy?" Chairman Kingston, the other lawyer on the Board, dived in.

"It's not!" replied O'Sullivan, unsure of Kingston's point.

"So what, that doesn't alter the fact that pregnancy is planned." Mike was back in the fray.

"We do pay for all the girls who have morning sickness at present," continued Ron Kingston trying to argue with Don O'Sullivan but appearing most uncertain about what he was trying to refute.

"Well, that makes it even stranger," added Don. "It's okay to be sick early in pregnancy. We'll pay for that. Just so long as you don't feel sick in the last month. If that happens, we won't pay! This stuff is crazy!"

"I've just thought of a good example of how inconsistently we act," Kingston interrupted, as if anyone really needed to have their inconsistency pointed out. "If a male went to have a vasectomy, wouldn't we pay him sick leave?"

"Yes."

"The problem is that if we make these rules so liberal the teachers will start taking advantage of us," added another voice, getting closer to what the board members really feared.

"That's ridiculous!" fumed O'Sullivan. "This teacher, Mrs. Grazio, applied for twenty days of sick leave. She has accrued sixty-three days. That's hardly trying to take advantage of us. If we are considerate with them, they'll be considerate with us; if we try to push them to the limit, they'll try to fleece us of everything they can. And rightly so! In their position I'd do exactly the same thing if treated the way we handle them. We only end up losing in the long run!"

"I think this discussion is getting us nowhere," cut in Chairman Kingston, fearful of being taken on another carousel ride, "and I do think there are some other very important considerations we're not looking at. There are the legal and political implications of deciding either way. One of the things I've been most fearful of, if we were to approve Mrs. Grazio's application, is that we could be flooded with a large number of retroactive requests from women who've previously taken maternity leave, trying to collect some sick pay for the times they took without pay. Now, irrespective of how justifiable the sick pay claim is, I don't think we can afford at this time to run the risk of having ourselves bombarded with a pile of such applications."

"What would happen if Mrs. Grazio decided to take this issue to court?" asked Gerald Bomford. "Because I understand we are being given strong legal advice indicating that in the courts we'd be most likely to lose!"

"Well, I'd be much happier for the courts to make a definitive statement," replied Kingston. "If that happens we'll just have to pay, but they also would probably define a date from which the law would be effective and that will save us from an overreaction of ex-maternity leavers who want to claim back sick pay!"

"You can't overlook the fact, however, that she has appendixed a letter from her doctor, indicating that he's advised her to cease work until after the birth," added Eddie Rhodes, keenly wanting the application approved so that his teachers would not be made more alienated. "What's more, Mrs. Grazio has acted in a more direct way with us than most do. She could have not bothered with this application and then, each morning of the next three weeks, simply called in sick and we'd have been obliged to pay her, that would have been horrible. We'd have had to scurry at the last minute to find a substitute, and her students would have spent each day with a new teacher, with very little continuity of instruction. All in all, she's done the best thing from the school's perspective. Now we're going to penalize her for being honest."

"That may all be true, but everyone knows these days that a doctor will write any letter for anyone. They don't look at anything much other than the patient's wellbeing," replied Kingston, ignoring completely what Rhodes had said about the problems of failing to reward responsible behavior on the part of the teacher.

"There's another side to this," added Mike. "A proposal exists in our current contract negotiations requesting sick leave for pregnant teachers, and it would be a most unwise strategy for us to change policy during the negotiation phase."

"It's also almost 11:30," added Ron Kingston, eager to end the debate. "It's far too late in the evening to be debating policy. We're all too tired. There are so many aspects to this whole thing that we really need a clear mind to think it all through. Before long, we'll probably even be asked to give males maternity, no, I guess it would be paternity, leave for purposes of child rearing."

At this moment I felt relief. At least Kingston appeared to have the sense, I thought, to realize that as a board they were not thinking clearly and that they should leave this complex policy issue and application until another date. No sooner than I'd had this thought when I heard Kingston say "I'm going to put the motion. Dr. Rhodes, please read it for us."

"Moved by Mr. D'Onofrio and seconded by Mr. Hewett, that the board of education deny the request of Diane Grazio for sick leave for the balance of the school year effective May 18. All those in favor say . . ."

The sick leave application was rejected.

While sitting through this event I felt that the board had gone completely crazy. The emotions were strange and the way the discussion took place was completely incoherent. People seemed to be acting contrary to what they were saying and nobody was using the responses or reactions of others as a significant guide to what they would do or say next.

Much later, when I came to think about this event with more detachment and clarity, I noticed several intergroup dynamics operating simultaneously, which I confidently speculate influenced powerfully what took place that night.

First the board as lowers banded together to resist the onslaught of their uppers (public). To survive, they suppressed their normal within-group conflict. They also did not fight back with the public but compliantly took the beating their uppers were delivering them. They absorbed the intergroup conflict and took it within their own group.

Second, once the public had gone, the board returned to their more familiar upper position and switching from their previous lower location began to behave with as much incoherence as they had been treated when they were lowers, taking out their own within-group conflict and putting it onto their subordinates.

Third, the parallelisms between the two groups when they were uppers were very striking. It was as though the board had introjected the irrationality of the public and then proceeded to act it out in their own behavior towards their subordinates.

Fourth, the board seemed quite indifferent to the fact that Mrs. Grazio's application and behavior had made things easier for the school system and had increased administrative efficiency. They responded in a mechanistic way, appearing unconcerned that their actions might have more negative than positive consequences.

Fifth, the board acted as though they were unaware that their position, rather than providing a protection from exploitation by the teachers, which was their stated goal, would instead ignite and fuel deviousness amongst their lowers.

Sixth, without any devious or exploiting actions on the part of any teacher, the board proceeded to act as though the only way teachers would relate to their uppers was through exploitation. Hence the board, without any information whatsoever, created a fantasized self-fulfilling prophecy that included seeing in their lowers the very thing about themselves as lowers they refused to acknowledge, namely their own deviousness. The whole evening began with the board's refusal to be explicit about how devious they intended to be over the next grade alignment battle and here they were now setting things up so that the only logical action of the teachers would be deviousness.

Seventh, the board as uppers simply ignored the insight that the superintendent's office, their middles, could bring to bear on their deliberations. They didn't stop their middle from talking but they might as well have for they took no notice of anything the superintendent's group was offering them.

Eighth, on the other hand, the superintendent's group was not very forceful with the board. As middles they seemed to adopt a characteristically tentative posture towards their bosses. Although they did express their opinions fully, they were presented with such tentativeness that they seemed easy to reject.

The Scapegoating

The board of education should have gone home after their irrational discussion about pregnancy. They should have gone to sleep for twenty-four hours and all taken a month's vacation in order to restore their individual sanity to build up some reserves to confront their collective insanity. But they didn't. Instead they drifted into the final item on their agenda and, in my opinion, engaged in the most destructive and convoluted decision-making process I've ever observed in any group at any time. The agenda item was the superintendent's annual salary increase. The final action taken by the board read like a jumbled-up jigsaw puzzle. "Terminate the superintendent's contract in eighteen months, but advise him of it tonight. Vote him a salary increase of $1,000 and tell him it's a vote of no confidence." Into the bargain, the board members most in favor of Rhodes pushed hardest for his dismissal and those most against him worked to avoid his being fired.

I'm not sure that I understand everything that happened that night nor that I can capture on paper all that I do understand. I do know, however, that the board went absolutely crazy and in the process scapegoated their superintendent. I'd like to tell this story to capture how those unresolved intergroup tensions of earlier in the evening crescendoed, converged, and were released on one individual, Eddie Rhodes.

The board had avoided for several weeks debating the question of a salary increase for Rhodes. They had given his two immediate subordinates five percent increases three months earlier, bringing Don O'Sullivan's salary precariously close to the superintendent's. Republican Julia Langdon had grown tired of the Democrats' obvious refusal to consider Rhodes' financial situation and had been adamant that it be discussed this evening, even though she was going to be absent. That was the first mistake. She should have been present since she was one of Eddie's strongest supporters. The second mistake was having it appendaged to such a complex meeting. Julia, had she thought about timing, could have realized this meeting was going to be a bloodbath and that Rhodes was a potential victim. But she too was being bull headed and not thinking straight.

It was 11:30 before the board got to what they euphemistically referred to as "the Rhodes situation." The superintendent was invited to make a statement to the seven board members present. He'd given a lot of thought to what he wanted to say. He was nervous but hid it well.

"I'd like initially to bring to your attention my salary history. At my appointment in January 1969, I started on $23,500 and served at this level for one and a half years. For the year 1970–71 it was raised to $26,000 and then two years ago it was increased to $27,000, and I've been at this level for the past two years. In addition to that I have a travel allowance of $1,000 a year. I have no particular statement to make about my salary, except to say I'm glad you're considering it and to let you know that I, like everyone else, suffer from inflation. I'll leave deliberations about appropriate salary to the board."

The board listened to Rhodes in deathly silence. Most eyes were focused on a spot somewhere in the center of the table. Everyone looked bored. The atmosphere was intense and Rhodes must have felt the uneasiness as he broached his second topic.

Rather eloquently he indicated he was concerned about the fact he and the board had never sat down together to discuss mutual goals for the school system and appropriate criteria for evaluating their educational achievements. "In the absence of these shared goals, I simply do what I think is best and then afterwards I often learn this wasn't what you wanted. That puts me in an impossible position. I'd prefer for us, perhaps in this summer when things

221

are calmer, to sit down together and develop common goals we can all agree on." He also raised another sensitive topic. "Secondly, my current contract expires in eighteen months. I'd like that to be reviewed twelve months before that date. So sometime this summer I'd also like to explore a contract renewal."

By this point the room felt deadly. Chairman Kingston asked if anyone had questions. There were none. An awkward fifteen-second silence strung out for what seemed like several minutes. Rhodes fidgeted with a paper clip. His eyes were also riveted to that same spot in the middle of the table others had been focusing on. Kingston then asked him to leave. No one had even acknowledged anything the superintendent had said.

The moment he left, the room erupted. Craig Hewett was first.

"I don't care who the superintendent is, and regardless of the man or the qualities he brings, we must consider what is the maximum salary a town like ours can afford to pay its superintendent. . . ."

Before he finished Republican Kaufman cut him off. "I don't think there's any way we can justify setting a maximum salary for any position. However I do feel we should look just at salary tonight. The other things Rhodes raised are important issues, but they are not relevant for right now."

"I move that there be no change in the superintendent's salary," continued Hewett, as though Kaufman had never spoken.

"Seconded!"

"Craig, that's really unfair!" Kaufman ignored the motion. "We've recently raised the business manager's and assistant superintendent's salaries, narrowing the gap between them and the superintendent, but we refuse to even consider whether Rhodes should be paid more."

"Well, I just don't think anyone should get paid that much," repeated Craig forcefully.

"I agree with Craig," added Chairman Kingston.

Kaufman turned to Kingston angrily. "Well, I'd like to know why you gave raises to the business manager and the assistant superintendent?"

"Because our negotiations with school principals have raised their salaries to a level so close to the central administration we felt it would be unjust not to give them the increase." Kingston was sneering.

"Well you solve one injustice and simply transfer it onto Rhodes. That's horrible!"

There was a slight lull. Then in came Mike, tentatively but provocatively. "The main trouble is we are unprepared to face the real issues." Gerald Bomford tried to prod Mike into saying what those real issues were but Kaufman grabbed the floor back. He pushed the chairman further. "Well, if you are unhappy with the man we should not extend his contract! However we always confuse things. We must give him some nominal amount so that the status of the position of the superintendent will be significantly above that of his assistant, independent of whether Rhodes is good or not."

"Well, those are two separate questions, and I think we should deal with his salary and not whether the man is any good for the job," continued Ron. Rodney Saunders by now was sitting on the edge of his seat. He was determined to get involved. "Reuben, what do you think the superintendent is like?"

"Rodney, let's keep those questions separate," pleaded Chairman Kingston. But he was about to lose that battle. The fuse had been lit and already several of the board members were about to explode with the incubated emotions that they'd been storing up all night. Rhodes was destined to be the target.

Mike D'Onofrio took off on a long tirade. "I feel at a real disadvantage. I've said a number of times I really like Eddie Rhodes, the man, but this last week I've seen so many occasions where I've had a chance to doubt his competence. The real issue now is what do we intend to do with Rhodes, for however we act tonight the handwriting will be on the wall. I, for one, want to say that I just don't feel that the superintendent's at all competent. . . ." Whereupon Mike proceeded with a convoluted and lengthy rundown of how the superintendent's office had been reluctant to give him some information that he'd wanted so he could construct a case for his ninth grade relocation campaign. The superintendent had felt that Mike would distort any information he was given in the light of his current removalist obsession. However, with pressure, D'Onofrio had extracted what he wanted, but he was still angry over this event. Early that evening when Mike had got himself trapped in the wrath of the public, D'Onofrio had lied to try to get the superintendent to take some of the heat. Wisely Rhodes had refused. This had upset Mike even more. He could see in Rhodes what he didn't want to see about himself. "The problem with the man is he just won't answer your questions straight."

Mike's outburst triggered a "let's dump on Rhodes" routine. Comments like the following occupied the next ten minutes.

"Well, I feel annoyed that here the superintendent, after four years in the job, suddenly decides we should develop some goals. What's he been doing all these years!"

"I like the man, too, but he just doesn't seem able to communicate. His position on Main Street is poor. So is his relationship with teachers."

No one paused to question whether these accusations were correct. Their mere statement was accepted as verification of authenticity. Nor did anyone pause to say "I wonder what it is we're angry at?" Instead the anger was accepted as justified, and most considered that the accusations being directed at the superintendent were valid. In reality, what had happened was that the whole previous week had been so laden with tension, uncertainty, and disorientation that now, more than anything else, what was most needed was a way to ventilate that emotion. Any object would have sufficed for the focus of the outburst. For this moment Rhodes proved to be a most satisfactory object.

It was also particularly easy to use him in this way because the board Democrats had done it so often in the past that they didn't even need to think about how to articulate their hostility. It just oozed out in the well-practiced forms.

Republican Gerald Bomford had never been part of a "dump on Rhodes" festival, and he was finding this whole thing to be distasteful. He wanted to stop what was going on. Watching him, it was obvious that he was distressed and that he was struggling about how best to cut it off. He could have said, "Why are you so angry at Rhodes?", or "Are you sure your statements are justified?" But he feared this would simply trigger another nauseating outburst. He was looking for a way to slap the group over the face and bring it to its senses. A method occurred to him. "If you feel this way about Dr. Rhodes, how come you're not asking for his resignation?"

Gerald was forceful. They ignored him. It would take more than this to stop the anti-Rhodes ritual.

Gerald got angry. He was determined. He faced another choice point. Escalate his point that if the board felt this way about their superintendent, they should fire him. Or look for another way to jar the group to its senses.

Bomford didn't think. He went for the former, little appreciating that *how* he was choosing to fight with the board was shaping the future of the superintendent so powerfully. Bomford's disgust was with the board. He could have fought with them directly. Instead, he did it indirectly, using a discussion about Rhodes as the vehicle for his battle. This, of course, was the very thing he was angry at the other board members about. He fell into the same trap. Like the others, he made Rhodes the ball in his power game. "Has the superintendent been told about these faults?"

"Yes!"

"Has there been an upgrading of his performance since then?"

"No!"

"Well, it's time then that we told him to leave!" Gerald's conclusion hung like a pall over the room.

Kingston made a last desperate attempt to avoid debating Rhodes' future. "Even if the man were doing a good job, I'd want to argue that he should be given no pay increase. He's getting as much as the town can possibly afford." No one grabbed the chairman's bait.

Bomford was feeling uneasy. Perhaps he had left something unsaid. "It seems to me that the superintendent is searching both himself and us for some clear idea of what we want from him." He could have made the point more pungently that the board was equally at fault for the superintendent's shortcomings. Gerald was still too tentative.

"He knows what we wanted," shouted three or four voices in unison. "Anyway he should be giving the board direction, not the board giving him direction. That's what he gets paid for. And too much. Nobody pays us! Why should we give him direction?"

The meeting went on like this for some time. It was a circus. First one Democrat would lead, then another. They seemed never to tire. Round and round, hypnotized by their own lamentations.

Republicans Kaufman and Bomford watched. Eventually, forced to distraction, Reuben Kaufman tried to stop the cycle. "It sounds to me as if the majority of the board is unhappy with Eddie Rhodes' performance. On the basis of that, I would agree to act upon his contract and decide to terminate it tonight. However I feel that there is a critical principle involved in not raising the superintendent's salary when all other salaries have been raised. I'll do you a deal! If the board will agree to increase the superintendent's salary at least to $28,000, then I'll go along with the idea of moving Rhodes on and terminating his contract."

"No deal!" boomed Hewett, with no time for thought.

Kaufman was annoyed. He considered his offer to have been eminently reasonable and now his conciliation had been so mechanistically rejected. Kaufman began to feel there was something sinister in the Democrat's position. They seemed determined to give Rhodes no increase, and at the same time as they were insulting him they'd also be lowering the dignity of the superintendency. He feared they would continue to harbor anti-Rhodes feelings, refuse to review his contract, and then a month or two before it was up, simply move him on. This made Kaufman's blood boil. It seemed intolerable to fire the superintendent, but to do it in such a way that he would have no place to go and have no time to look for alternatives was preposterous. For Kaufman, giving Rhodes no increase at this time had to be viewed as the equivalent of his dismissal. He said as much.

This stopped the Democrats. At last. I felt some relief. Then instantly the mood in the room changed. The rage vanished. In the resultant vacuum another range of feelings came rushing in. The place suddenly was like an empty funeral parlor. It was unreal. People switched emotions so quickly. They started expressing sympathy for Eddie Rhodes, as though he had died. They began to remember his good points.

"He should be able to get a decent job somewhere. He's got some important skills."

"With all Julia's connections in the state, she'll get him fixed up okay."

With this change in mood, Chairman Kingston began to think aloud that maybe a salary increase would be a good idea. "At least it will be a supportive gesture on our part and should help him preserve his dignity as he leaves."

Someone commented how awful it is to have to dismiss a public figure. All this was going on, even though there had been no debate, discussion, or even any formal motion with respect to the superintendent's contract.

Craig Hewett eventually broke this group mourning by thrusting a jab at D'Onofrio. "One thing's for sure, Mike, you're one person who's going to have to make a decision about where you stand with respect to the superintendent this time. You've ducked it every other time, but now you're caught."

"Yeah," chimed in Saunders perceptively. "What I'd like to know is whether you are mad tonight because you've had a bad week or because Rhodes performed poorly over the last two or three years."

Mike snapped back angrily at both Craig and Rodney. When he'd cooled down a little, with face half turned towards the doorway, he said reluctantly, "I want everyone to reject everything I've said about Rhodes here tonight. Perhaps Rodney is right. I've had a really bad week." Loud laughter! Mike was now about to get the same treatment they'd been giving Rhodes.

"That's like putting false evidence before the jury and then asking them to ignore it!" They were mocking Mike who was looking duly embarrassed.

After a few minutes, Lodell went back to the original topic. "I still don't think we should give Rhodes any increase."

Kaufman, bitingly quipped back, "Despite the shortcomings of the man, he's head and shoulders above both the previous superintendents that you, Matthew, had worked so hard to defend." Lodell simply laughed off the incongruence Reuben Kaufman was pointing out, and before he could be pinned further on this point, someone came to his rescue by another outpouring of sympathy for Eddie.

In the next ten minutes or so there emerged what I feel can best be described as a "moral imperative". It grew out of Gerald Bomford's initial exchanges and the position that both he and his fellow Republican, Kaufman, now found themselves in. To them it seemed clear that the Democrats, although not yet acknowledging this, had developed a consensus that Rhodes had no future in Ashgrove. This realization led Bomford to start arguing with himself internally. "If they're so strongly for getting rid of Rhodes, he'll eventually go; but I'll bet they procrastinate to the point where he'll be left with nowhere to go. Then we'll dump him with cruel jest. If this is inevitable, and it certainly seems so now, the right thing for us to do is to tell him now that it's all over and give him plenty of time to find a reasonable alternative." This logic seemed impeccable and brought with it some moral tugs and an imperative to act. Gerald felt these forces and he went into high gear. He concluded that the only constructive thing that could now be done would be to force the early decision not to renew Rhodes' contract and then tell of this immediately. And with this, Gerald started. "I think we should discuss the Superintendent tonight. But it *must* be done tonight." Kaufman, realizing what Bomford was doing, joined in the attack.

Most moral imperatives mock reality. This one was no exception. Here we have the curious twist that the two board members most supportive of Rhodes became the strongest voices for his dismissal. The question was no longer should Rhodes be given a salary increase or should his contract be terminated, but rather whether the forces of morality would win. With almost a religious fervor, the two Republicans pushed their position.

226

This startled Democrat Hewett who began to wonder aloud whether Rhodes should be dismissed at all. Kingston too began to move towards a more balanced view. "Maybe we should even look at ourselves and all the ways in which the board operates. Perhaps there are things we're not doing right and we're blaming the superintendent for them."

"I don't think that would do any good," offered Reuben Kaufman, keen not to lose the impetus of this new initiative and fearful that this might just be an effective ploy to delay the inevitable dismissal until Rhodes' contract had expired. "The superintendent's been given his chance to do what the board expected him to and didn't take it. So now I'm for moving him on. I certainly never wanted it to be done this way, but if it's inevitable it must be done and should be done soon, preferably now."

Those advocating the superintendent's dismissal at this moment were Bomford and Kaufman. All of a sudden, Mike D'Onofrio, always a sucker for a good moral imperative, began to join the Republicans. "Perhaps we should act; it certainly seems as if the feeling against the man is getting stronger." Craig Hewett cut him off. Here was the eternal turncoat at work again. D'Onofrio had been taking the low road all night. Now it seemed like he was going to wrap his actions in someone else's morality and present himself as walking the high road. This was too much. "What the hell are you trying to protect now!" This wasn't a question. It was an outburst.

Mike replied, "The integrity of the superintendent and of the board." This was too much.

Chairman Kingston began to cringe. There seemed little alternative to him. Everything had gotten too bizarre. "Perhaps it would be best if we were to table this whole thing until another occasion."

"No," objected Hewett. "We should vote on the salary now and tell the superintendent tonight of what the outcome is."

More than an hour had transpired since Eddie Rhodes left the room. It was almost 1:00 A.M. and he was sitting alone in his office across the passageway trying to distract himself. Slowly it dawned on him that his fate was in the balance. He began to feel inside the stirring of a discomfort so pronounced that it had no name. He knew, by the length of time the board was taking, that the worst would occur. He was beginning to feel numb. There was an inevitability to it all. He comforted himself with the thought that soon the ordeal of uncertainty would end. Too much ambivalence can be soul destroying. He sat alone, an incubation of a human misery, soon to be freed from uncertainty. Knowing would be cathartic.

The major dynamic within the board was now settling into the intersection of two overlapping forces; one articulated that the board must attempt to be fair to Rhodes; the other emphasized that the integrity of the position of the superintendent should be preserved. The first had become so twisted that by taking a decision tonight *not* to renew Rhodes' contract, the demands of fairness would be fulfilled. Dismissal had become defined as *the* ethical act, so long as he were advised of it immediately. The other could be fulfilled by voting a salary increase, done as a gesture to the office of the superintendent, not the man who occupied it. As such, it would be an affirmation of the board's continuing support for the office of the superintendency. It also provided a veneer that affirmed that there was nothing wrong with the board or the superintendency. It was simply the mere unfortunate placement of an unsuitable man in the seat of the superintendency. Such is the nature of scapegoatings.

No one was in control of events anymore. If they weren't going to postpone the decision, all that was left now was for the formal actions to be taken. Everything had been said. The turmoil of the earlier week had clearly taken its toll. There had been that bruising session with the public, some five hours earlier, over the ninth grade. And there was the illogic of the pregnancy debate. And the fatigue. All this converged on this moment. No one was in any way master of his destiny. Each person was being carried along on the powerful rush of the undercurrents. It was hard to see which way anyone was headed, let alone the impending boulders they were bouncing into as they crashed towards an implosive decision.

"We must now take action," announced Kingston. "We have three things to vote on. First, if we want to give Rhodes a salary increase. Second, if so, how much? Third, whether we'll terminate his contract." No one said anything.

First, salary increase. Those in favor of an increase—Bomford, Kaufman, Saunders, and D'Onofrio. Against—Lodell and Hewett. Carried.

Second, the amount of the increase. Those in favor of $1,000 increase— Bomford, Kaufman, and D'Onofrio. Against—Saunders, Lodell, and Hewett. A tied vote. Broken by Chairman Kingston who voted *for* the increase.

Last, the contract termination in eighteen months time. In favor—Hewett, Bomford, Kaufman, Lodell, and Saunders. Against—a lonely and confused vote from Mike D'Onofrio.

No sooner had the vote been taken than the room burst into a scene of angry tempers. Rodney and Mike started a clash about whether they'd predecided to dump Rhodes that night; Lodell fumed at D'Onofrio about his vote; Hewett and Bomford started at each other. All of a sudden, in the confusion of it all, someone remembered that no one had taken minutes of the meeting, nor was the dismissal vote legal because the superintendent's contract had not been an item of the agenda. These were valid concerns, but things had gone too far and no one was caring about formalities. It was quickly agreed to simply record the salary vote and then to tell the superintendent of the spirit of the board's action.

Reuben Kaufman suggested Rhodes should be told tonight.

"Couldn't we wait until tomorrow?" pleaded Chairman Kingston. "I'm really tired and I'd prefer to do it all in the morning."

"Knowing this board, I'd tell him right now; it'll be out in the street by the morning," encouraged Kaufman, making a direct reference to Lodell's tendency to leak anything of a confidential nature immediately to the public.

Ron Kingston reluctantly agreed and set off to the superintendent's office. The others stood around and talked, very disoriented by the mixture of feelings that now hit them. Some felt good, some felt bad, some felt guilty, some didn't know what they felt.

Inside Rhodes' office, the two men exchanged confused pleasantries, weighed down by a mutual awkwardness. Eddie accepted the news quietly and with gentlemanly poise. He was bitterly disappointed and hurt more than anyone could imagine, but he managed to muster enough empathy for Kingston to acknowledge that this was hard news for Ron to have to convey. They talked for a long time, going over and over the events of the evening. At 2:45 A.M. Ron left.

Eddie sat alone in his office. He never looked at his watch but by dawn he'd dispiritedly dragged himself home to his empty apartment, longing for the comfort only sleep could bring.

He slept lightly. By the time he rose, midmorning, he knew, irrespective of what choices were available to him in the future, he wanted no more of Ashgrove. He would take his flight. Already he was beginning to feel better.

Since no formal dismissal action had been taken, Eddie resolved to be bold. By writing a letter to all board members indicating that there would be no circumstances under which he'd be willing to stay at Ashgrove beyond the end of his current term, he could avoid the town history or the board's minutes ever recording a dismissal action.

He went to work, summoned his secretary, who also was a good friend, told her the story and dictated his letter. She tried to convince him to refrain, but Eddie was resolved. He decided to tell no one else of his action because he knew, in time, the whole story would be on the streets of the town, and he wanted to be sure of protecting everyone except board members from being blamed for the leak. Eddie knew that Lodell would tell the story.

Within a couple of days, each of the board members received the following letter.

May 4, 1973

Mr. Ron Kingston
Chairman, Board of Education
420 Main Street
Ashgrove

Dear Mr. Kingston:

This will serve to inform all members of the Ashgrove Board of Education that I would not consider a renewal of extension of the three-year agreement currently in effect. It goes without saying, however, that during the time I remain under contract as superintendent of the Ashgrove Public Schools I will continue to perform the duties of the office to the best of my ability within the resources made available to me.

I trust that in the time remaining the board and superintendent will work pleasantly and effectively together.

Sincerely,

Eddie Rhodes
Superintendent of Schools

The next few months sped quickly by in Ashgrove. Not one of the board of education members even acknowledged to Eddie Rhodes that they had received his resignation letter. It had leaked into the press but when board members had been approached for comment most of them were simply unavailable. The whole town went calm. It was as though all the turbulent emotions of the previous months had been exploded out of the system. Or had they just gone underground!

You may recall that on the grade realignment issue the Democrats had decided to effect the ninth grade switch for the 1974–75 school year during the summer. It was placed on the agenda for the July meeting and despite the earlier struggles it was passed without even a fight. Gerald Bomford tried to stir the old troubled waters. His efforts didn't even create a ripple. Voting was done mechanically and on party lines with Republicans voting against the removal.

In noticing this I was really struck by how human systems, like volcanoes, seem to build up pressure to the point where a release is essential in order to maintain the system in its current form. As the pressure builds there appears to develop a concommitant fear or expectation that the system will really change this time. Things will be different after these forces have been played through. Then there's the explosion. And everything returns to normal. As if nothing had ever happened. For the first time I had a keen sense of how stabilizing these emotional eruptions are for a social system. There are casualties. People get hurt. Everything is different as a result. But it's also the same, too.

In the years since I first went to a power laboratory I've shown a lot of people my Montville document and told stories about Elites, Outs, and Ins. Most people have been skeptical about whether people or groups really behave that way in "the real world". I've been confronted over and over again with disclaimers like "I know myself and I know had I been at Montville I would not have behaved the way Richard or Anthony or Steve did. What's more, Montville was such a closed society. It was artificial. Everything was speeded up. Lived out in extremes." I've never really known how to address these responses. It's been easy to agree that each individual would have done things differently. However, I've tried to argue that qualitatively, the behaviors would have been much the same, that individuals would have gotten locked into similar psychological prisons, that the convoluted forces of dynamic conservatism and the social comparison processes would have been just as convoluting and blinding. The external forces might have been different but the essence of these would be just as potent.

I've been successful in convincing very few people, and I suspect they knew it long before they met me anyway. Usually my argument gets brushed aside with claims that if I were right, these things would also be going on in every organization, all the time. I've responded that they are, but that the problem is most of us are so close to these events as they occur in our everyday experience that we don't see it all happening to us. We don't see how the structural encasements of power or powerlessness shape our views of reality, our understandings of the social dynamics around us, just as the Montville actors didn't see them.

I'm firmly convinced that in this one May Day board meeting at Ashgrove, we can find all of the Montville-type forces converging and playing themselves out with a power that defied the capacity of any Ashgrove actor to comprehend what was going on in anything other than a very limited way. I do not pretend that I've captured everything that was important to know in appreciating Ashgrove's 1973 May Day. However, I know this picture is much more expansive and complete than anyone at Ashgrove can put together and it's certainly more than enough to convince *me* that if we look, we'll find Montville lurking behind, beneath, within or above any piece of social reality we experience.

Reversals

I am coming to the end of my Ashgrove story. Because it's finished? No! Because it never ends! In a way there's nothing more to tell. It continues to be the same. And probably always will.

"Why then have you told your story? Do you have no answers?" I hear my critics loud and clear. "No, I have no answers." For I now know that every solution simply produces a new problem, which raises new questions that demand new answers. Every attempt to escape from one structural encasement leads into another. And the new answers are really no different than the old ones. And one prison is really no better than another. It's all the same. A harsh realization!

In the years since I went to Ashgrove, I've been asked a thousand times what advice would I offer to someone caught in binds like those of Eddie Rhodes or Principal Brook or the board of education. My only reply has been to tell my final Eddie Rhodes story or my final Mike D'Onofrio story.

In the months immediately following the May Day board meeting, I realized it was time for me to start thinking about leaving Ashgrove. This meant I had to cease being a silent observer and to offer the major groups involved some report of my findings. This had been part of my original agreement with everyone. To this end, I decided to bring together the board of education, the superintendent's office and the four principals to give them a summary of what their school system and what their behavior as groups looked like through my eyes. This promised to be a difficult task because I suspected they'd disagree with my pictures and because I'd placed a lot of limits on what I could say in order to preserve the confidentiality of my sources.

We all assembled one summer evening. The mood was tense and I felt very much on the spot. I knew that in the history of Ashgrove these three groups of people had never been in the same room together before. Since they fit the standard configuration of uppers, middles, and lowers, I was justifiably afraid that these particular hierarchical dynamics would get played out in the interactions between the board, superintendents, and principals respectively on this evening. I chose to present my findings in this upper-middle-lower framework, hoping that insight might lessen the probability that the dynamics in the room would be destructive. When I came to talk about how a group could be an upper, a middle, and a lower at the same time, Eddie Rhodes became very interested. Previously he'd talked to me at length about how he felt the Factory had it in for him and wanted to drive him out of the town. As Eddie began to understand this upper-middle-lower framework, he started to wonder whether maybe his fear of the Factory grew primarily out of his lower paranoia. In addition he'd always made sure he never talked to the Factory about educational issues "because" as he said, "as superintendent I must protect myself from any kind of political pressure." Now he began to wonder if this might have been unnecessarily restrictive and that this perspective was due mainly to his being caught in a mentality of middleness between the political and educational concerns above and below him at the same time. He also began to suspect that, since the upper encasement restricts the passing up of accurate information, maybe the intensity of the Factory's political force over the ninth grade removal was based on simple ignorance.

Eddie asked me explicitly what he should do. I replied "many of the things you feel you shouldn't do seem not to be working for you or the system. Maybe these 'should nots' are merely a way for you to remain trapped in a particular structural encasement and at the same time keep you blind to the realization that you've been caught in a psychological prison."

"Okay," he replied, "what should I do?"

I answered "What do you think you shouldn't do most in this school system?"

"Talk to the Factory!"

"Then why not go and talk to the Factory," I suggested. "At least that way you'll learn what it is you're avoiding." I added "I can't see what harm could come from simply talking with him. You don't have to discuss political issues."

Concurrently, though unknown to me at that time, the Factory was also putting out feelers through other channels that signaled his interest in meeting with Rhodes. It so happened the Factory had become very disturbed about the idea the board was forcing him out of Ashgrove, though Eddie had no idea of this.

Two weeks later, Rhodes and the Factory met at a truck stop some fifteen miles out of Ashgrove. Rhodes arrived armed with all his statistics and reports and a very open mind. He was ready for anything.

The exchange started with the Factory saying how disappointed he'd been that the board had dismissed Eddie Rhodes. "I think you've been a good superintendent, but they've given you a really hard time."

Eddie was amazed. "I thought I was being thrown out of the town because you didn't like me."

"To the contrary. I think you're a good superintendent!"

These two men who'd fought publicly and interacted vigorously on school issues through the media and emissaries but never privately had a direct confrontation were now sitting down face to face. Rhodes meticulously laid out with his adversary the whole situation of the school crowding and the outmoded buildings from beginning to end. The two men ate and talked, argued and discussed, and by the end of three hours the Factory concluded, "You've convinced me. I think to shift the ninth grade would be wrong. You know, neither Maloney nor I really care where that grade is housed. What we've cared about is the fact that people at the high school keep screaming about the need for more space and as far as we could see they've had enough space all along. We felt by removing the ninth grade we could shut them up for a while. However, I've never realized before that the main reason we were short on space there was because of this flexible program that that school offers. Now I see it's not just a space issue. It's also a program issue. It's because we're committed to this type of program that we need the extra space, right? I've never understood that before. If you look at the number of students alone, they seem to have plenty of room."

In that moment Eddie Rhodes knew that he'd won a major victory. By the time they parted, the Factory was firmly committed to not moving the ninth grade. Within days the superintendent's office started to receive phone calls from different Democratic members of the board indicating that they had been rethinking this issue and were now willing to support a rescinding of the July realignment motion.

A Democratic caucus was held and all, save Lodell, agreed to act to keep the ninth grade in the high school.

A few months later, in December, the ninth grade issue was placed on the board's agenda once again. A large group from the town and the schools filled the public gallery and created an aura of expectation and confrontation. This time the Democrats had kept quiet about their intention to rescind their earlier actions.

Craig Hewett clamly moved, "The board of education rescinds its action of July 1973, and resolves to leave the ninth grade in its senior high school." The event flowed like clockwork. Each board member was asked to make a statement on his or her current personal opinion and then the vote was taken. The only continuing opponent, Mathew Lodell, was absent due to illness, so the vote was recorded as a unanimous act.

This time there was no clash, no dissension, no public anger. Everyone seemed happy.

To this day, it amazes Eddie Rhodes that he didn't have the wisdom to go through the ninth grade situation with the Factory earlier. In hindsight it seemed so simple, though Eddie dismisses it quietly with a smile and a "but then I didn't realize I was imprisoned in the structural encasement of middleness."

Debate was intense in the Ashgrove Democratic party during the summer of 1973. The topic? Whether Mike D'Onofrio should be renominated to run for the board of education that coming November. Board Chairman, Ron Kingston, D'Onofrio, and Reuben Kaufman were all completing six-year terms and faced the prospect of re-election or retirement.

Kaufman came quickly to the decision not to run.

Ron Kingston, after long deliberation, decided also to withdraw from educational politics. His law practice and family life had become overtaxed during the last two years of his chairmanship, and Ron felt strongly that he had to revise his time priorities.

That left Mike D'Onofrio. Despite his springtime protestations to the contrary, he was running as hard as he could. Privately, he hoped that his attempts to remove the ninth grade would have rebuilt his bridges sufficiently to cause the party leaders to redraft him for the ticket. Kingston's withdrawal would also help his cause, so Mike thought, for three completely new board members would introduce a significantly unknown factor, which might intimidate the town fathers into choosing him just simply because he was, despite his unpredictability, at least somewhat known.

Mike approached me privately to ask for my help. "I know you've got all the information I need, Ken, in order to get re-elected. If only you'd tell me, I can work out who I should put pressure on."

I was angry at Mike for approaching me this way. I told him I could not do this for it would violate completely all my agreements with everyone. He wouldn't accept my position and worked hard to try to convince me. Eventually when he realized I wouldn't give in he asked how my upper, middle, lower had relevance to his situation.

"The only advice I can give you Mike, is to say that the things you're working so hard to force happen are working against you. If you were to do some of the things you feel go most against the grain for you, you might hear how trapped you are in one structural encasement or another. When once you've trapped yourself, you've also trapped those whose behavior you're attempting to change. The harder you push them, the more entrenched they get and the more struck you get. Go in other directions and it may produce some more flexibility to the system and for you too and maybe you won't spend all your time locked into the one prison that's gotten you so depressed."

At party nomination time, Mike alternated between despair and hope, somewhat paralyzed by the conflicting emotions. He'd learned to recognize that he'd become caught in the drift of opposing political currents and that

234

his political future had been snatched entirely out of his own hands. It was now a toy to be played with by the town's master puppeteers. He couldn't change things anymore. Fate was in his favor. D'Onofrio was unexpectedly given the nomination.

The Democratic party, however, was keen to use this election as a way of getting the board to be more fiscally conservative. A budgetary hardliner and well-tested, headstrong, conservative was chosen to replace Ron Kingston.

The election was held in November, and as predicted, two Democrats, including D'Onofrio, were returned together with a minority Republican who stepped into the vacancy created by the departure of Reuben Kaufman. Overall, this election brought a more conservative flavor, the plan of the town fathers.

Immediately after the election, the board's top priority was to choose a new chairman, a coveted position for those who had future political aspirations. This event was to occur publicly at the November 13 board meeting scheduled exactly one week following the election, though clearly it promised to be a highly preorchestrated decision.

Everyone seemed to assume that the chairmanship would go to a Democrat so there was no lobby amongst the Republicans for one of their group to be presented as a candidate. Of the Democrats, there were two people who desperately wanted the position, Craig Hewett and Mike D'Onofrio. These two men, four or five years earlier, had been the best of friends. Craig had helped to settle Mike and his wife into Ashgrove when they initially arrived, reaching out and befriending them in a time and manner that D'Onofrio desperately needed. As a by-product of this friendship, after Mike had been on the board for a couple of years, he'd encouraged and eventually helped engineer Hewett's entry to educational politics. However, the last two years of bitter political battle had generated a deep rift between these two men that brought discomfort to them both, but it seemed irresolvable. Now they were to be pitted in deepest battle.

Mike had aspired to the chairmanship two years before when Ron Kingston had acquired the post. In that election, Hewett had been Kingston's strongest supporter and had been joined by Lodell and Saunders. That had left Mike with the lone Democratic support of Luise Taylor. However, with the three Republican votes and his own in an open floor battle with the full board, D'Onofrio had felt he could have pulled off a victory. Within the Democratic caucus, back in 1971, however, he had lost four to two. With that, he had the choice of remaining loyal to his party's wishes and demonstrate party solidarity or else run the risk of alienating his colleagues and trying for a conquest on the floor. Mike had vacillated on what to do for quite some time, but at the critical moment found all initiatives wrested from him, as Republican Julia Langdon placed his name in nomination. Embarrassed, somewhat afraid, highly anxious for his future in the party, he withdrew and thereby assured Kingston's success.

For two years D'Onofrio had harbored some resentment towards the processes that, in his perspective, "robbed me of the chairmanship that was rightfully mine," had he been prepared to "play the game tough enough." Now that he'd successfully maneuvered his way back onto the board, he wanted to try again for this position of prestige and power. To me, this seemed inconceivably ambitious given that over recent months, Mike had been perhaps one of the lowest status persons on the board and in the town politics. On the surface it would appear that he had no hope at all. Only weeks before he looked like he wouldn't even be nominated.

On the other hand, Craig Hewett had been Ron Kingston's friend and mentor over the past two years. Together, they had enjoyed great fun and camaraderie in operating the affairs of the school district. As a virtual, though undeclared, deputy Craig seemed the logical choice to replace the retiring Kingston. He had the capacities, connections, and the poise to slip easily into the chair. His only possible obstacle looked like being this obstinate D'Onofrio. But that seemed hardly cause for despair!

On the Thursday immediately after the election, and five days before the chairmanship vote, Craig called Mike and asked if the two of them could meet early that evening. At 5:15 they repaired to a private corner of New Bedford to deliberate the future. Craig took the first initiative.

"Mike, I want to ask you to do a very special favor. I'd like to be chairman of the board of education and I want to ask you to nominate me for that position on Tuesday night." D'Onofrio tried hard to hide his dismay by asking what votes he was assured of. Craig continued. "I've spoken to Luise Taylor and Rodney Saunders. They both said if you want to nominate me that they will support me."

That piece of information was demoralizing to Mike who had privately hoped that Taylor's and Saunder's votes would be the two he could count on to add to the Republicans to wrap it up for himself. He felt uncertain about Lodell's vote and knew for sure Hewett would get the support of the new board member. Taken aback, he suggested to his old friend and current enemy, Craig, that he'd like time to think about it and then would call him back.

They parted.

Mike felt that unless he could gain the post this year his chance of ever doing so would slip by. He didn't yet believe he had no chance, though he hadn't spoken to people adequately to be fully certain of that. After a few hours of deliberation with himself, he called Hewett to tell him the news. "Craig, I've decided I will not be nominating you. I want the position myself."

Hewett feigned surprise. "Mike, you really confuse me. I felt confident you'd be willing to do this for me. I'll call you back and talk about it with you further."

The two opponents hung up. Hewett never delivered the promised phone call. Neither of them even spoke to each other between that Thursday night and the evening of the next Tuesday when the critical vote was to be held.

236

Mike knew that Luise Taylor's vote was critical and whoever could capture that would probably win. Craig, however, desperately needed Democratic votes. He had little chance of any Republican support. Although D'Onofrio had managed to alienate his opponents during the recent months of toeing the party line, there seemed to be much more chance of his collecting the Republican support than Hewett, who'd always, almost by definition, placed himself against the Republicans' position. D'Onofrio called Luise to ask her where she stood. She replied, "Mike, I'd be happy to support you for chairman. However, if you don't run for the position and want to nominate Craig Hewett, then that's fine by me. I'll then support that. I do think, however, we should caucus and decide this before Tuesday."

"Thanks, Luise, I'm really glad to know of your support. I'll call you back later." Mike began to hope again. That news was critical.

Unfortunately for Craig, he had upset Luise on numerous occasions during the past two years, especially over the way he and Kingston cooked up half-baked schemes, forced them on the other Democrats in caucuses, only to have them backfire. She still felt angry about the Patrick Sheehan and athletic director event. Craig had been more hurt by how he handled that than he ever expected or even now understood. Matthew Lodell was also privately willing to vote against Hewett in response to having felt pushed around during that event, though he was particularly concerned to do what the town fathers felt would be best. Hence, Mike was not about to depend on Lodell's vote.

That left Rodney Saunders. If Mike could be sure of his vote, that would tie it up three to three in their party and then the chances for him were great because of the Republican support he felt confident he could draw. If the informal count was three to three, it would be very much to D'Onofrio's advantage to avoid going into a Democratic Caucus. If it went into a caucus and it was all tied up at three votes, each, someone like Mayor Maloney would enter the scene and prevail on them all to support the candidate of his choice. Mike was most uncertain as to how Maloney would jump—he guessed in Hewett's favor. He felt if it came to a big, behind-the-scenes fight, that his previous lack of support for his party would be politically lethal. Above all, D'Onofrio feared that the town politicians, and Mayor Maloney in particular, would support Hewett and this would be strong enough to swing sufficient votes away from himself.

When Mike spoke to Rodney Saunders, Rodney echoed similar sentiments to Luise Taylor. Mike was delighted. He now had the three votes he desperately hoped for. D'Onofrio was now certain of what he must do. He had to try to avoid a caucus and keep the whole chairmanship as low key an issue as possible. So began the long wait.

Mike was committed to doing nothing. That appeared to be his most promising strategy. The problem was this tactic meant he was having no contact with anyone. And four days had yet to pass before resolution would unfold. Someone else might have been able to work with such a strategy but not

D'Onofrio. Eventually, by late Sunday afternoon, he could tolerate the silence no longer and decided to actively seek contact with someone who might be in the know. He had to make it appear casual though, and so with an uncharacteristic nonchalance, he visited a local coffee shop to see whom he could find. There, to his relief was the Factory, the chief, invisible political power of Ashgrove. Mike approached him and for some little time the two men talked. The news was good. The Factory and Mayor Maloney had concluded that they wanted D'Onofrio to be chairman and were working on the idea of having Hewett withdraw and nominate Mike as a show of party unity. The only problem was Hewett was not accepting this decision.

Maloney, sensing all was not well, called for a caucus one hour before the commencement of the formal board meeting where the vote was to be taken. Everything was still in a state of flux. Craig Hewett was refusing to go with the decision of the Factory and the mayor. He wanted the position. He was as anxious as ever to continue to fight and as the caucus opened he was still declaring himself as a candidate, but without very much support. He was hoping against hope that the two political power figures, whom he knew liked and supported him more than D'Onofrio, would come to his aid at the last moment and swing one of those three votes that Taylor, Saunders, and Lodell would cast. Then the victory could be his for that would tie it up three-three which Maloney could break by casting a vote in his favor. The remaining three Democrats would then change their allegiance to produce a block vote, which he could then win six to three or at worst five to four, if D'Onofrio in revolt, broke from the party and voted with the Republicans.

The Factory and Maloney, however, were not proving to be too responsive. Craig could not ascertain why. It seemed ironic and confusing that the election had caused a drift towards a more conservative board yet here the chairmanship was about to be put into Mike's hands, the most liberal and unpredictable Democrat. But those master politicians understood the shrewdest subtleties of this game. They had figured that in the past Mike D'Onofrio had been the most vacillatory figure in their party. By having him chairman that would be one way to rigidify his behavior. In the final analysis, to have him in the chair meant there would be five firm Democratic votes on the floor of the board room. If Hewett were chairman, D'Onofrio could continue to defect and regularly tie things up four to four by voting with the Republicans. Certainly Hewett as chairman could then resolve the issues in the Democrats' favor; but if Mike became committed to corroding his party he could shrewdly maneuver the critical issues to be voted on when one Democrat was absent and hence enable the liberal Republicans to win. The politics went as follows. By elevating Mike to chairman, they could control the board easier and assure that this conservative board would in fact act in a more conservative manner. This is why in that caucus, Craig Hewett was having no success in his last minute battle to snatch the prize from Mike. Seven-fifty-five P.M. arrived with no decision reached and suddenly Craig stopped fighting. In high confusion they all dispersed to travel the three blocks to the board meeting.

There was an air of great expectancy, for the superintendent and the public had all been kept guessing about how the chairmanship would be resolved.

Luise Taylor, as board secretary, took the chair. She declared nominations for the board chairmanship open.

Within a second Craig Hewett was speaking. "Madame Chairperson, it is with great pleasure that I nominate my good friend and colleague, Mr. Mike D'Onofrio, for chairman of the board. I can think of no person more deserving of that position or more suited to that role."

"Seconded," flashed Matthew Lodell.

"I move that nominations be closed," added Rodney Saunders, in rapid succession.

"Seconded," by Gerald Bomford.

A routine private ballot was taken and then Luise announced, "Mr. D'Onofrio, I invite you to occupy your new position."

"Thank you, Ms. Taylor. As the chairman of the board of education of Ashgrove, I would like to make a few introductory remarks. First, . . ."

Two months after D'Onofrio became chairman he received a phone call from the Factory. "You know, Mike, I don't think it makes sense for us to have to get ourselves a new superintendent of schools this year. Our educational program has been going through so much change these past years, it's time for some stability."

"I agree."

"See if you can talk Rhodes into staying."

Three months later a unanimous vote was recorded by the board of education to offer Superintendent Rhodes a further three-year contract and an additional $1,200 salary increase. Rhodes accepted.

In May of 1980 a retirement dinner was held to honor Dr. Eddie Rhodes who was stepping down from the position of Superintendent of Schools of Ashgrove, which he'd occupied for twelve years.

Postlogue

Ashgrove and Montville have profoundly influenced my life. I visited them because I wanted to search for an understanding of one basic psychological/sociological paradox. I left them with an intense questioning of the very fabric of my own inner realities and of social reality in general. I encountered Montville and Ashgrove at one point in time and space in my own individual life journey. Now I find that the ghosts of those two social systems have permeated into all domains of my life pilgrimage, my journeys into the inner crevices of my being, my place in the social activism (or lack thereof) of our times, my role as a conservationist of social values that are important to me, my belief (or disbelief) in the integrity of academe, and my ambivalence about the overall worth of my profession.

I started this book with the desire to study a phenomenon. I end it with the humble recognition that it is not possible to separate out such phenomena from the very essence of social life itself and that my mind is able to comprehend only the smallest part of the whole social complex. Who I am, who I've been, and who I'm in the process of becoming are all a part of the dynamics I feel I bumped into and attempted to articulate in my Ashgrove and Montville quests. It all penetrates to the core of my being. This is not to say there's not a great deal more in that core as well. I know there is. This is like a speck of sand. But it's an abrasive speck for it has scratched the surface, shaken the foundations of my inner epistemology, and called into question virtually all of the fundamental principles on which it appears my life had been predicated prior to this time.

In this moment, I do not feel that I've resolved my original paradox. Nor have I answered the initial question that provoked my quest. However, I have come to appreciate why my paradox exists and why it's such an important phenomenon. In addition I do feel that my question has become greatly enriched; it's now a more complex question and it penetrates deeper into the inner reaches of the individual identity theme and into the further horizons of social theory.

There are several scattered comments I need to make in order to gain closure on this manuscript. Some of these have implications as summaries of theoretical concepts. Others deal merely with my own affects.

241

Fact or Fiction?

As I've talked about Montville and Ashgrove, people have repetitively asked me if the stories were true, whether they all really happened that way. This has been particularly potent when friends have suggested things like, "If I'd been an Elite, I'd have never done. . .! How come they were so blind?" Of course, these comments are being made by those of us who were not subjected to the Kenloch pressures at that time. Had we been there in Montville, the chances are very high we'd have behaved similarly. Maybe not identically, but equally bizarre! This is not because we're stupid but because the social forces are so powerful they constrain and significantly determine our realities.

I can respond to the "are these stories true?" question by an unequivocal assurance that I've attempted to capture as faithfully as possible the events as I saw and interpreted them. This is not to say that I got it all. There were other realities at play to which I never became attuned, that some other investigator might have unravelled and made more focal. Also, I've had to eliminate or summarize a great deal of material to compress Montville and Ashgrove into one document. I've undoubtedly used the "predefined contours of my mind" to filter and summarize the Ashgrove and Montville worlds as I saw them. While I certainly tried to stretch my investigative capacities to extend beyond my precalibrated biases, I'm more than willing to acknowledge that I may not have been successful.

Certain events, situations, locations, and personages have been fictionalized to protect the "innocent" and "guilty" alike. Names are pseudonyms and I've been careful to disguise or distort certain critical events a little. I request that anyone "in the know," especially from Ashgrove, not interpret what's captured on these pages as exactly how it all happened. Almost all of it is my best representation of what actually occurred—but some if it isn't. I deliberately fictionalized about five percent of the events to minimize the possibility of anyone being hurt. I'm telling no one which five percent is made up. If you are from Ashgrove and you disagree with what I've said please feel free to think that this falls into this fictionalized category.

The central question is: "Are these stories true?" To this I wish to respond by quoting my favorite line from *Roots*. One of the children, when told the Kunte Kinte story of the old African slave, asked with wide-eyed disbelief, "Is that really true?" To which Tom Harvey responded, "It isn't whether it's actually true that matters; it's that it is filled with truth." I will not claim that Montville and Ashgrove represent *The Truth*. But for me they are *filled with truth*.

Structural Relativity

In the whole of this quest, the most revealing moment for me occurred when it became clear that any group or individual could be caught simultaneously in all three of the structural encasements. The idea that the hierarchical intergroup was a relative phenomenon rather than a static property of the social structure was an overpowering concept for me. This gave meaning to why someone such as Superintendent Eddie Rhodes could be experiencing himself as an individual while others would be seeing him as the focal representative of the superintendent's office. He was looking at himself from his inner perspective while others were viewing him from their own intergroup vantage and could understand and interpret his behavior only as the operative structural encasements predetermined. It reached farther than this, however. This concept of relativity of upness, middleness, and lowness made it possible for Dr. Rhodes to be experiencing himself as a middle, torn by the encasement that grew out of his concerns for those above and below, while an upper group would look at those same behaviors as expressing the blocking and resistance of a lower, and a lower group would look at those same behaviors as expressing the indifference, incompetence, and arrogance of an upper. Each action could have multiple and divergent meanings depending on the perspective from which it was experienced.

For me, this concept of structural relativity helped greatly in untangling the multilayered realities embedded in Ashgrove. In addition, it drove home to me that mostly I experience myself in a middleness mentality, torn by polar tensions that pull on me. Ask me why I behave the way I do and mostly I'll respond by focussing on those various and opposite pulls and how they intersect and get balanced out in my inner being. However, others looking at me are probably going to experience my behavior through the filters of either upper or lower structural encasements. Rather than seeing me as a "middle torn by tension" I may be viewed as "suspicious, blocking, uncooperative, or rebellious" by some and, at the same time, as "manipulative, uncaring, blind, and insensitive" by others. Who sees me what way will undoubtedly be dependent on what power dynamics are being played out at that time.

I suspect that most of us see ourselves in a middle position most of the time. We experience ourselves as feeling and responding to those opposite pulls. However, I equally suspect that others, when relating to us where there are power differentials, see us through either upper or lower structural encasement filters.

Personal Impact

The diagnostic methodology of nonintervention took a great toll on my emotions. I was never, no matter how hard I tried, able to be dispassionate about what I observed. For example, at Montville, I was so overwhelmed by the system craziness that I saw getting put into Anthony, transforming him slowly into the village lunatic, it was all I could do not to jump into the power laboratory, "go native" (as we Anthropologists call it) and shake everyone till they understood what was happening. In the review period for Montville, a mock court was held to determine whether Anthony or the society as a whole had been crazy. I took on the role as Anthony's defense and with all my passion attacked the society as being insane with Anthony being the only one who'd been wise enough to really understand. This, of course, was a gross oversimplification. However, it did speak to my need to release pent up emotions before I could move to a more detached interpretation of Montville's events.

Similarly at Ashgrove, I can recall to this very day the livid emotions I had when at the May first meeting the board of education decided to fire Rhodes. The day after I was still so emotionally agitated and angry that I could do nothing of a constructive nature. I remember walking around the city green for several hours, kicking stones and leaves, in an obvious attempt to dissipate my abrasive emotions. It had been extremely hard for me to sit through that board meeting without breaking out of my researcher role. I wanted so badly to jump on the seat and yell at them all how crazy their behavior looked from my perspective. I guess the emotional energy I expended in stopping myself from doing that took its toll. That next day I snapped impatiently at friends, cursed the President of the United States a few times more than usual, and needed a lot of open space, independence, and time to be alone.

I was always very conscious of how much pain I potentially was causing people, not by my conscious intent but as a consequence of the role I'd taken on and my determination to minimize my impact on the system.

In Ashgrove, there was a large number of occasions when pressures on individuals in the system were so strong that they simply had to find some way to gain release from the resultant tension. Since I possessed a large mass of critical information that could help lessen people's conflicts if only they could get their hands on what I knew, I was regularly seen as a potential vehicle for helping individuals to cope with unbearable conflict.

Several people at Ashgrove also needed desperately information that would help them to feel accepted and convinced they were doing the right thing. One of the difficulties at Ashgrove was the large amount of ambiguity. Many people had struggled for years with little knowledge of whether they were liked or viewed as competent. The resultant ambiguity was somewhat soul destroying. I, as a person and as a researcher, because of the breadth of the data I'd gathered, provided a unique opportunity for offering that confirmation. And yet, there I was adopting a stance that assured that individuals would be unable to ever gain that from me. My unwillingness to speak simply reinforced the system's ambiguity with respect to them and their performance.

I recognized the pain I caused people by my silence. This hurt me too for I wanted in the worst possible way to give expression to the humanistic dimension of my own personhood and yet felt compelled to refrain because I perceived my study would be destroyed if I stepped out of my role. My expectation was that if I gave in to pressures people placed on me for information, my credibility and hence my potential objectivity would be washed away.

Probably the most stressed three individuals during the period of my study were the superintendent, Principal Lewis Brook, and Mike D'Onofrio. These three were the people I felt most pained over refusing to share with them my findings on a day-to-day basis.

Eddie Rhodes never once asked me directly for information. However, when we spoke about the school system, he opened up to me so personally that I could always see clearly the sharp anguish produced by his not knowing things that I knew. I always found this characteristic strongly seductive for not only was I aware of his pain but I felt keenly the fact that I had the capacity and the information to make that pain more tolerable for him. An additionally seductive aspect of this relationship I had with Eddie Rhodes was that this voluntary opening of his internal life was highly uncharacteristic for him. In almost all of his relationships with people for a large part of his life, and to his own detriment, he'd struggled to separate out the personal dimensions. I wanted to encourage him to continue this increased openness but felt that in my own actions, I was in no way rewarding this new behavior of his. My refusal to step out of role with the superintendent was difficult for me to handle personally.

Lewis Brook always stirred in me the widest range of emotions. There was hardly an occasion when I saw him, either individually or in group settings, that I didn't have a strong affective response. It was always of interest to note also that those feelings I had for him mirrored in some way the nature of the overbearing forces that were impinging on him. I often found myself, for example, feeling angry when he felt angry, or disappointed when he felt organizationally impotent. My role of silence seemed to make things worse for Lewis. He felt isolated and cut off by everyone else and he experienced me as just one more person who refused to let him know what was going on.

One of the critical features of Principal Brook's position was the fact that because of this feeling of isolation he was always looking for cues about what was going on elsewhere in the system to help him construct his sense of social reality. He would tend to take my questions and the way I phrased things, as somehow a signal of things that might be occurring elsewhere. Hence after many questions, Lewis Brook's response, rather than providing an answer to what I wanted to know, would be "Does that mean such and such is happening?" I always felt the need to remind him that I didn't feel I could specifically address what he'd asked. However, there were occasions when it became absolutely imperative for me to fill in some minor gap in his knowledge just so that he wouldn't make grossly inappropriate deductions from the way I had asked my questions, many of which may have been nothing more than an idiosyncratic element of my non-American version of the English language. When I refused to engage Lewis in dialogue on those occasions when he questioned me, he always graciously acknowledged the restrictions of my role but clearly felt, and usually expressed, intense frustration with my silence.

My relationship with Lewis was turbulent. He was always outwardly cooperative but he often didn't trust me, especially in the early days. One day I asked if I could look in his personnel files. He said, "Sure! Next week." About two months later he showed me another set of files with the comment, "You can now look at these if you wish. I know this is what you really wanted to know. These are the really sensitive papers I pulled out of the personnel files that I didn't want you to see when you first asked. I now trust you enough to show you this stuff."

I've spent a lot of time pondering, with feelings of guilt, the extent to which I may have made life more difficult for Lewis Brook and the extent to which I should feel responsible. Across the years, I've managed to rationalize most of it away. However, even as I write this now, I feel a small twinge of discomfort within.

Mike D'Onofrio was always a ball of tension. Hence, he was eager to know how people viewed him. From the first day of my visit to Ashgrove, he wanted to know what I thought of him. After board meetings he would ask me during casual conversation for my evaluations of what he'd said on different themes throughout the evening. He looked to my approval as one way of coping with some of the tension he was juggling within. I always refused to reply, much to his disgust.

During one interview, after I'd been asking him questions for an hour, Mike slammed his fist on the tape recorder and demanded that we stop. "I've given you one hour of my time answering your questions. Now you give me an hour of your time and answer my questions!"

He used the most legalistic mode he could and focussed on things like, "Do you think I'm a man of honesty?" I refused to answer him on the basis that I felt it violated the spirit of my research agreement. This made him extremely angry and he accused me vehemently of being unwilling to see his side of the situation—a justifiable accusation from his perspective. With my refusal, he accused me of being "worse than Nixon" and "pulling the Fifth Amendment more than any American would." He even pleaded with me to recognize that he was facing great psychological turmoil and as a friend, I should be willing to help him out. Both Mike and I knew his political future was in the balance and that I could give him information that could turn things around for him. He felt my silence to be intolerable. As we said good-bye that day we both felt the wrench keenly. I did nothing of a constructive nature for several hours. I knew I had hurt Mike deeply. I'd failed to respond to his human suffering and as a fellow human I felt that hard to accept. I couldn't reconcile myself as to how much turmoil I had created for Mike that day and how my attempts to be nonintervening proved to be probably an intervention of the most powerful form.

On one occasion I was challenged publicly as to whether I'd kept my promised silence. I tried to assure my challengers that I'd kept the spirit of this but on a couple of occasions had not blankly refused to talk, but discussed my noninteractive role with the person concerned in an attempt "not to be inhumane." D'Onofrio from across the room yelled out, "You were inhumane to me!" The subject was dropped and Mike and I never discussed it again.

At one time Mike pressured me relentlessly in public to provide proof that something he was saying was correct. It wasn't. I steadfastly refused, leading to a vigorous and messy public fight between the two of us. While hating this fight, it served my purposes well because it clearly demonstrated Mike didn't have me in his pocket, something he often tried to imply for his own political gain. For some long months he and I were somewhat estranged. When all the tension was over and Mike had been elected chairman we made our public peace. It was done with a simple gesture. We never discussed it. Given that we both understood the political nature of things, we just played it out. On Thanksgiving, just days after D'Onofrio's political recovery, he and I went to the football game between Ashgrove's high school and Carlo Esposito's team. Sure. Ashgrove lost. Again. We stood together under the goal post and for two hours everyone and his dog filed by and greeted us. Together. It was a wonderful symbolic statement. Mike and Ken had mended their fences.

Mike never changed, however. One day in April 1980, I got a desperate call from him telling me that Eddie Rhodes' retirement dinner was being held the next night, that I had been invited to make a speech in his honor. "Not much. Just a few words. Eddie knows and he's thrilled!!" I was very touched. But I was in Washington, D.C., and it was going to be inordinately inconvenient to rearrange my schedule to be present. Mike wouldn't take no for an answer. Of course I was flattered and wanted to go, especially when Mike told me I would be the only one to speak. I went. As usual Mike had misrepresented the situation to me. There were hundreds of people present and every conceivable politician from the state down to the local PTA all wanted to pay their tributes.

I was very glad I went however. Although Eddie Rhodes is not the real name of the superintendent, I've always called him that. It's been our inside joke. We embraced and as we choked in our joy at seeing each other again, he paid me the highest professional compliment I've ever received. "Ken, the first six years here at Ashgrove were hell for me. The last six years were wonderful. You do understand don't you, you really do understand, your study turned the school system around for me!" I was overwhelmed. Proud. And humble. And very joyful. Seeing Eddie and being in the bosom of Ashgrove again, six years later, provided the necessary stimulus for me to be able to complete this book.

A Final Catch 22

After Montville and Ashgrove had been written, one of my friends sympathetically, but forcefully, suggested that he suspected I had constructed this particular framework for understanding the social processes of groups in conflict because it would help me deal with something taking place within my inner being that was very disquieting to me. I was shocked at the prospect. Not that I thought it couldn't happen, but because I'd been so faithful in trying to monitor my inner reality so that if this happened I'd be aware of it. This critic suggested that one way for me to explore this would be to see if I had greater empathy for one of the Montville groups or one of the Ashgrove groups. As a tool for opening this topic up, I sat down and rank ordered who I liked most through to least in Ashgrove, fearful that this would reveal a systematic pattern that would indicate a critical bias.

In the final ranking there were seven who stood out at the top of the list. I found it difficult to differentiate my overall feelings towards these seven people. To my relief, of the seven, three were board members, two were from the superintendent's office, one was a principal, and one was a teacher. That was fascinating. At one general level I felt contented that at least using this index I'd not fallen into the trap my friendly critic had suggested. His comment, however, left a nagging reaction inside me that would not go away. I resolved to look at what were the types of things that triggered my warm feelings for these particular people and when did those feelings surface most. There a pattern emerged. I found myself drawn to these people predominantly when they were operating in roles that placed them in the middle position.

This observation became overwhelming to me. Now it was all clear! I had fallen into the trap of my own theory. For my theory is a theory of middleness.

Who but a person trapped by the encasements of middleness would try to explain a social system in its totality giving equal credence to the realities represented in the polarities. Who but a person overcome by middleness would take the tensions of the system and struggle with them so intensely in his inner being. Who but a middle would try to explain this all, write a book so others could understand the processes as well, but be able to offer so little insight on what to actually do with the realities explicated. Who but a person entrenched in middleness would even believe that by knowing and understanding more our experience will be enriched.

At this moment I'm only too aware that I'm a person of primarily a middle mentality. For almost all my life I've been coopted by middleness processes. What else would have enticed me to spend twenty years of my life in school and the pursuit of knowledge? What better expression of the obsessiveness of a middle mentality. I search for the meaning of life. I read books but they write them faster than I can read them. So I take speed reading courses. Why? All with the vain middleness belief that somewhere in the pursuit of knowledge I'll find meaning. And now I even take years out of my life to write about it all.

At this point, I'm forced to acknowledge that this whole document is an expression of a middle mind set. I'm forced to ask, what might an intergroup theory look like through the eyes of a lower? Or an upper? The answer is I don't know. It seems to me that lowers don't write theories, at least not from lower perspectives. While in their lowness they're more inclined to run the revolution. Uppers don't write theories either. While in their upness they're too busy perpetuating the status quo and making sure they continue to keep control. People only write theories when they're in a middle mentality. Even Karl Marx. The ultimate middle. And it's only when in a state of middleness do people read about them.

What happened to me when I first realized this? First, my mind ceased functioning. Then I wept!

Notes

Prologue

1. This pattern is observable in structures ranging from the modern bureaucratized military to agrarian settings of antiquities where peasants, on being promoted to the rank of overseer, would become even more tyranical toward former comrades than the owner himself. Freire (1972) argues that this occurs because in the condition of oppression the only model of "manhood" that is internalized is that of the oppressor (pages 23–24).

2. I refer to this process as trajection, the dynamics of which will be explicated in a later paper. It is similar to the Sullivanian concept of paratactic distortion and is central to understanding the displaced attribution process embedded in ethnocentrism.

3. It is the process of linking various sensations with one another in time and space, delineating boundaries around events and objects, and then formulating relationships between them that is at the heart of object relations in psychoanalytic theory (Klein, 1932) and in the biological and organizational perspectives on open systems theory (Katz & Kahn, 1966).

4. Freire (1972), expanding on this issue, points out that the process view of reality enables us to see man as a conscious being, whereas the product view of reality conceives of man as the "possessor" of a consciousness, an empty "mind" passively open to the reception of deposits of reality from the outside world (the "banking" concept of man).

Montville

5. *A Methodological Note.* At the Montville laboratory there were three regular Anthropologists and one Anthropological photographer. I participated in the role of an Anthropologist.

We three Anthropologists attempted to deploy our resources so that each of the three groups was always being observed. We tended to stay with a group for approximately one to two hours and then rotated to another group. This was often influenced by which groups were meeting together and what was taking place in these encounters. When two or more groups were meeting, more than one Anthropologist would be present, thereby making it possible to double-check one's perception of what was going on. Our rotational scheme was designed to help keep us maximally in touch with the whole system and to minimize overidentification with any one group.

The Anthropological photographer moved through the society at a much higher rate than the rest of us, taking a pictorial record of events. He also acted as a liasion to keep the other Anthropologists constantly informed as to where groups were located and generally what they were doing.

At each point of Anthropological rotation, we would attempt to take a few minutes to update each other on what was happening in the various parts of the society. At each meal we would try to spend a significant period of time together to assure updating. For approximately two hours each evening, after the participants in the laboratory had gone to sleep, we would get together to reconstruct as fully as possible the events of the day.

Most of our data consisted of observations of what was actually transpiring and written or taped records of what was being said by people. Occasionally interviews were conducted.

There were two other major sources of data. The first of these was what was occurring within our own experiences as Anthropologists as we lived out our "parasitic" role on the system. For example, there were times when we felt very vulnerable as Anthropologists, especially when the society became highly aggressive. Then it would always seem dangerous to carry any money, because that would make us prime targets for anyone who became desperate enough to need to thieve in order to gain food. There were also times when I became anxious about the prospect of my Anthropological notes being stolen. When I felt this anxiety I knew that Montville was straining at the seams with information deprivation and overall deception. In these moments, it was evident that a set of Anthropologist's notes would be a very valuable source about what was happening elsewhere in the system. Another major introspective domain was that in order to survive myself, I had to be willing to reflect the values of the group I was observing. Hence, as an Anthropologist, like others at Montville, I sometimes missed out on meals. There were occasions when I too was hungry and knew what it felt like to be angry at those who were instituting deprivations. In this regard I would operate temporarily on the values of the group I was assigned to observe. If they were stealing to eat, I too would steal to eat.

The second major source of additional data was the two-day debriefing phase. During this time, participants introspected publicly, providing their reactions to events they previously had struggled to keep hidden. They were also available to Anthropologists for in-depth interviews.

In the account provided here, I've restricted myself to material that was verifiable through multiple data-gathering modes. Editorial license has been taken in presenting the story from the omniscient author perspective and in fictionalizing small aspects of certain events in order to constrict the volume of this account.

6. Description of Pursewarden by Lawrence Durrell in *Mountolive,* New York: Dutton, 1958, page 219–220.

Ashgrove

7. Methodological Issues at Ashgrove.

a. *Reducing the Impact of My Biases.* I used the methodologies of Organizational Diagnosis (Alderfer, et al., in press; Alderfer, 1980; Levinsion, 1972; Mirvis and Berg, 1977; Smith, 1976) and Participant Observation (Filstead, 1970; McCall and Simmons, 1969; Hammond, 1964; Bruyn, 1966; Diesling, 1971) in this study of Ashgrove. My major fear in using this qualitative approach was that I might become coopted by individuals or groups within the system, thereby corroding my objectivity.

There were five major orientations I developed to help define my role so as to maximize my objectivity. There were a few occasions when this meant that access to information was less than optimal, but as a general rule I tried to take the choices that would heighten objectivity and avoid cooptation even if it meant temporarily diminishing access to data. Those five major orientations were: seize the initiative over whom and when I'd make observations; minimize my impact on the system; constantly collect data from multiple parts of the system; minimize "performing" behavior on the part of Ashgrove people; and, maintain a marginal role as a researcher.

1. *Seize the initiative over whom and when I'd make observations:*
I wanted to take the prime initiative around who I would interview and when, what meetings I would attend, and what I would observe. Hence, I requested of people information about what was going on, where and when, and problems different people may have around granting me access to meetings, etc. However, I never allowed myself to feel compelled to respond to any specific invitations to observe or interview because I wanted to avoid being seduced into any individual's or group's perspectives. It seemed most probable from the outset that I

could come to feel highly accepted in one part of the system and less accepted in another part. I was afraid that if this were to happen, the personal pulls on me to respond to friendly and encouraging invitations to observe or collect a disproportionate amount of data from one group at one time would be strong. I knew this could powerfully distort my perspective. The pulls were certainly there. At times I felt much more accepted in one part of the system than in others. However, whenever I felt myself becoming particularly comfortable in one setting, I forced myself to quickly move to a place in the system where I felt less accepted and more uncomfortable. I'm sure this lessened bias but at a cost. One major cost of this autonomy of mine was that as people learned of my investment in being independent they were less inclined to tell me of what was going on and when. This meant that I had to increase my level of energy in order to find out when meetings were to be held or what the agenda was.

2. *Minimize my impact on the system:*
I wanted to minimize my impact on all parts of the system with which I was interacting. To do this, I refused to answer any questions of a content nature about my study. I always indicated, when asked questions about what I was thinking about or uncovering in my research, that a reply at present would be premature and that, as agreed in my contract, I would not indicate to any part of the system my findings until the end. The only things I would willingly discuss were issues related to my role, what parts of the system I was gathering data from, and topics relevant to confidentiality. If people asked how my study was going, I would reply with trite comments such as, "Fine," or "I'm working hard," etc. If they asked whether people were being cooperative, I'd reply, "Yes." If they asked whether I was getting anything, I'd reply "I'm finding it most fascinating." All of those responses were, in fact, an accurate reflection of where I was almost the whole time. However, I felt it was important to give all groups and people similar responses and to give nothing of what I knew away. This, I hoped, would protect me from becoming overly identified with one particular group or any individual.

3. *Constantly collect data from multiple parts of the system:*
To avoid bias of my outlook, I attempted to balance the people I was speaking to during any time period. Thus, if I spoke to the superintendent or his assistant on one day, I would make sure that before I spoke to either of them again, usually two or three weeks later, I would spend time with teachers, board members, students, and principals. I adopted the same principle with all groups.

4. *Minimize performing behavior on the part of Ashgrove people:*
Another behavior of mine that became critical in defining my role was the fact that I gave the appearance that I was constantly writing. In the very early stages I had the sense that people were performing for me. They looked to see if I wrote down what they'd just said. In time this diminished; but it helped greatly if I always was writing, if not recording events, at least doodling. This made it of no value to look at me for cues about their behavior and helped reduce the performance phenomenon.

5. *Maintain a marginal role as a researcher:*
It seemed imperative that I work at maintaining the marginality of my role as much as possible. This was particularly hard because I, like all others, had needs for inclusion, to be liked, to be perceived as a person of worth. The more marginal I was, the less possible it seemed that these important dimensions of me could be satisfied. There were three major things I did to help my marginality without denying my own personal needs.

The first of these was to talk with Ashgrove people about my role regularly. I often felt very uncomfortable and frustrated with my noninteractive stance. Others, too, felt similarly about my role. Whenever there was the slightest suggestion from others about frustration they felt with my silence, my distance, or my "non-get-atableness" I'd talk about that with them. I'd share some of my frustrations about feeling compelled to be that way for research purposes, and that I needed to be mutually interactive, etc. I encouraged them to do likewise. These discussions were always therapeutic for those I talked with and myself. The sharing of the dual frustrations about my role became a way of developing a significant rapport with different people without abandoning the essential elements of distance that role demanded. These role discussions always made it easier for me to continue to operate and for others to accept my distance. They also made it easier to reduce my distance as a person while at the same time retaining my distance as a researcher. In the latter stage of the study it was clear to everyone that because of the highly politicized nature of the system I held data that could make people feel confirmed or disconfirmed and the fact that I was refusing to step out of role to use this information increased the frustration level of those with whom I dealt. Hence, discussions around my role occurred much more often in the latter phases of the study. I also sensed an increase in anxiety about who I was or what I was about. As time went on people became very concerned about what sort of a person I really was.

A second thing I did to help retain marginality was to always dress in my regular clothes—casual academic. Hence, I never really looked like anyone in the system. By dressing this way, when with the board, superintendent, principals, or teachers, my dress was always much more casual, my hair longer, and my difference highly visible. In interactions with the students, my dress usually proved to be neater, and my age confirmed my differentness from them.

The third thing I did was to struggle to minimize verbal and nonverbal cues about my own responses. I tried to keep relatively poker-faced during group observations, for example, and whenever possible to refrain from laughing during humorous situations, etc. Sometimes this was humanly impossible. I steadfastly held to the issue of refusing to give anyone any information about what I was finding during the data-gathering stage.

b. *Data-Gathering Issues.* There were five major types of data in the Ashgrove study that I sought out:
1. Perceptions and behavior of individuals around events in the system,
2. Perceptions and behaviors of groups in intra-group situations,
3. Perceptions and behaviors in inter-group situations,
4. Historical and documentary data, and
5. What happened to me as the researcher within the system.

The major methods for gathering the data were:
1. Individual interviews,
2. Observations of intra-group interactions,
3. Observations of inter-group interactions,
4. Observations of structural features of relationships and emergent patterns of interactions in unstructured settings (for example, during informal discussions),
5. Informal discussions with individuals or small groups insufficiently structured to justify the term interview, and
6. Observations and introspections on the forces impinging on my life in the context of the system.

There were three basic principles that I adopted in data gathering.

The first was to vary the sources of my data quite regularly. Hence, I would not overuse any particular person or group.

The second principle was to vary on a regular basis my forms of data gathering. Hence, I would follow group or inter-group events by a series of interviews or some informal observations to try and gain a different perspective on the interactions through a different methodology.

The third principle was to seek out multiple sources and multiple methods from the same sources to gain as broad and complete a perspective as possible.

c. *A Researcher's Power.* Although in my early interactions with the school system, everyone led me to believe that my research could do little harm to anyone concerned, it quickly became obvious to both them and me that this was not so. People gradually came to believe that I had reached the point where I potentially could confirm or disconfirm so many people's stances. From this perception I derived a great deal of power within the system. Within a one month period I'd gathered enough data from multiple sources within the system, a large part of it offered in confidence, such that I was aware of the ramifications of things going on in the system that no other one individual knew about. People wanted the information I had, and yet there was no way for them to get access to it. The generation of this power of the researcher's role produced two types of forces. (1) It meant that it became increasingly important for everyone to keep on my good side. While there were no overt risks, from my perspective, of ever breaking out of my role and telling all, this always existed as a possibility in the minds of those with whom I interacted. Also, since I was retaining a minimally interactive stance, giving no cues to anyone as to what I knew or didn't know, it was possible (at least anticipated in the minds of many) that I had the goods on everyone. Most seemed to respond as though I were somehow untouchable and hence, on occasion, I became the object of considerable deference. There seemed almost to develop a form of "be kind to Ken," especially in the public domain, although as time went on more and more people began to express private frustration at my silence and unwillingness to break from what they described as my aloof role.

(2) The second force that emerged was that it seemed to become somewhat risky for those involved not to level with me. Since all knew that I had gained access to a large mass of data, but no one really grasped what I knew or what I didn't know, to not volunteer information that they thought I might need became a risk in and of itself. As one board member said at one point, when someone wanted to throw me out of a meeting I was observing, "You've got to be kidding. I've told him everything by now so he might as well know it all. He's got the goods on us anyway. We'd be fools to alienate him now!" Not to continue to let me have the full inside story meant that I might end up getting a distorted picture. Since I held the key, at least in the perceptions of many, to a lot of people's hopes to find out how they were seen within the system, it was dangerous not to let me know all.

As a result of these two forces at play, there were a large number of times when people used me and the apparently friendly relationship between them and me, for the purpose of "scoring points." To be seen confiding information in me became somewhat synonymous, in the perceptions of some of those observing the confidences, with—"He must be aboveboard; look, he'll tell it all to Ken." That seemed to be used as one way to make mileage with adversaries. Another was to interact with me publicly in such a way as to draw a friendly response from me. That potentially was synonymous with— "Ken thinks he's a good guy, hence he must be okay."

Most of my power derived from my silence and the uncertainty that silence generated. Later, especially after I'd provided feedback to the board, the superintendent's office, and the principals, most of my systemic power disappeared. It was clear then, that either I was not able or at least I was not going to use in a destructive sense any of the "goods" I had on people.

The nicknames generated for me during the study reflected my developing power. In the early days I was referred to as "The Outsider." Later, it became "The guy who's always writing." By the end, with an obvious reference to Watergate, I was called, "The Australian Plumber."

References

Acton, H. B. *What Marx really said.* New York: Schocken, 1967.

Alderfer, C. P. "Group and intergroup relations," in *Improving life at work.* J. R. Hackman and J. L. Suttle (Eds.), Santa Monica, Calif.: Goodyear, 1977.

Alderfer, C. P. The methodology of organizational diagnosis. *Professional Psychology.* 1980, *11*, 459–468.

Alderfer, C. P., Brown, L. D., Kaplan, R. E., and Smith, K. K. *Group relations and organizational diagnosis.* New York: Wiley, In press.

Alinsky, S. D. *Rules for radicals,* New York: Vintage, 1971.

Blake, R. R., and Mouton, J.S. Comprehension of own and outgroup positions under intergroup competition. *The Journal of Conflict Resolution,* 1961, *5,* 304–310.

Blake, R. R., Shepard, H. A., and Mouton, J. S. *Managing intergroup conflict.* Houston: Gulf, 1964.

Bonhoeffer, D. *Letters and papers from prison.* Edited by E. Bethge. New York: MacMillan, 1972.

Bruyn, S. T. *The human perspective in sociology.* Englewood Cliffs, N.J.: Prentice-Hall, 1966.

Caute, D. (Ed.) *Essential writings of Karl Marx.* New York: Collier Books, 1967.

Cleaver, E. *Soul on ice,* New York: Dell, 1968.

Cooley, H. C. *Human nature and the social order.* New York: Scribner, 1922.

Coser, L. A. *The functions of social conflict.* New York: Free Press, 1956.

Dahrendorf, R. *Class and class conflict in industrial society,* Stanford, Calif.: Stanford University Press, 1957.

Dalton, M. *Men who manage.* New York: Wiley, 1959.

Dentler, R. A., and Erikson, K. T. "The functions of deviance in groups." *Social Problems,* 1959, *7,* 98–107.

Diesling, P. *Patterns of discovery in the social sciences.* Chicago: Aldine, 1971.

Drucker, P. F. *The New society: The anatomy of the industrial order.* New York: Harper, 1950.

Durrell, L. *Mountolive.* New York: Dutton, 1961.

Einstein, A. "On science," 1918, unpublished address, cited in R. M. Pirsig, *Zen and the art of motorcycle maintenance.* London: Corgi, 1974.

Erikson, E. H. *Identity: youth and crisis.* New York: Norton, 1968.

Filstead, W. J. *Qualitative methodology.* Chicago: Markam, 1970.

Freire, P. *Pedagogy of the oppressed.* Ringwood, Australia: Penguin, 1972.

Freud, S. *Group psychology and the analysis of the ego.* New York: Bantam, 1960.

Goffman, E. *The presentation of self in everyday life.* Garden City, N.Y.: Doubleday, 1959.

Goffman, E. *Interaction ritual.* Garden City, N.Y.: Doubleday, Anchor Books, 1967.

Hammond, P. E. *Sociologists at work: essays on the craft of social research.* New York: Basic Books, 1964.

Haskel, B. G. "Disparities, strategies and opportunity costs." *International Studies Quarterly,* 1974, *18,* 3–31.

Janis, I. L. *Victims of groupthink.* Boston, Mass.: Houghton-Mifflin, 1972.

Jung, C. G. *Answer to Job.* Princeton, N.J.: Princeton University Press, 1958.

Jung, C. G. *Memories, dreams and reflections.* New York: Vintage Books, 1965.

Katz, M. B. *Class bureaucracy and schools.* New York: Praeger, 1971.

Katz, D., and Kahn, R. *The social psychology of organizations.* New York: Wiley, 1966.

Klein, M. *The psychoanalysis of children.* New York: Delta Books, 1932.

Kohn, M. L. *Class and conformity: A study in values.* Homewood, Ill.: Dorsey, 1969.

Kopp, S. B. *If you meet the Buddha on the road, kill him.* New York: Bantam, 1972.

Laing, R. D. *The politics of the family.* New York: Vintage, 1969.
Laing, R. D. Public presentation on philosophy at Yale University. New Haven, 1973.
Lao Tsu, *Tao Te Ching.* (600 B.C.) Translated by Gia-Fu Feng and J. English. New York: Vintage, 1972.
Levine, R. A., and Campbell, D. T. *Ethnocentrism.* New York: Wiley, 1972.
Levinson, H. *Organizational Diagnosis.* Cambridge, Mass.: Harvard University Press, 1972.
Lorenz, K. *King Solomon's ring.* New York: Crowell, 1952.
Marx, K. *Manifesto of the communist party.* (1848) Translated by S. Moore, Moscow: Foreign Languages Publishing House, N.D.
Marx, K. *Economic and philosophic manuscripts of 1844.* (1844) Translated by M. Milligan. London: Lawrence and Wishart, 1961.
Marx, K. *The holy family.* (1845) London: Lawrence and Wishart, 1956.
Marx, K. *Capital.* Vol. I (1867) Translated by S. Moore and E. Aveling. Edited by F. Engels, London: Lawrence and Wishart, 1961.
Marx, K., and Engels, F. *Selected works.* Vol. I and II London: Lawrence and Wishart, 1962.
May, R. *The courage to create.* New York: Bantam, 1975.
Mayo, E. *The social problems of an industrial civilization.* Cambridge, Mass.: Graduate School of Business Administration, Harvard University, 1945.
McCall, G. J., and Simmons, P. *Issues in participant observation.* Reading, Mass.: Addison-Wesley, 1969.
Mechanic D. Sources of power of lower participants in complex organizations. *Administrative Science Quarterly,* 1962, *7,* 349–364.
Michels R. *Political parties.* New York: Dover, 1915.
Miller, E. J., and Rice, A. K. *Systems of organization.* London: Tavistock, 1967.
Mirvis, P. H., and Berg, D. N. (Eds.) *Failures in organizational development and change.* New York: Wiley, 1977.
Nietzsche, F. W. *Thus spoke Zarathustra: a book for everyone and no one.* Baltimore, Md.: Penguin, 1961.
Oshry, B. *Notes on the power and systems perspective.* Boston: Power and Systems Inc., 1976.
Oshry, B. *Power and position.* Boston: Power and Systems, Inc., 1977.
Oshry, B. *Middle power.* Boston: Power and Systems, Inc., 1980.
Parsons, T. *Essays in sociological theory.* New York: Free Press of Glencoe, rev. ed. 1954.
Parsons, T. *Social structure and personality.* London: Free Press, 1964.
Pirsig, R. M. *Zen and the art of motorcycle maintenance.* London: Corgi, 1974.
Porter, L. W., and Roberts, K. H. (Eds.). *Communication in organizations.* New York: Penguin, 1977.
Rice, A. K. Individual, group and intergroup processes. *Human Relations,* 1969, *22,* 565–585.
Rogers, D. *110 Livingston Street: Politics and bureaucracy in the New York City school system.* New York: Vintage, 1968.
Sarason, S. *The creation of settings and the future societies.* San Francisco, Calif.: Jossey-Bass, 1972.
Sayles, L. R. *Behavior of industrial work groups.* New York: Wiley, 1958.
Schutz, A. *On phenomenology and social relations.* Edited by H. R. Wagner. Chicago: University of Chicago Press, 1970.
Serrano, M. *C. G. Jung and Hermann Hesse.* New York: Schocken, 1966.
Sherif, M. *Outline of social psychology.* Rev. ed. New York: Harper, 1956.
Sherif, M. Superordinate goals in reduction of intergroup conflict. *American Journal of Sociology,* 1958, *63,* 349–358.

253

Sherif, M., and Sherif, C. *Social psychology.* New York: Harper & Row, 1969.

Shapiro, D. *Neurotic styles.* New York: Basic Books, 1965.

Simmel, G. *Conflict and the web of group-affiliations.* New York: Free Press, 1955.

Smith, K. K. The values and dangers of power conflict. *Contemporary Australian Management,* 1975, *3,* 19–23.

Smith, K. K. Some notes for OD consultants: learning how to interact with client systems. *Australian Psychologist,* 1976, *11,* 3, 281–289.

Smith, K. K. An intergroup perspective on individual behavior. In J. R. Hackman, E. E. Lawler, and L. W. Porter (Eds.), *Perspectives on behavior in organizations.* New York: McGraw-Hill, 1977, 359–372.

Smith, K. K. A political perspective on "openness" in interpersonal relationships. In R. T. Golembiewski, *Approaches to planned change,* Vol. 2 New York: Marcel Dekker, 1979.

Sumner, W. G. *Folkways.* New York: Ginn, 1906.

Tillich P. *The courage to be.* New Haven, Conn.: Yale University Press, 1952.

Van Maanen, J. "On the understanding of interpersonal relationships," in *Essays in interpersonal dynamics.* Edited by W. Bennis, J. Van Maanen, E. H. Schein, and F. I. Steele, Homewood, Ill.: Dorsey, 1979.

Wells, L. (Jr.) The-group-as-a-whole. In C. P. Alderfer and C. L. Cooper (Eds.), *Advances in experiential social processes,* Vol. 2. London: Wiley, 1980.

Woodward, B., and Armstrong, S. *The brethren.* New York: Simon and Schuster, 1979.

Wilden, A. *System and structure.* London: Tavistock, 1972.